Modern China Series

Can China Rule the New World?

Tian Guang

Chen Gang

ISBN: 978-1-948915-22-9

NORTH
AMERICAN BUSINESS
PRESS

Seattle, WA
Atlanta, GA
Toronto, Canada

North America Business Press

May 2018

About the Modern China Series

China, as one of the oldest civilized regions in the world, has emerged as something of a "new world" because it is working to embrace its own essence and heritage and link them to viable economic strategies. In the last 25 years, China has made tremendous strides by doing so. The country and her people have every right to take pride in these accomplishments. With these successes under their belt, many Chinese leaders and intellectuals anticipate continuing growth. China's plans and strategies, furthermore, are often based upon this premise.

There is tremendous interest in the US on the Chinese economy and business environment. China has emerged as a global super power, and scholars and businessmen in the US are keenly interested in learning how this is going to continue to affect them and how they can do business with China. In response to growing interest from international and Asian scholars, North American Business Press is pleased to announce our Modern China Series (MCS) books, which is first of such series in the US and has garnered tremendous interest both in the US and around the world. With our first book reaching stores in September 2011, this initiative is aimed at developing relationships between NABP and Chinese scholars who desire to promote their academic and applied business writings to the rest of the world.

We have had overwhelming demand for the Modern China Series from both authors who would like to publish in the series and people who would like to read the books. Currently, there are ten books published in the series and, additionally, we have a couple of dozen books that we are considering for the series. The books have been viewed by tens of thousands of people from the U.S. and the rest of the world.

We have published books relating to several areas revolving around the Chinese business environment. We have a few that focus on the best practices in marketing in China; a couple relating to "best practices" in doing business in China; and a few on the outlook of the Chinese economy. The market for the Modern China Series is huge. There are tens of thousands of scholars that are keenly interested in the continued growth of the Chinese economy and the implications that will have on the business world. Even more significant are the millions of businessmen that are interested in the impact that China will continue to have on the global economy. It is difficult to pin down the exact demand for the series, but it is very large.

We have big plans for growing the Moderns China Series. This has the potential to one of the most significant economic/business series ever produced. We are very selective with the books that we will add to the collection, but we encourage any scholars who think they have unique and interesting perspectives on China to submit their books to us. From the readers perspective, we are committed to producing high quality books on a regular basis so that readers should expect a steady stream of insightful books to be coming out for many years to come.

This initiative is headed by Dr. Robert Tian, a renowned researcher and academic, who spearheads our efforts in partnering with foreign authors and administering day-to-day operations of this series. Dr. Tian, a Vice-President with North American Business Press and Editor of this series, spends much of his time in Beijing, Shanghai, and other Chinese cities, focusing on developing and managing our interests with authors and universities. Below is the list for the books we have published:

1. Enterprise Strategy: New Horizon authored by Zhang Xiuyu
2. Governance of Private Enterprises in Modern China authored by Zhong Qin
3. The Art of War and Enterprise Strategy Management by Fu Shouzhi
4. Marketing Issues in Modern China edited by Robert Guang Tian et al.
5. The Footprints of the Academician authored by Fu Zhouzhi
6. Marketing and Economics in Modern China (I) edited by Xiaoguang Qi et al.
7. Marketing and Economics in Modern China (II) edited by Wang Tianjin et al.
8. An Islamic Heritage in China authored by Ma Zhanming
9. Environmental Anthropology in Modern China authored by Wang Tianjin et al.
10. Can China Rule the New World? Authored by Tian Guang and Chen Gang

Can China Rule the New World?

Tian Guang

Chen Gang

Table of Contents

Preface

Those who underestimate the potentials of their rivals often suffer. As a result, Western economic leaders need to consider the economic progress that China has made in the recent past and realistically project its future achievements. Currently Chinese intellectuals and economic leaders envision continued growth and clout. In this book, some of these thoughts are discussed in order to provide clues regarding the contemporary Chinese mindset. By understanding the perspectives of Chinese leaders, those in the West will be better prepared to meet the future.

In the early 19th century, the more "developed" and astute European countries regarded the United States as backward and dependent upon the old World. The people of Britain, who controlled a mighty and growing empire, acknowledged that America possessed great resources, but assumed that the wisdom and savvy of the Europeans overshadowed the New World and would continue to do so. In short, Americans were not taken seriously.

Despite such European chauvinism, American intellectual Ralph Waldo Emerson wrote what has come down to us as "The American Scholar" (1837) which predicted that if America threw off the leadership of the Old World, it could rise above it. History proves that Emerson was correct and the late 19th and 20th centuries emerged as an era when the United States and North America assumed a dominant position in the world.

Today, the New World seems to have become the new Old World because the United States embraces a paradigm of economics and economic growth that has dominated for many years. And like the 19th Europeans who Emerson rebutted, many Americans (and other Westerners) continue to think that their paradigm and dominance will continue far into the future.

China, the oldest civilized region of the world, in contrast, has emerged as something of a "new world" because, like Emerson's America, it is working to embrace its own essence and heritage and link them to viable economic strategies. In the last 25 years, China has made tremendous strides by doing so. The country and its people have every right to take pride in these accomplishments. With these successes under their belt, many Chinese leaders and intellectuals anticipate continued growth. Plans and strategies, furthermore, are often based upon this premise.

The example of Ralph Waldo Emerson and America in the 19th century reminds us that underestimating others is unwise. As a result, taking China seriously is a wise strategy. The authors of this book examine the views of a representative sample of Chinese intellectuals. Such analysis does not imply total agreement; it is merely presented to help the reader to understand how many Chinese leaders perceive their options and how these opinions impact their behavior. The comments presented in the book reflect common views held by the overwhelming majority in China to alert non-Chinese people to what many Chinese think, as such they do not necessarily represent the authors' views.

Currently China is facing a list of import tariffs levied by the U.S. Trump administration, agitated by the country's $375 billion trade surplus with the United States while in the side of service trade with China, US enjoys a very handsome surplus. In response, it has hinted at relaxing rules on some American imports and suggested dialogue rather than escalating a potential trade war. The gung-ho attitude of President Trump is that the U.S. would welcome trade wars with various (if not all) trading partners because for decades the U.S. has had the short end of the stick in all its international trade deals. Many would dispute this, because the U.S. as the world's largest economy has had more economic clout than any of its trading partners and can press for arrangements to suit. Mr. Trump, stable genius and business colossus, does not see it this way. In his opinion, any trade war will be resolved in U.S. favor and consequently, the U.S. economy will be the winner. This is a simplistic view by any measure as thought by most Chinese scholars.

The World Trade Organization (WTO) does not share Mr. Trump's view and has cautioned that a US-China trade war could have severe impacts on the global economy, beyond the two main protagonists. Current U.S. plans would see tariffs worth $50 billion applied to some Chinese imports with China set to retaliate against U.S. exports. The Chinese Premier Li Keqiang said at a press conference after the conclusion of the annual legislative session that there will be no winner in a trade war should it happen between China and the United States. The Chinese Deputy Commerce Minister Wang Shouwen held a press conference in the afternoon on April 4, 2018 to accuse the United States to impose tariffs on Chinese products as irrational practices and announced tariffs on $50 billion of U.S. goods equivalent for retaliation. The video gained over 20 million thumbs up on the Internet in just 2 days. The situation is unprecedented, and this is representing China's public opinion.

On April 5, 2018 the U.S. threatened to expand its tariffs on Chinese imports to $150 billion, after a strong countermeasure for China. Subsequently, China's Ministry of Commerce, the Foreign Ministry and other departments quickly responded on April 6, 2018 saying that if the U.S. ignored the opposition of China and the international community but adhere to the practice of unilateralism and trade protectionism, the Chinese side will follow through as China is ready to respond to the further escalation of the U.S. side measures and has drawn up very specific countermeasures.

In responding to the later threat from Mr. Trump to raise tariffs on $100 billion of Chinese imports, one of the leading newspapers in China, The Global Times, publishes an Editorial on April 6, 2018 entitled "Even if Sino-US Trade Goes to Zero, China Will not Retreat" indicating that the latest threat from Mr. Trump to raise tariffs on $100 billion of Chinese imports has been met by a faster and more determined response from China's ministry of commerce and foreign ministry. China's two ministries have said they want to "listen to what they say" to the U.S.

government, which is a strategic defiance of the other's outburst and harsh words. At the same time, the two departments not only said they would "go to the bottom", but for the first time they used the phrase "at any cost", which is extremely unusual.

The editorial indicates that the Chinese are now assuming that Washington is apparently lack of capital to start a trade war with China, but also to uphold the tariff. We are sure that we have fully capable to let U.S. in a trade war with China suffer the same loss and to let U.S. pay its own economic and political costs, which cannot be so little. Consider the White House said the new $100 billion tariff plan China can retaliate in a very broad area, except for U.S. exports to China, its service exports, and its highly profitable investment in China are all in the line.

The editorial claims that China and the United States have roughly equal trade strength, but the future is in China. A trade war would be painful for China's economy, but it would also push China's economy to a faster transition and create a "new China." While America's loss will be in the future, with many of the world's top companies slipping out of the first camp because of the loss of the Chinese market, and America's modern agriculture will be hit hard. After the full start of a trade war, China will never shrink back, and the strong will of the whole society to stand shoulder to shoulder with the government and share the difficulties will be completely unmatched by the U.S. side. Root cause is that the trade war is the provocation, China is on the just side, and we are safeguarding the rule of the multilateral trading system and based on the rules of our own rights. All Chinese know that the only choice we have is to try our best to deal with the U. S. and to learn from it. Our weakness will only embolden Washington to inflict more harms on ourselves.

The editorial addresses that we will do whatever to fight back against any trade crackdown by the U.S., and this is not something that the Chinese government will say usually. This is not only the decision of the Chinese government, but also the common choice of the whole society. Over the years, China has been under constant threat from the US. In addition, Chinese people have accumulated thousands of years' experience of "do not make trouble, but never fear anything." This time the will of the Chinese is clear: if Trump and his team are willing to, it can lead to a trade war with China to make the mutual investment between the two countries to zero in the direction of the play, China is ready to face all the challenges, to keep up with all its steps, until Pacific becomes the line of international trade barrier.

The editorial indicates that relevant Chinese authorities are ready to fight a trade war. They have developed sophisticated and detailed responses, many of which are already very specific. The relevant teams of the Chinese government can resolutely repel the attacks of Washington, defend China's interests and defend the multilateral system with confidence. There are concerns by most Americans as their everyday life is closely related to Sino-US trade, with the upgrading of a trade war with China, all Americans could be impacted by the unprecedented "trade war epic," it is time to let Americans make the choice between supporting Trump's reckless action or making him account for that.

On April 10, 2018, Chinese President Xi Jinping delivered a keynote speech at the opening ceremony of the Boao Forum for Asia Annual Conference 2018 and promised to further open China to the world by further widening market access, improving the investment environment for foreign investors, strengthening protection of intellectual property rights, and taking the initiative to expand imports. The Chinese people cheered for Xi Jinping's keynote speech, saying that the speech highlighted China's confidence and courage. Although the Chinese authorities addressed on April 11, 2018 that the speech had been prepared long before American President Trump’s attempt it functions as the most powerful response to his plan to launch an unpopular trade war, and draws attention to China's strength as the leader of the new world.

Clearly, the differences exist among peoples in the world, and we are unable, if is not impossible, to cover all the various opinions and statements about China and its role in the world by different peoples. Here, the key question is whether China can become the largest economy in terms of economic aggregate, and whether it can truly become the world leader in terms of its comprehensive strength. Even with the potential for comprehensive strength, how should China be the world's biggest? What will happen to the world after China really becomes the No.1? Will the international political landscape be restructured? Will the new international economic order be established? How does China come to be the world leader? Can China serve the world with strength?

We summarized and presented the Chinese scholars' views on the role of China in the world with the strong belief that it is good for Americans and people from other countries to know what the Chinese scholars think. Yes, there are some arguments or opinions that are not in line with the Americans or people from other countries, but they are simply what the Chinese scholars believe. We are in the position that we should let the world learn the voice from the Chinese scholars so that the rest of the world will have a better understanding about China and her people.

Acknowledgements

This work is deeply indebted to many Chinese scholars who did much to inspire it; we have referred hundreds of their articles and books published both in Chinese and in English. We thank Dr. Gao Jian, Dr. Liu Yu, Dr. Luo Kanglong, Dr. Ma Jianfu, Dr. Ma Zhanming, Dr. Wu Hexian, Dr. Xu Zonglin, Dr. Zhao Peihua, Dr. Zheng Muqiang, and Professors Li Dekuan, Wang Tianjin, Yang Tingshuo, and Zhang Shaoping, for their insightful comments on and constructive suggestions to the initial manuscript, without their encouragements and supports this book may not be able to get published in time.

We thank our student Ms. Dai Qinqin who had participated in the project in the earlier stages and based on which we had published a book in Chinese on the same topic. Our students Ms. Wang Ying, Ms. Li Wei, Ms. Yu Hong, and Mr. Wan Yongan helped us collected data and conducted some technique editing works. Mr. Yan Jimin, a professional translator, helped us translated considerable amounts of Chinese documents. Thanks also go to Professor Zou Lan for his willingness to write the foreword for our book.

Finally, we would like to thank the Academic and Scholastic Publishing Foundations of Shantou University and the Center for Social and Economic Behavior Studies of Yunnan University of Finance and Economics for their support to the publishing of this book.

Foreword

When China Becomes No.1 Again

Zou Lan

Dr. Tian Guang is my former colleague at the Research Institute of State Commission for Restructuring Economy as well as my time-honored friend. He has taught in the USA for a period after taking up advanced studies there. Dr. Tian and his colleague recently fulfilled their book manuscript to discuss if China can rule the new world, in which some thought-provoking questions are raised according to the situation that China's economy has risen back to the No.2 in the world approaching to the No.1 where China had stood in for more than one thousand years but lost for hundreds of years.

These questions make some Chinese people who are arrogant for the situation reflex deeply that what opinions China and the entire world will have if China becomes No.1 one day. If so, will China act as "world policeman" like America does? Prof. Dr. Tian talked with me about this book and requested me to offer a foreword for their book. After carefully reading the manuscript, I have similar feelings about their deep thoughts and the preliminary conclusions they have reached, so I wrote down some thoughts too.

The per capita index of China is still low as the No.2 in the world. In 2012, the GDP of China became No.2 in the world after the USA, leaving Japan far behind. The international statistics are below:

No.1 the USA: GDP $15.09 trillion (about $50300 per capita)

No.2 China: GDP $ 7.3 trillion (about $ 5613 per capita)

No.3 Japan: GDP $5.87 trillion (about $30890 per capita)

No.4 Germany: GDP $3.58 trillion (about $44710 per capita)

No.5 France: GDP $2.78trillion (about $42710 per capita)

No.6 Brazil: GDP $2.49 trillion (about $12500 per capita)
No.7 the UK: GDP $2.42 trillion (about $39000 per capita)

The reason I ranked 7 countries patiently is that the UK was the first country who took over China to be No.1 in GDP, and then the USA took over the UK. The rank had some changes 4 years later. According to the data WB released about all the countries' GDP in 2016, the GDP of the entire world has increased to $74 trillion, in which No.1 the USA accounts for 24.32%, No.2 China accounts for 14.84%, No.3 Japan accounts for 5.91% and No.4 Germany accounts for 4.54%.

The statistics are below:

1. the USA ($18.03trillion)
2. China ($11 trillion)
3. Japan ($4.38 trillion)
4. Germany ($3.36 trillion)
5. the UK ($2.86 trillion)
6. France ($2.42 trillion)
7. India ($2.09 trillion)
8. Italy ($1.82 trillion)
9. Brazil ($1.77 trillion)
10. Canada ($1.55 trillion)

The ranks have changed including the dropping of Brazil, with India rising from far below No.7 to No.7, the UK rising from No.7 to No.5 and France declining by one step. There are some positive predictions that China will become No.1 someday. Not to say that becoming No.1 in the world is totally different with being No.1 in the world again, linear prediction is not reliable as all know. History is not like logic which can be predicted and reasoned. Both China and the world are changing. Brazil was quite weak in the 15th century because Portuguese had not come yet. At that time, China was in the 5th year of the reign of Emperor

Hongzhi of the mid Ming Dynasty and was still strong, holding the position of the world's largest GDP.

However, a Spanish fleet led by Columbus entered the Carribean, which indicated that the balance of strength between Chinese and European economy began to shift. It finally led to the UK becoming the second No.1 because of industrial revolution. Brazil is No.6 but its GDP per capita is far more than China's, so the No.2 position does not deserve to be showed off. The country is rich enough while people are not. Even if China's GDP exceeds the USA, the GDP per capita will be just 1/4 of the one of the USA as China's population is about 4 times as many as America's. There's nothing to be proud of for Chinese.

But it is true that as for China, being No.2 in GDP is an important turning point in its tortuous developing history since modern times. The former No.1 fell to the bottom and then bounced back to No.2. There is no doubt in the world that China is the boss between the Han and Tang Dynasty during BC and 8th century as everyone agrees that the USA is the boss now.

According to Paul Bairoch, China's GDP accounted for 55% of the GDP in the world in 1750 (the 15th of the reign of Emperor Qianlong), India's GDP accounting for 24% and the five countries in Europe (the UK, France, Germany, Russia and Italy) accounting for 17%. China was at the top of the list stably for 900 years from the Tang and Song Dynasties to 18th century.

Until the Yuan Dynasty, Marco Polo at Apennine Peninsula which is on the other side of Eurasia, went across the Eurasia even longer and harder than the Tang Monk did. The flying distance from the Atlantic coast to the Pacific coast is about 11600 km but the Tang Monk travelled from Xi'an through Uzbekistan, Afghanistan all the way to India and if his destination had been in the New Delhi area, the distance would have been about only 6000km, which is only about half of the Marco Polo's travel distance.

Why did Marco Polo spared no expense to come to China? If you ask this question to Vasco da Gama, Christoper Columbus, Hernan Cortes of Mexico or Francisco Pissaro of Peru, they would give you the same answer, that is money, gold and wealth. During the period of Han and Tang Dynasty, it was called the China dream.

If the same question is asked to the African and Arabian refugees who are desperate to reach Europe from Africa at the risk of deadly storms or those who went in illegally to Europe or the USA from Wenzhou, Zhejiang province or Fuqing, Fujian province in China, the answers would probably be same as the Europeans centuries ago and people chasing the American Dream for hundreds of years.

China had been the most powerful country in economy from A.D to 18th century with a proportion of the total world economy which never had been under 20%. China's GDP accounted for 32.9% in 1820 (the 25th of the reign of Emperor Jiaqing) when the Golden Age of Three Emperors just passed and Jiaqing, the son of Qianlong has just been the emperor for 25 years.

When the parabola reaches its vertex, it tends to decline in a sharp curve. The proportion mentioned before fell to 17.2% in 1870, to 8.9% in 1913 and to 4.5% in 1950. Such freefall drop was due to domestic and international factors. As for the domestic factors, decay of the imperial system of China had been deep in its soul and hard to change. The reign of the Emperor of Xianfeng was from 1850 to 1861 and the one of Emperor of Tongzhi started from 1861. Taiping Heavenly Kingdom burst out from the end of 1850 to the beginning of 1861 and failed in 1872. After that the armed conflict between the Hui and the Han in Weinan, Shanxi in 1862 resulted in large-scale severe conflicts between the two religious groups. Confronting two internal disorders during the same period made the old great empire be wasting away at time-lapse speed while the industrial revolution in Europe and the USA were speeding up. This comparison helped make the scales of history tilted to Europe.

According to Angus Maddison's research, China's GDP only accounted for 6% of the world GDP when it was invaded by the Eight-Power Allied forces but the five Europe countries' GDP accounted for 54.5% (the UK 18.5%, France 6.8%, Germany 17.9%, Russia 8.8%, Italy 2.5%), the USA's came up from behind accounting for 23.6% and

Japan's GDP accounted for 2.4%. These seven countries' GDP in total accounted for 80.5%. The results, certainly, are just estimated from statistics about the national economy. China was at Han and Tang Prosperity at the early and medieval ages of the historical parabola when we can hold heads high in Asia.

During that time, China was quite strong in every aspect, with sustained prosperity of economy and the Silk Road. Businessmen from all over the world crowded in for pursuit of the celestial empire's prosperity. The Middle Kingdom embraced and was tolerant to all the foreign cultures. When China was in the traditional agricultural economy, Chinese people's nature of diligence, frugality and pragmatism as well as the technological progress represented by the four great inventions made up the basis of China keeping the No.1 position in economy and culture.

At that time, it was not necessary for China to have military strength around the world to make Northern nomadic people's armed forces restrained themselves because the Kingdom's deterrence was enough to keep peace in surrounding areas. Even so, the stratagem and tactics ideas in Sun Tze's book can still enlighten the military strategists from various countries in the contemporary globalization pattern.

The economy, culture and military are the basis of China's prosperity during Han and Tang Dynasties. The extrovert culture which can embrace foreign cultures, also the best values in the world, is able to export. To the foreign envoys who paid tributes, China accorded courteous reception to them, giving gifts, which valued much higher than the tributes, which was the best proof of giving preferential treatments to the surrounding peoples and being willing to befriend them. Japan, the Korean Peninsula and Vietnam's classical literature in the Chinese language and characters was also the evidence of culture and value influence.

Nevertheless, aggressive strategies can protect the national security and the military influence of the Middle Kingdom in the western regions extending to Central Asia can protect the interests of China and other countries on the Silk Road as well as the international trade among the countries. There were also brigands harassing the empire, but in general, the nomadic people in the north who coveted and attacked the Middle Kingdom were all wiped out and banished to the distance. The longest and most difficult expedition in the sword and shield weapon age was Gao Xianzhi's expedition from Xi'an through the Pamir Plateau to current Gilgit and Hunza area. He went on a unitive expedition to attack the enemy and finally triumphed.

Although it is said that Building the Great Wall basically reflected the national strategy of defensiveness, emperors and generals did not stick to the line of the Great Wall in Han and Tang Dynasties. It seemed like core zone, buffer zone, and marginal zone in a nature reserve. The area inside the Great Wall seemed to the core zone, the invaders would be wiped if they invaded. The area outside the Great Wall seems butter zone, it was not as critical as the above situation. As for the marginal zone beyond the Northern Steppe, the military nomad in that area could be left alone.

From Song Dynasty to Ming Dynasty, although the Middle Kingdom was still an economic great power, which could not input culture and value influence to the Japanese as before, Chinese culture still had a strong inclusiveness. A group of Jews were attracted by the friendly Chinese culture around Kaifeng and let down their guard to be assimilated into Chinese culture later.

For the military accomplishments, Song and Ming Dynasties banned the maritime trade as the strategy of defensiveness, which led to the result of losing the powerful position among neighboring counties. In the reign of the emperor of Yongle in Ming Dynasty, the coming of Philippine's Sulu Island king was perhaps one of the few cases which the overseas rulers came to China. China once gave north military nomad a lot of money in exchange for the peace in the border area. Certainly, culture and art in the Southern Song Dynasty, the Northern Song Dynasty and Ming Dynasty continued to grow to the top in the era of imperial autocracy, because military achievements were looked down in those epochs.

It was boom in economy and culture instead of military achievements supporting the constant rising of GDP, with Northeastern

Jin forces harassed often the Song Dynasty. Both the Northern Song Dynasty and Southern Song Dynasty gained the peace by paying to the northern military nomad. Although Ming Dynasty has been prosperous ever, it was still toppled by the military nomad outside the Great Wall. The defensive function of the Great Wall building since the Han Dynasty was thoroughly lost from then on.

It seems that the prosperity of the period of Kangxi to Qianlong Emperors was the last radiance of the setting sun, because when Jiaqing, the son of Qianlong, was in his 25th in reign, China's GDP reached the vertex in the history, according to The Long-term Performance of China's Economy written by an English scholar Angus Maddison. After the vertex of the parabola, there came the falling.

Without any effective strategies, with culture decayed but still great wealth generating in the economy, the regime of late Qing Dynasty was swollen into arrogance. However, when facing the foreign powers surrounding, it could not agglomerate people's hearts and power or deal with foreign affairs and international trade properly, which led to national humiliation. Additionally, the regime of late Qing Dynasty also had paid innumerable indemnities to Japan, the United States, Russia, etc., which happened to help Japan develop faster particularly.

The claims and property paid to Japan because of Sino Japanese naval battle was about 3.6 million liang (6.34 million ounce) of silver, equivalent to 510 million yen. The money was 3.4 times of Japan's actual military expenditure, 6.4 times the total annual fiscal revenue in Japan and Japan's fiscal revenue for 7 years. When the war bonus arrived, the Japanese government and the common folks were filled with exultation, and the foreign minister Mutu Munemitu said happily: We have never thought of getting hundreds of millions of silvers before these claims. The total income in Japan is just 80 million yen. At the idea of getting 510 million, the Japanese government and people felt very rich.

What did Japan do with the massive reparations? 10% for the Japanese royal family, 10% for education, 80% for industrial construction and for the acquisition of improved military equipment. Most of the reparations were used to enhance the economic strength, a small part was used to improve the educational and training of militarism economic operators and military. The huge amount of money stirred up the appetite of the wolf. After the war of 1894, Japan's economic and military strength expanded rapidly, which provided the basis for Japan to invade China fully in 1930s.

Before World War II and after the World War I, the Chinese economic development and national strength began to pick up when the European and Japanese imperialist powers were scrambling for hegemony. This golden period was interrupted by the Japan's invasion. The trend of national strength falling again had not rebounded until 1950s. China's GDP rebounded to 5% in 1978, and then the proportion of China's GDP in the world had a significant increase, reaching 10.7% in 1995. It is not difficult to see that China's position in the world's economy had experienced a "U" development track, which had two turning points in 1820 and 1950. According to Angus Maddison's calculation, the proportion of China's GDP in the world will reach 20% in 2020, and will be the No.1 in the world in the future.

Another part of China, Taiwan, had also entered the way of industrialization and international trade leading to economic take-off after the difficult transition and reform in 1950s. Both sides of the Taiwan Straits pulling in the same direction showed that if getting rid of outside interference and implementing internal reforms, the ancient Chinese nation's vitality, can still be invigorated. The driving force of Chinese traditional farming economy to the society and economy had been exhausted by 1820. The accelerated development of the industrial technology revolution began in 1782 because of Watt's invention of steam engine. But after 40 years, the industrial revolution began to phase in after thousands of years of farming and it played a key role in promoting the social and economic development.

This is the substitution of a wave of innovative technology brought by intellectual development to the leading role of physical labor in the economic development. However, on the level of national strategy and military strategy, our country has not had any visible global strategy for decades. If it is worth mentioning, the second-strike force formed by the development of the strategic missile has provided China with a nuclear umbrella. In addition, in the early stage of reform and opening, the naval strategy in 1980s has been reemphasized.

The strategic nuclear missile is only the last deterrent because it is the ultimate weapon at vital important moment. It is defensive, is the last resort. If the opponents with the same strategic nuclear missiles do not want to face the same lethal bombings, they will be very cautious to decide to push the nuclear button.

And the Navy, in accordance with the different level of equipment, can be a tactical force, and can also be upgraded to strategic force through the layout of the strategic nuclear submarine. Between the two levels, the warship combat group, especially the aircraft carrier combat group, has the two major functions of tactics and strategy and it can also be between coastal defense and blue water freely. The military and national strategy is the basis for China to move towards a world-class power. We need to redefine the national development strategy and the corresponding global military strategy, according to China's new status in international economy and politics.

Qualifications of the boss: economy, culture and military power

When China was a leader in the long past, the entire world could not be integrated yet. Even the emperor in the Imperial Palace didn't know how many square kilometers of territory there was. And even with the industrial revolution, the news that the UK beat Napoleon in the Waterloo war in June 18, 1815 and thus became a world leader, was sent back to Britain the next day by pigeon from financial institutions of Rothschild. Now it only takes 2 hours from London to Waterloo in Brussels suburb by high-speed rail. Traffic and communications were still backward then. Military forces were naturally unable to effectively be dispatched to the distance. Han Yu, as a vice ministerial level official in Tang Dynasty was banished by the emperor to Chaozhou, Guangdong to be the local administrator, he relied on the cart to go to the place in months.

The ancient Chinese military motto "When the soldiers are meeting attacks in faraway places, they do not have to obey the orders of the emperor" implying that the command can make his own decision upon his on-site observation and judgment, does not appear out of nowhere. In the era with no mechanical power vehicles, detailed military instructions could hardly be transmitted to five hundred miles or even thousands of miles away only by horses or Beacon Tower to communicate with each other. In 1449, Tumu Fort incident that the emperor Ming Yingzong was captured which caused a loss of 500 thousand troops and horses occurred in Huailai county in less than 100 kilometers away from the Beijing city. Such events cannot happen in the contemporary information age. Because it is possible to pinpoint the enemy leader thousands of miles away, relying on information and modern military technology.

Anyway, there was no need for a world police officer. The police taking care of their own regional business would be enough. It was the time of the traditional society and the sword and horse war. The fastest force was the cavalry of the nomadic people. But it was difficult for a cavalry to stay in one place for a long time without a stable logistics base. It was not possible or necessary for them to move around the world and attack or deter the rivalries like the current American fleets do. And now, if we apply the American way as the world's big boss, the boss must be world policing. However, the US has interests extended to the entire world needing to be effectively protected. Being the boss needs to have good statements and in good names. If the argument is not convincing, the words will not ring true. The Chinese ancient people knew this truth long ago.

Marshal Lin Biao once said, “He who convinces by virtue wins, and he who compels by force loses”. If the definition of virtue is universal, such as the three basic principles of liberty, equality, and fraternity, it will be recognized by the mainstream of the world. It is worth thinking that Marshal Lin, a person who had been serving military service for all his life, could come up with such a conclusion. If something is started in the wrong name, it will not succeed. The process of European powers' colonization began to collapse in the 19th century and collapsed entirely after the second World War in the mid-20th century, which firstly solved the problem of equality between the colonies and the colonizers, and secondly it gave the colonies liberty. As for the fraternity issues, the Chinese ancient saying that if the food is enough, the virtues are known and when you have more, you can take better care of elders and children.

At the anniversary of 9·11, the Americans spent so much time to read out more than 3000 names to show respect for the victims. The President of the United States and all the high officials respectfully listened to the names read out by the representatives of different families, rather than let everyone listen to the so-called important instructions by politicians. The Vietnam Veterans Memorial in Washington is engraved with the names of every fallen soldier in the battles. As for the MIAs in the battles, no matter how many years have passed, when there is any clue leading to discovery of the remains of MIAs, they will be send back to US for burial, at the expense of US. And the soldiers buried in Arlington National Cemetery, regardless of the military rank, are equally treated. Such respect for people is humanitarian.

The legal system in the United States may be that the rich can lessen the punishment, but the probability of injustice to the innocent is quite low. It is relatively fair. The number of Nobel prize laureates in the United States is more than any country else in the world. I do not have any specific figures, but by the end of 2008, the statistics of two universities in the United States showed that the number of scholars who won the Nobel prize in Columbia University was 88, and that in University of Cambridge was 86. The University of Chicago has 10 Nobel Economics winners. The number of Nobel Prize winners in University of Chicago alone exceeds the total number of Chinese Nobel Prize laureates.

No matter what their motives were, people who entered and stayed in the USA by legal means or illegal means were as many as or more than those who have settled in China as they came from Central Asia and Europe between the Han and Tang Dynasties. Because in AD 1000, the global population was about 65 million (now roughly equivalent of French population); the maximum Chinese population then was estimated at 16 million (slightly higher than the actual population of Shenzhen city now). Now much more people want to migrate to the USA, than to any country else.

It is said that 16 million people in New York metropolitan area came from more than 180 countries and regions in the world. 36% of the city's population is foreign immigrants (2000 census), whites are 37%, blacks are 28%, Latin Americans are 27%, Asians are 10%. The new Yorker speaks more than 170 languages, mainly English, followed by French, German, Russian, Chinese, and Japanese.

The population of such a city and the number of languages spoken are roughly enough to illustrate the attractiveness of the United States to the global people. The products of the USA sell to all over the world, although its manufacturing industry is now declining, the planes a lot of people take daily now are Boeing, many of the cell phones people use now are Apple. The Hollywood movies, the Broadway shows, and pop songs are fashionable in the world market. These imply the American culture and values, are accepted worldwide, which is soft power

If the behavior of world police is like that of Imperial Japanese army which was burning all, killing all, and looting all, it will not be long before someone kicks him aside. The world police have done a lot of terrible things. For example, Chile's Allende administration was toppled in 1973, In Nicaragua Sandino was assassinated in 1934, Mohammed Mosadegh administration in Iran in 1953 encountered a coup, and conflicts happened in Cuba in 1963 and so on. In recent years there has been an incident invading Iraq under false excuses. There is a strong anti-American sentiment in the world, which is closely related to all these. Of course, the world police do so, indeed, for American interests. The US will not tolerate the troubles that prevent it policing the world.

However, when the United States does do something in bad, the excuse it use is are seemingly plausible. The Central Intelligence Agency, for example, was involved in the subversion of the Allende regime, saying that the leftist regime threatened the rich and the capitalism. When hunting Sadam, it said Saddam harbored Al Qaeda and in Iraq there were mass-destruction weapons threatening Israel. The United

States did not say directly that US was going to topple him. Even if US does, US will find a good excuse to wrap it up. In the final analysis, the United States, of course, has the right to pursue its national interests. Sometimes it is really a zero-sum game.

Even so, the United States still has a strong appeal to a lot of people in the world. There are people who pursue Americans' richness, who admire the opportunities offered by the United States, who like the tolerance of the USA, who want to go to the United States to get scholarships for their studies, and generally appreciate the values of the USA. It said that convincing people by virtue wins, compelling people by force loses. But it is not necessarily an immediate loss, and one may not be able to protect oneself without power and force.

So being the police in the world also needs all the power. According to the information of Spanish media Rebellion, the United States has 737 bases overseas by 2005, including Guantanamo in Cuba, Okinawa in Japan, in Germany, in Iraq, and in the Pacific Islands. The newspaper said that in 2005, the United States distributed 38 large and medium-sized military installations in the world (mostly the air force and naval bases equipped with bombers and fleets), almost the same number of 36 naval bases and British military bases in 1898. The Empire of Rome in its prosperous era (117 BC) needed 37 large bases to monitor its vast territory, from England to Egypt, from Spain to Armenia. Perhaps the best number of large bases and garrisons for an imperialist power longing for the rule of the world is between 35 and 40.

There is no meaning to the base without personnel. In the fiscal year 2005, the American military deployed 195975 servicemen in military bases abroad, the number is same as the number of non-combat men and women working for the Department of Defense. In addition, 81425 foreign workers were employed worldwide.

The newspaper article continued that in 2005, the total number of military personnel in the United States deployed the world, including the military bases at home, was 1840062, the civilian staff for the Department of Defense and subsidiaries was 473306, and the local contract workers were 203528. According to the statistics of the

Department of Defense, there are 32327 barracks, parking aprons, hospitals and other facilities of the USA overseas, and 16527 rented facilities. These facilities took the area of 687527 acres (1 acres for abroad is equal to 6.072 mu), both at home and abroad at a total of 29819492 acres, making The Pentagon the world's largest land owner.

The report also said that although the figures were surprising, there was still no mention of the total figures of the American military bases in the world. For example, a 2005 report about Al Qaeda did not mention any garrison in Kosovo (a province of Serbia), although there is a huge camp Bernd Steel built in 1999, which is operated by American company KBR, a subsidiary of Halliburton. The report did not either include the USA garrison in Afghanistan, Iraq (May 2005 106 barracks), Israel, Kyrgyzstan, Qatar, and Uzbekistan, and from the "9.11" event the American forces has set up a large military base system in the Persian Gulf and Central Asia. In the preface, the report also apologized for saying that the military facilities provided by other countries were not included, but that was not entirely true. The report included 20 military facilities in Turkey, which are owned by the government of the Turkey and are also used by the United States.

In this way, a huge amount of money is needed to support such huge overseas military bases, military and foreign employees and these bases are just the fixed ones.

The deployment of China's PLA includes the Beijing military area command, the Shenyang military area command, the Nanjing military area command, the Wuhan military area command, the Guangzhou military area command, the Chengdu military area and the Lanzhou military area, covering only the Chinese mainland. Only recently this was changed in the military system reform in China. In the United States, the military commands are set up in accordance with the map of the world.

Militarily, the USA divided the entire world to various parts ruled by different commands: Pacific Command, Central Command, Northern Command, Southern Command and European command. The United States and Canada, Mexico, Cuba, belonging to the Northern Command;

Mexico South America and the Caribbean islands to the Southern Command; the whole of Europe and the Soviet Union was under the region of the European Command; Egypt, the Middle East, the Caucasus region under the central command; China, Mongolia, Pakistan, South and Southeast Asia and East Asia to the Pacific Command Department.

If China is the boss of the world and must be the policeman of the world, it will not only need to estimate global deployment, but also divides the world into their own designated regions according to their own geopolitical and geo-military needs like the United States to meet the needs of all the regions and all the troubles.

The understanding of geopolitics of Chinese ancient scholars may not be less than the present experts. Gu Zuyu (1631-1692) once pointed out the important significance of Central Asia to China's territorial defense: To protect Qianlong (Shanxi and Gansu) it is necessary to secure the Hexi Corridor, and to protect the Hexi Corridor, it is necessary to secure the Xiyu (the Great West). Before the War of Resistance against Japan, the Turpan county magistrate Zeng Wenwu also pointed out a clear picture of the Great West. In his master work 《A History of Chinese Administration in Great West》(Zhongguo Jingying Xiyu Shi),he concluded that if Pamir is not in China's hands, there will be no Shule(today's Kashgar), and there will be no Xinjiang if without Shule. A slight move in one part may affect the situation and the importance of the region to the border defense can be easily seen.

In fact, in addition to these, the United States also has many fleets of aircraft carrier's cruising around the world's oceans. At present, there are 12 large aircraft carriers in the United States, of which 10 are deployed in the United States. The Pacific Headquarters has the Third and Seventh fleet, their main patrolling areas including the Pacific and the India Ocean. In the West Coast, there is the Third Fleet deployed in the United States, the headquarters in San Diego, California where the First Aircraft carrier group is deployed while the Seventh Fleet is deployed in the West Pacific region, the location of the headquarters of Yokosuka in Japan, with a "Kitty Hawk" as the flagship of the fifth battle group.

The Atlantic Headquarters has the Second Fleet and Sixth Fleet, the main patrolling area is the Atlantic and the Arctic region, the location of the headquarters at Norfolk Naval base in Virginia on the east coast of the United States. The Fourth, sixth, eighth aircraft carrier group are stationed here. The second fleet deployed on the east coast of the United States, the location of the headquarters of Virginia, Norfolk Naval base; Sixth fleet deployment in the Mediterranean region, the headquarters is in the port of Gaeta in Italy, where the second aircraft carrier group is stationed.

The times spent patrolling of the American fleets were not even for each ocean. Basically, the deployment time in Indian Ocean accounts for 3 / 4 or half of the total time in the year, and the time of deployment in the Mediterranean accounts for 3 / 4 or 4 / 5 of the total time in the year, while in the Western Pacific region, that is, the East Asian and Southeast Asian region's deployment time is uninterrupted all the year round. The United States also has the air force that can cover the global airspace, as well as the strategic missile forces, which are subordinate to the Army, the Navy and the Air Force respectively.

In addition, the American has an international vehicle: The North Atlantic Treaty Organization (NATO). It was an international military alliance to deal with the Warsaw Pact Organization in the Cold War, led by the United States and ally of the United States. Many of these countries in Western Europe were recipient countries of the Marshall plan after World War II. The United States helped the economic revival of these countries, ideologically consistent or very close to the United States, so they guarded against the Soviet Eastern European Group during the Cold War. The total military and economic force of these countries may not be less than the United States' total strength.

After the founding of NATO, it was basically the solo of the United States. Only in the Twenty-First Century, the financial resources of the United States were difficult to support NATO, US began to have more NATO allies to participate in the military operations. For example, in Libya the European allies of NATO took the offensive while the United States was on the second line, standing by.

Talking from Marshal Plan to the economic capabilities. Without the strongest economic capacity, it is impossible to support Marshall's plan to attract allies. In addition, the United States can deal with two wars at the same time, including economy and equipment, and the ability to mobilize personnel. Without these, it is impossible to be everywhere around the world and once the national interests are under threat, there will be no immediate dispatch of military forces protect the interests.

In jurisdiction, the laws of the USA observe the so-called Long Arm principle that is no matter what happens, anywhere in the world, civil or criminal cases, whether or not involving American or Americans, as long as there is minor relationship to a party and legal person in the United States, such as a small foreign company in the United States having some temporary services in the USA, the laws of the United States have jurisdiction. If a plane is over the United States, the United States can also get jurisdiction. In one case, in the United States, heard by the Supreme Court in 1959. The subpoena was sent to the person on plane when the defendant was in, over the area which the court has the jurisdiction.

This so-called long arm is really a long arm. But this is determined by the international influence of the United States. Imagine that when a landlocked inland small country or not land locked weak country also claims long arm jurisdiction, how can they enforce their law? As a result, Americans often extend their domestic laws to international affairs. Therefore, when someday China has a GDP more than the USA and is close to the USA in GDP per capita terms, it will still be a question whether China has the ability, willingness, or enough experience and financial resources to take over what US does currently.

Whether the old policeman is willing to be taken over is another big problem. Because the role of the world police has expanded the international interests of the United States. It can control the lifeblood of the international trade and economies, cost of resources can be set low, and the finished products and services can be sold at a higher price. There is a double interest between one bought and one sold like this. Besides, young students from all over the world are eager to study and stay in the American colleges. American universities have become the world's best talent harvesters. The top talents educated by foreign governments or families have been attracted to the United States by scholarship, which has provided US with valuable contribution to science and technology and culture in the US. Using the talents of the world to support America for longer is also the advantage of the United States as a world police.

It is Hard to Be the New No.1

The biggest premise of discussing about to be the new No.1 and world policeman, is that the original No.1 is willing to hand over. If it does not want to, what we say here will be just a empty talking. At the 2012 American presidential election, both candidates, Obama and Romney, were complaining about China as if China was the one to be blame about all the social and economic problems in the United States. No one knows how the original No.1 will react when the tremendous global benefit is going to be lost.

The Snowdon affair in 2013 exposed the fact that the U.S. does not trust any other allies expect for UK, Canada, Australia and New Zealand. Only these four "brotherly states" in the Anglo-American tradition are not being monitored by the United State intelligence. Germany, the important ally of the NATO, is still unable to avoid being spied on. The U.S. declined to sign the agreement of not spying on each other and even monitored the phone calls of Germany Chancellor. Recently, after the German double agent selling intelligence to America, Germany has uncovered another American espionage. The United State even does not trust its longtime ally so it is much less possible for America to give up the No.1 position. The U.S. can't be willing to give up the benefit of being the No.1.

It is not realistic that as the world No 1, it only wants to pursue its own development without bothering the international policing. Strong as America is, it still was attacked by the radical religious extremists and terrorists on September 11, 2001. What's more, even an enterprise should better take the social responsibilities to the consumers and the public when it grows strong. One becoming the world No.1 must take more international responsibilities. Even if the No.1 can be completely self-sufficient, without any external business, it still has the international duties. And a total isolationist No.1 is impossible after the industrial revolution changing the world and economy.

If someone depends on the international resources and markets to develop, it will be necessary to help his less fortunate "neighbors" to develop themselves. This is the responsibility of the international community. If the rogue states make trouble, he needs to reach out to the people in need and get things right. If the rogue countries provoke deliberately, scrambling for the benefits, he should teach them a lesson as well. Comparing to the No.1 role of the U.S., a new No.1 has also to play a role of the world police.

The problem: a new No.1 must set up worldwide 38 police headquarters and 699 police stations (38 of the 737 overseas American bases are large military one), to deploy nearly 200,000 "police force" and 81,000 local staff. In addition, there are many local troops of the United States' allies to help, such as NATO and Japanese troops as the hitmen in the East Asian region.

Additionally, this "police" has the Seventh Fleet and the Sixth Fleet patrolling in the western Pacific, Mediterranean and Atlantic every now and then. Wherever the disturbances are, there will be the patrols monitoring and as the deterrents. If troublemakers are still not willing to stop, they may be disciplined on the spot. There are ten US aircraft carrier fighting groups guarding the three coasts of the United States so it can dispatch one or two to where it is necessary.

Moreover, over the years, the United States has been the ally to the European countries after the Second World War, and friend with Mobuto Sese Seko of Congo, Anastasio Somosa de Bayle of Nicaragua and Augusto Pinochet of Chile, and with Saddam Hussain of Iraq and Usama Bin Laden in Afghanistan. It shows the United States needs to place its own interests first, without ideological differences. The moment US feel some a friend, he is a friend. The moment the US changes the mind, he is an enemy. And the enemy will be a friend overnight if there is the need.

There is a famous quote of governance in China, "To resist foreign aggression one must stabilize the country". The meaning of "stabilizing the country" is social stability, reducing the distractions to the resistance. The good condition of stability for a country is powerful, its people in good living and willing to work for the country. In other words, the state decision is made on the wishes of the mainstream people. Only in this way, the government can rest assured of domestic affairs and commit to solve the international problems.

If he is a tyrant at home, who is not only losing all money in gambling and affecting normal life, borrowing or even lavishing money, but also beating children and wife after heavy drinking, when he goes out and help his neighbor for justice the next day. Will the neighbors believe that he is a good guy?

Now that to be the world police, it is necessary to know the world. Chinese history has one ancient stupid king saying, "Why they don't eat meat paste?" when there was a big famine in his kingdom and many starved to death. The king obviously had no knowledge of common people and their livelihood. If such person goes abroad to be the "police", he will be just an easy target. He could not solve the problem, but he himself will be part of the problem.

The military and scholars in the United States have in-depth study of all countries in the world, covering not only politics, economy and culture, and deep into folklore and anthropology subjects. Without necessary knowledge, one goes to the world irritating and angering many people and probably one does not know why. An unwelcome person will not do the job well.

Also, when the new No.1 is the world police, it cannot be weak. If there is a trouble with a far-reaching implication, there will be no room for hesitation to stop it. He must be tough in trouble shooting. And there will be no more practices of "foreigners above nationals" in this country, with nationals first in priority. If your own people are despised while foreigners given preferential treatment, when you go abroad to police, nobody will respect you.

When your own development is not to the benefit of your own people, but at the expense of your workers and people, and people in the world will be afraid of you copying the sweat shop model to other parts of the world. When in your country a lot of the students are fooling around in studying and examinations, the economic growth will be unsustainable. And the No.1 in economy will be lost some time later.

When the illegal enterprises in your country use melamine and drainage oil to make dirty money and are not punished, the No.1 position in economy is nothing either. When some officials in your country do not serve the people and business but do their job as businessmen, distorting and bribe taking, hindering business growth and jobs, the No.1 position in economy is nothing, either.

If all these irregularities are eliminated by deep and comprehensive reforms and the country becomes No.1 in economy, still a so what? It is also necessary to have the ability and experience to be the police of the world. China is far from ready in many aspects to be the world police. Suppose that the new world police come from a different culture background other than Christian or Anglo-Saxon background, there should be a soft Eastern way instead of the arrogant way. However, the universal values should be included while the Eastern hypocrites do not.

It is also worth mentioning that, at present, international trade, international finance, agricultural technology, industrial technology and high technology, and international judicial practices are basically the rules formulated by the United States and the West. Their domestic standards and practices are almost the international standards and international practices. If the new No.1 has no achievements in these fields but can be a follower, even he is the new No.1 or new world police, it can only be a phony.

Unless the international police do better than the USA and can avoid the shortages, the USA has (arbitrary, pursuing American interests in the name of the public, utilitarian pragmatism, and so forth) and make best use of the advantages of the USA (allies everywhere, bases, resources, the professional skills to cope with the mess), add the new strengths (Whether there is a strong point or not, it needs to be confirmed by itself and the world). Otherwise, give up the idea of being the No.1 and world police.

The international situation is now "one superpower and multi powers" But the multi powers are also in dynamic changes. Russia has begun to recover from the decline from world's No.2 as Soviet Union, and its strength now is not weak. Europe now is still a strong power, although it has some serious problems now, it still can influence the world situation. Japan had been No.2 for a while, but it is always strong in economy but weak in international politics, dependent on the USA.

The trend of development in the world is dynamic. Britain was the world's No.1 200 years ago, but the title had already been lost to the United States. Brazil was not on the country list in 1492, but it is now the seventh in the world. Japan was still in the position of the world's second biggest economy, only a few years ago, but now China has taken the place of Japan. One is developing while others are also working hard. Therefore, any slack, complacency, and any major error in any internal and external policy may make China a second Japan.

Aging process will drag on our country. With the population of China, it is difficult for us to adopt the way in which the United States absorbs many immigrants to make up the shortage of labor. Therefore, it is the only feasible way to improve the educational quality of the whole people, improve the farmers' ability of scientific farming and intensive management, and improve their technical quality and ability, to improve the efficiency of the material production sectors. At the same time, we also need the reform of government functions, reduce redundancies to improve the efficiency, limit the negative impact on economic growth.

But, we should be confident that Chinese civilization is resilient and vigorous over the long history. We should have enough wisdom to guide our country through history and the world mist to make a brilliant new chapter in history. The present world is interdependent. So even if the USA is really the No.1, it could not be correcting in everything. Imagine a powerful executive council composed of several powers, like the United Nations Security Council. Is it possible to really have an effective world policing that is basically detached from the superpowers' private interests, to keep global peace?

Therefore, China had better be not arrogant upon becoming the economic No.1 as the per capita GDP is lower than the US. Even if

China per capita GDP exceeds US, China still should learn from US about how US can maintain the top position for more than one hundred years.

As the No.1 in economy, the overall No.1 and the other countries might be politer to him. In the global village, if he still supports in general the world police to maintain peace, to give the No.1 a helping hand when the One needs help. The economic No.1 in one aspect could protect its own peace without trouble in vicinity, and can also help his friends or good neighbors not be bullied, and these friends must not be rogues. In times of trouble, these friendly neighbors will also be willing to support him, and the behavior patterns in the village are also approved by other countries. It is like to be the assistant of world police, helping him when he is right and criticize the police when he is wrong.

In the process of developing from the world's second largest economy to the largest economy, China should learn more about improving people's living standards and protecting their rights to make China more respected, which means strong economy, cultural tolerance and influence, and strong military power to beat the enemy. To protect the country safe, keep the peace, and joining in the international community to help punishing the villains and pursue justice. If China takes the responsibility of being No.1 in the world as well as the world police, it might take half or one century more on the trainee and assistant job. The USA standing for the West and China standing for the Asia, a G2 of USA and China supplemented by the other powers of the world will be probably feasible.

Being the No.1 but not seeking hegemony, improving external relations and internal growth that no one else dares to offend, assisting the world police to uphold justice, and persuading with other allies the world police when the police goes too far. Perhaps this is the most feasible international role for China after becoming the No.1 in the world.

Part I: Various Conjectures

Chapter 1:

Can China Become the No.1?

Nowadays China's economic aggregate has jumped to the second in the world, which has shown the world the peculiar effect of "the rise of China." The international community approves the development of China's economy. Under this premise, when will China's economy overtakes the United States? This has become a hot topic that is widely discussed, which has formed as a pattern sensationally raised up by the prophets every occasionally.

Can China become No.1? In fact, this question was put forward shortly after the fiscal crisis. Because the development of China's economy has witnessed remarkable progress in recent years, especially the special ability to resolve the financial tsunami. In September 2009, the former assistant principal of Peking University as well as the Dean of Guanghua College of Peking University, Professor Zhang Weiying said with great confidence that after the financial tsunami, it is now impossible to rely on export to stimulate economic growth, however, China's economy can still maintain its rapid growth. It may even replace the United States in the next 30 years and become the largest economic entity in the world. Although the total economic output in China was only No.3 in the world at that time, but will the situation change in the next two years?

On April 7, 2011, the Social Science Press conducted a seminar titled "Rise of BRICS and Global Development and Governance" in Beijing and a press conference on the "Blue Book for Emerging Economies" in Beijing. This conference discussed the developments and changes of emerging economies and the new trend of global development and governance reform. At this conference, A Blue Book of Emerging Economies titled the BRICS Economic and Social Development Report (2011) was formally released. In this Blue Book, it predicted that China's total economic output may surpass the United States by 2020, and then will rank first in the world, while India's GDP will rank the world's top five (Lin and Zhou, 2011). If only you praise yourself, others will not believe. Therefore, only the Chinese people say that the Chinese economy will be the first, this cannot convince the people of the world. At the same time, let's listen to some voice from the foreign media.

The International Monetary Fund predicted in 2011 that the proportion of the United States and China in the world economy will also change by 2016. China's proportion will increase from the current 14% to 18%, while the United States will drop from the current slightly below 20% to 17.7% which will be lower than China a little bit and thus be the second in the world. Of course, the International Monetary Fund is not the first one to make such a prediction. Nobel laureate Fogel predicted that China will become the world's largest economy by 2020.

A UK magazine Economist published a monograph about the assumption that China and the United States will have 7.75% and 2.5% GDP growth respectively over the next 10 years, with inflation rates of 4% and 1.5% respectively, then China's GDP will surpass the United States by 2019. At the same time, World Bank economists predict that China's economy will overtake the United States and the EU in 2030 and become the world's largest economic market, by that time, China, the United States, the European Union, India, Japan will behavior like “five dragons" to promote the world economy. As you see, there are so many foreign agencies that have predicted whether China's economy will exceed the United States or not （Yin and Yang, 2011）.

Can China become No.1 or not? This is an objective question. We need to consider the actual situation in China. In situations where opportunities and challenges coexist, are opportunities more than challenges? Or are challenges more than the opportunities? This will affect the question. In addition, we must also consider the history of

China, such as the origin of China's peaceful rise. Since ancient times, China is a peace-loving country, and has always adhered to such diplomacy as "not seeking hegemony." Well, one of the questions we are discussing is "can China be No.1?" Is this contrary to the national guidelines and policies? This needs our thorough discussion. Finally, we also need to consider a subjective question: Does China want to be No.1? Just like the "demand" that occurred in economics, people must have the willingness to buy first, then the purchasing power, to become a real "need" eventually. When we talk about whether China can become the world leader or not, the truth is the same. Therefore, only when both subjectivity and objective have been reached can we draw the conclusion.

Can China rise peacefully?

Dr. Zhao Jingfang is an associate professor working at the Crisis Management Center of the National Defense University, she said that China's economic strength has been enhanced continuously in these recent years. The crisis which China has encountered in the surrounding areas has been increased steadily. Obviously, it is going to be more difficult for China (to) rise peacefully. This is a strategic environment that cannot be ignored for China. When facing the strategic environment that has changed and is still changing rapidly, we must overcome our theoretical misunderstandings about the peaceful rise and adjust the current strategic thinking and tactics in time. This is what we must do. Only in this way will China pass the undercurrents on the broad road of peaceful development. Undoubtedly, it will depend on not only the economic and diplomatic forces but also the military development when China rises peacefully. Therefore, it is not just the rise of economy and diplomacy, but also the rise of the military. Only relying on this kind of multiple rise can China realize the complete peaceful rise. In other words, without the support of economic and diplomatic forces, the peaceful rise is hollow and false, without the guarantee of military power, the peaceful rise will be fragile and unsustainable (Zhao, 2012).

When talking about the economic development of China, the international community changed their words immediately. They disseminated various "threat theories" concerning the rise of China and even exaggerated the economic development to the political and military levels. They believed that China will inevitably end up on the path of hegemony in the war. In fact, whether Chinese or foreigners, their historical studies on China are far from enough for those who think so. China is neither a militant nation like the United States nor a colonial expansion like Europe throughout the history of China. Even before the Opium War, China never had such a thought to keep its position of number one in the world through the war. These are inseparable from the history and culture of China.

Of course, it should be a peaceful rise if possible. So, what is the rise? It has the meaning of accelerating the national economic development. However, when we say the rise of China, here the meaning is different, the rise we are talking about means the rise of comprehensive national strength and then affect the world's forces, order and code of conduct (Yan, 1997). In the history of China, China has had her rise on several occasions: the first one was the unification of China governed by the Qin Dynasty and this is the first unification for China; the second rise was the establishment of the Tang Dynasty and then its flourishing life occur; The third one is the Ming Dynasty, Zheng He's voyages was the landmark event, Zheng He brought the Chinese civilization to the Middle East and North Africa. The fourth rise came to us after the Cold War (He, 2005). All these 4 rises are mild and friendly; thus, we can say that China is a "state of ceremonies" which is not "war" or "killing" at all.

In the history of China, the Confucianism that represented by Confucius, was regarded as the "golden rules" of governing the country since the Han Dynasty. At that time, people ignored all other theories except the Confucianism. Confucianism needs us to be "courtesy" and "benevolent," to govern the country, it advocated to govern with virtue and gentleness. In modern society, these are just "governing the country with virtue" and "governing the country according to the laws."

Nowadays the strategy is more enlightened and equal, some bad ideas have been abandoned. One should not impose on others what he himself does not want, we are all good friends no matter where you live, this kind of ideas have been known by Chinese. The previous emperors of China also keep Confucianism as their ways to govern the nation. For example, when we see the portrait or sculpture of the Chinese previous emperors, it comes to our mind immediately that they all look like people believing in Confucianism.

The political concepts are different under different civilizations, only China was never interrupted during the past 2000 years, and the Chinese nation was the only nation that did not advocate military force. In comparison, the westerners believe in the theory of original sin of human nature, thus they uphold the domination by law, they also advocate the "law of the jungle." The brilliance in the Roman Empire, the France domination in Europe during the Napoleonic times and the powerful United States after the Cold War, all these illustrate that Westerners have a very strong idea to dominate the citizen by the military force （Chen, 2004）. There is good news, the Confucian ideology and culture represented by Confucius, is moving into the world and being accepted by more and more countries in the world under the current complicated cultural background, which is helpful to bring human beings into a peaceful and new era.

In the contemporary era, we are more likely to fall into a perceptual way of thinking. That is, we basically explain the international relations and diplomatic strategies according to the western model. We stubbornly believe that it is a normal phenomenon to struggle for supremacy. Because the Westerners thinking is: You are already so powerful, why not go seeking hegemony? They think it is unbelievable and weird for a country if not go seeking hegemony after becoming powerful.

However, the Chinese leaders have declared constantly that this way of thinking should be given up. For example, Premier Wen Jiabao held a speech entitled "Investing in China" at Harvard University on December 10, 2003. For the first time, Wen Jiabao represented the Chinese government and explained the theory of China's peaceful rise to the world publicly and transparently. In this speech, he said that China is a country that is rising peacefully. In his speech, Wen Jiabao also pointed out that the path, mode and the value orientation during China's rise will be based on peace. This is the first time that the top Chinese leaders to use the phrase "peaceful rise," which marks China's peaceful rise as a fundamental national strategy (Zhang and Jiang, 2011). On July 1, 2016, General Secretary Xi Jinping declared at the celebration of the 95th anniversary of the Chinese Communist Party: "We hope to promote the relationships with all other countries, to promote to establish a new type of international relations under the win-win cooperation, and to promote the formation for human destinies community and benefits community." The human destinies community will not only bring benefits to China but also to the world. China's development and strength are not threats but opportunities for other countries. At the just-concluded 19th Chinese Communist Party Congress, General Secretary Xi Jinping appealed once again that all people in the world should work together to build a community of human destiny and to establish a world of lasting peace, universal security, common prosperity, inclusiveness, cleanliness and beauty.

China is a sincere country and is ready to develop with all other countries in the world in a prosperous manner. "One Belt, One Road," this strategy is the best proof. "One Belt, One Road" refers to the principle that we must uphold our common business, and build our beautiful life together and then share it. It is not a soloist of a certain country, but a chorus of the countries along the line. When rising peacefully, China also allows other countries to get on the "convenient car" to support the common development of all countries and to build a shared garden.

Obviously, the rise and development of China will not threaten any country or any people. If some countries or some people in the world still support the "China threat theory," we had better ask them shall we return to the poor and weak era and return to the humiliation era when all others were attacking us? Is this what you meant? Is this what you recognized as "safe?" If so, where is the fairness of the world going? "If one can be stable in all his life, nobody would want to be displaced", this sentence is particularly suitable to show China's current situation. The Chinese people are peace-loving and dislike of the war, which has been handed down from generation to generation and cannot be changed in the future. Moreover, we are quite happy to continue like before.

Of course, when we cannot rise peacefully and when our rise is suppressed, we cannot and will not give up our rise. In other words, if we are unable to rise peacefully, we will also consider the other ways. Therefore, for China, apart from the strategic thinking for rising peacefully, the most important thing is to consider whether we ourselves have the strength and ability to rise peacefully, that is, whether we will have enough military strength when the wars happen. We are convinced that China's military strength will become stronger and stronger, and it is impossible for the Western countries headed by the United States to attack China to guarantee the stability thoroughly around the near areas (Zhao, 2012).

Opportunities for China's economic development

"Well going wagons depend on the leading horses." These three wagons driving the growing of China's economic are three horses belonging to the same wagon, is "export" the leading horse or "investment" the leading house? Different theorists have different opinions, there is no distinct answer. However, this is positive that it has never been said that the wagon "consumption" is the main force driving the growing of China's economy. Therefore, China's future economic development opportunities will emerge: consumption. In recent years, what we have always emphasized is to stimulate domestic demand while growing stably. However, where does the largest part of domestic demand come from? Consumers in China can be grouped into two smaller ones at the two ends and a big one in the middle, while the middle one will serve as the principal breakthrough forces to increase the domestic demand.

Nowadays the people in the middle class do not consume too much, where did the money go? Savings? No! Just take a look to the China's

CPI then you will see, it is well known that the money will be devalued if you just put it in the bank. Such a small savings rate simply cannot make up for the current inflation losses. Where did the money of people in the middle class go? Would not go away? Even though the wage level is not high, but it is enough to maintain a livelihood, why the consumption is not very active? In fact, it is not difficult to find out the reasons. Let us look to the education, which is the biggest spending for the general working-class people. Nowadays the education has become completely different than what it was before, it has been "commercialized." Not to mention all kinds of malpractices in China's education system, one can have a look at the education fees. The tuitions and charges that a high school student pays is as high as dozens of thousands. The education should be one of the public welfare, but it has now become a tool for profit. Chinese citizens have nothing to do but to tighten their belts, not to spend money on other stuff anymore, just for their children's education and thus they live frugally, except this, what else can they do?

Let us look at the China's real estate, which is more serious than the education. In fact, the house is just a place for people to live in, but in China, people buy houses and then sell them to make money from the houses. Those real estate investors or speculators, they may say: China's stock market is not making money, if you do not buy a house, where will you put your money? Finally, let's look at the social security. Everyone may get sick and die. This is unavoidable. The people in the middle class must prepare for their own post-retirement living arrangements, especially in the face of catastrophic illness, which will make it even more troublesome if there is not enough money available. After considering the above three points, for most people, most of their savings they made in their whole life are now empty, no further money to spend on other consumption. What to talk about the domestic demand? Even if you have demand, but if you do not have the ability, it is useless. Therefore, the middle-class, there will be some potentiality that can be exploited, it will become a fantastic opportunity for China's economic development. This depends on the actions taken by those policies makers.

In addition to the working-class people, there is another large group that we cannot ignore, that is the peasants group. China is a big agricultural country. The "three rural issues（agriculture, farming and peasants）" are what we have been trying to improve and we have achieved remarkable results. To increase the peasants' income, this is another important measure for the CPC Central Committee to stimulate domestic demand. Moreover, to accelerate the urbanization will also help increasing the income of Chinese peasants. During their spare time, peasants will find opportunities to work in the nearby town or county, this is so called "migrant workers." This group has a key role in urbanization. By perfecting the household registration system and employment system gradually, urbanization will go faster! It was said that China's urbanization lags far behind the industrialization, so there will be a variety of "labor shortage." Then, this "shortage" is going to be another historic opportunity for China's economic development.

If we want China's economy to develop further, it is not enough to rely on the hard power GDP solely. Therefore, the soft power culture will be served as a key role during promoting economic development. In the late 1980s, the dean of Kennedy Political Science School at Harvard University, Professor Joseph S. Nye Jr. found that the soft and hard power of the United States is not symmetrical among its overall strength, which is harmful to the United States. Then the concept of soft power was put forward strategically. China paid close attention to this kind of soft power theory. Chinese scholars and politicians agreed with the basic theory of Joseph Nye and accepted it congruously, they agreed that culture is an important source for the soft power and it also served as a very important role during the development of a country. He believed that the sources for soft power are also expanding constantly as time go on. For example, in this era of internet information, how to master and control the information? This kind of ability is also very important for a country's soft power (Wang, 1993; Ni, 2001).

It is quite unbalanced between different regions for China's economic and social development. It is developed much more well in the eastern area than the western area. According to the statistics, it covers over 60% of the country's large cities, industrial production bases and export processing bases within 200 kilometers of the coast in China's eastern region. The coastal population in the east accounted for 36.1% of the China's total. From 1979 to 2008, it absorbed 81.2% of the total foreign direct investments in our country. From 2005 to 2008, the regional GDP accounted for an average of 55.6% of the China's total, while the industrial added value accounted for 59.8%, Total exports accounted for about 89%. In 2009, the GDP of 11 provinces and municipalities on the eastern coast accounted for nearly 60% of the national total. In contrast, economic and social development in the western region will be much worse. According to the statistics, 12 provinces, special cities and autonomous regions in the western region of our country account for about one-third of the population of the country and 71% of the land area. However, due to natural, historical and social reasons, the economic development in the western region lags behind. Per capita GDP is only equivalent to two thirds of the national average and less than 40% of the average level in the eastern region. The western region not only has a large population, but also has abundant resources and great market potential. Its strategic position is important. To speed up the economic and social development in the western region and bring its economic and social development at or near the eastern region level is undoubtedly a very huge economy for China Development Opportunities (Ji, 2011).

The soft power culture in China can be said to be a "fertile soil" to be excavated. If it is effectively used, it can be transformed into a powerful real productive force. The value created by the American cultural industry has already exceeded the total value of heavy industry and light industry. How can Chinese culture go to the world? In the eighth chapter of this book, we will elaborate the grandness and limitations of Chinese culture completely and provide some concrete opinions on the developments and constructions of China's cultural soft power.

It is far from enough to reply on its own internal strength alone for developing China's economy. Because under such a global trend, the development of a country is inextricably linked to the world environment. Undoubtedly, peace and development are the main themes for current time. Therefore, relatively speaking, the external environment for China's future economic development will still be favorable. Although there are the hegemony and threat from the United States, the global public opinion is still justice. If the United States wants to act willfully, all the people in the world will not agree. Even the native citizens of the United States oppose the war, after all, no one wants to live a tense day in the war.

As for the opportunities for China's economic development, the above enumeration is not complete or comprehensive, and we have never thought of enumerating it endlessly. In short, only when the internal and external environment meet the development needs, can economic development be better. However, the fact is usually not satisfactory, everything does not exist perfectly. Therefore, after talking about the opportunities for China's economic development, the following discussion will certainly concern the challenge of China's economic development. This is a stereotype, but it is also necessary to solve issues completely. After all, every coin has two sides, and we cannot see the trees out of the woods, which makes the taboo of academia.

Challenges for China's economic development

Since we are talking about the challenges for China's economic development, let us skip those issues that are common to the entire world for a long time and let us talk about China's unique challenges with Chinese characteristics mainly. Only in this way can we know the gaps between China and the world more clearly and truly and clearly answer the question of whether China can become No.1.

China's administrative interventionism is an embarrassing economic phenomenon. Admittedly, this authoritarianism is quite beneficial to the economic development in certain aspects and can make up for the market defects. Of course, in a fully market-oriented economy, it is necessary for us to pay more attention to the rules of the market and appropriately reduce administrative interference. The experience told us that an economic development model characterized by an authoritarian system may be effective in completing the economic accumulation. However, as a non-balanced development model, it also pays a heavy toll on economic achievements. Such imbalances are: short-term behavior of economic development, disparity between rich and poor, corruption and civil rights issues. To be specific, the government represents some people's benefits in some ways, and most of these people that already benefited serve as officials. This is harmful to the market economy development.

There will be a series of internal problems with Chinese characteristics once the economy involves politics and power, and it is easy for the corruption to be turned up and grown rapidly by using the national power for private benefits. In China, all people know the real meaning of the word "relationship," however it may be unfamiliar for those foreigners, they do not know the actual meaning of this special word used by Chinese people, but we ourselves have a clear understanding. This is not intended to belittle or ridicule our own people. Instead, we want to warn or remind them that the market economy will exert its unique charm by reducing unnecessary administrative interference. Of course, the reduction does not mean the complete elimination. Necessary macroeconomic regulation and control are indispensable. A few years ago, it turned out to be a hubbub for Guangzhou Pharmaceutical regarding the Jiaduobao and Wanglaoji trademarks, because Guangzhou Pharmaceutical is a state-owned enterprise, while Jiaduobao is a private enterprise, and finally the trademark was given to Guangzhou Pharmaceutical according to the concerning laws, otherwise there would be a loss for state-owned assets. Professor Lang Xianping pointed out that "This is a win-win thing, Jiaduobao produces Red Pot Wanglaoji, and Guangzhou Pharmaceutical produces Green Box Wanglaoji, but now it actually became a zero-sum game. If all act in favor of the state-owned enterprises, who would dare to go with the state-owned enterprises in future?" This issue is worth pondering. It is going to be imperative to change the government functions!

In connection with the administrative interventionism, there is an phenomena known as "official standard, " which is also a major challenge to China's economic development. It is not very accurate to call it a challenge, it is a major obstacle, a "cancer" that affects social fairness and justice. Of course, the thought "official standard" has its historical reasons. The Chinese traditional ideology that lasts for more than 2,000 years is one of the reasons. When talking about the "official standard," some people say it is a kind of consciousness, some think it is a kind of culture, some think it is an ideology, and others define it differently. In fact, the meanings of "official standard" are referring these following two points: one is the official-oriented consciousness existing in people's minds and the other is the official-oriented phenomenon driven by the official consciousness(zhu,2008). In their minds, the officials' benefits are over all others, they protect the benefits of officials at the beginning and in the end. Fortunately, what we advocate now is "people-oriented" rather than "official-oriented." When the day comes, Chinese people will no longer be forced to demolish their houses and the private rights will no longer be misused. The people can accuse officials with no difficulties. By that time, China's "people-based standard" will be corrected truly.

When speaking about China's economy, we must talk about China's real estate, because a large part of China's economy comes from the real estate market, this phenomenon is just like: One piece of hair gets pulled and then the whole body will be affected. The necessary regulation for the real estate market cannot be relaxed, otherwise it is very likely to cause real estate blowout. On the face of it, China's real estate is so hot because of its large population and its scarcity. In fact, it is wrong to look at the problem if we just look at the appearance without seeing the inside. In fact, we have vast territory, and it is very easy to realize that let our Chinese residents have their own houses. However, the housing problem is so serious in China. The housing system problems are just the reasons. The "restriction order" issued by China's government is a best remedy for it.

Since ancient times, the Chinese have been paying attention to settling down for their own lives. The house is a recognized "symbol of stability." For most people, the house represents a kind of security. Under the guidance of such ideas, China's rich people started to buy houses madly and made money by selling houses. Then those "house slaves," who were mostly working-class people who will suffer finally. As a result, the polarization will be accelerated even further. The rich will use the real estate to seek more benefits, and the poor will have to pay a higher price for it. The most important thing to do is to control the real estate market strictly, to compress the real estate bubble, thus to slow down the economic development and to return to economic rationality. At the same time, the laws supporting real estate should also be further improved. Only when the legislation and law enforcement instruments are built, will the economy not be in ups and downs so that a country can move forward at a stable speed.

Compared with the American economy, most of the China's economy rely on the material economy. The development potential of the material economy is very limited, it does not have a huge vertical and horizontal extension like the virtual economy. Some of China's economic has been exploited and plundered by the virtual economy from the United States. Why do we say so? You can have a look at China's development model, "manufacturing power," "Made in China," this means China is a country that produces the material products, but the United States owns the virtual economy such as named brands, intellectual properties and so on, plus her own innovative technologies, as well as the monopoly of the United States dollars, so US will be able to gain the benefits with ease. Therefore, China still has a long way to go in terms of virtual economy.

It is both an opportunity and a challenge for China to speed up international exchanges and expand the economy abroad. At present, China has set up more than 12,000 overseas direct investment enterprises in 174 countries and regions, with a total number of over 4 million overseas workers. In 2009, China used a total of 90.03 billion U.S. dollars of foreign capital and its exports amounted to 1.216 trillion U.S.

dollars, ranking the first in the world. In 2011, China imported 254 million tons of crude oil. At the same time, China's overseas investments are still increasing. China's economic development is significantly dependent on overseas resources and markets. Therefore, if China cannot protect foreign assets, international energy and trade channels and overseas workers effectively, China's economic development and the economic benefits will be challenged heavily(Zhao,2012). To promote the overall open pattern and perfect the system of China's foreign trade is crucial to the opening of our country at this stage. President Xi Jinping proposed at the 19th National Congress that we shall focus on the "One Belt and One Road" construction, stick to the principle "building and sharing jointly," adhere to the principle "co-construction and sharing," and strengthen openness and cooperation, expand foreign trade and foster a new mode of trade format. To innovate the methods of overseas investment, promote international cooperation in production capacity and form a global trade, investment, production and service network and accelerate training international economic cooperation and competition. Only by keeping pace with the outward expansion of the economy, will the China's foreign economy and the people's interests be protected. This is also an important problem that needs to be paid attention to at the present stage of foreign trade.

As for the question "Can China become No.1 or not?" In addition to talking about the advantages of China, it is also necessary to ask the current No.1, that is the United States. The formidable opponent will undermine the competitiveness of China's economic development. The United States is a country with great natural resources. US has the third largest land area in the world, the fourth largest forest area in the world, the fifth largest land available per capita in the world, the 12th largest proven oil reserve in the world, ranking the fifth in the world and the coal reserve ranks first in the world. Moreover, US attitude to China's economic development will also affect the external development environment. On June 5, 2012, the United States published the "Report on the Development of Military Power in China," and on June 16 and 18, China's Shenzhou Ninth satellite got launched and docked with Tiangong satellite, this brought concern in the United States, Japan and South Korea and a new round of "China threat "argument. Another example: In 2015, China led the establishment of the Asian Infrastructure Investment Bank (AIIB), which was established to promote the interoperability and economic integration in Asia and to strengthen the cooperation between China and other Asian countries and regional cooperation. It was distorted by the foreign media as the Chinese version of the "Marshall Plan." In addition, to defend its supremacy, the United States suppressed the development of China. The United States reached a Trans-Pacific Partnership agreement (TPP) with 12 countries such as Japan and Australia etc. and set a series of rules and conditions for China to stop China from joining. It can be said precisely because of the irreconcilability between China and the western countries that China cannot obtain the identity of the "peaceful rise" in the international community no matter how it is advocated (Zhao, 2012).

In addition to the challenges discussed above, China also has the following problems such as the population aging, the extensive economic growth, the employment issues and the loss of cheap labor. All these problems will affect the future development of China's economy and China needs to change its methods for economic development, to strengthen independent innovation, to improve the employment system, to think of ways to avoid the loss of cheap labor.

The temptation to become No.1

Why do all countries in the world strive to become economic powers, and want to become the dominant global economy like the United States? Of course, because it is full of temptations to become No.1, it will own the economic power that other countries cannot catch up with. Otherwise, who would be so stupid to be the No. One in the world?

The United States financial hegemony brought enormous benefits to the Americans and has surpassed the benefits gained from the material economic growth in the United States. This is mainly due to the dominance of the U.S. dollar. Because the U.S. dollar is the world currency, if the United States issues it, products from all over the world can be bought with green papers by the United States. In addition, the government can get money globally by issuing the U.S. bonds and trading the American company stocks. And this was only a string of numb figures for the United Sates, which was increased by this means. The United States has always been very clear about its liabilities because this will in no way affect the U.S. economy. The United States has ever interfered with the exchange rate of Japanese Yen through its U.S. dollar supremacy. The "Plaza Accord" is the testimony. A "conspiracy" with regards to the Yen appreciation has caused Japan's economy to be unstable. All the countries today are worried whether their domestic currencies will be the next "target" or not. A couple of countries led by the United States are asking for the appreciation of the Renminbi, which seems to imply that these developed countries are doing the same as what they did before once again. China still can say no currently, but who can guarantee that China's economy can always say no to power? After all, the economic strength is the most important thing! Without economic strength, we can only live in miserable conditions where people are pauperized. Given the enormous benefits like the dollar's monopoly, will the Renminbi become the next world currency? We can only wait and see.

In addition to the economic benefits brought by the world currency U.S. dollar, the United States economic hegemony can also affect the rights and prestige of the international economic organizations. The United States never denies its "double standard." in terms of the trade policy. On the one hand, the United States has no scruples in giving trade subsidies to its disadvantaged industries. On the other hand, the United States insists on applying anti-subsidy barriers to its trading partners. Although this "pendulum" trade policy of the United States brought about some loss, it obtained lots of "relative interests" when it suppressed the opponent countries. This hegemony strategy that looked like "Kill 1,000 enemies and 800 self-loss" guaranteed the U.S. economic interests, and the position as the world economy leader was kept (Cheng,2005). The United States is more afraid than any other country to be surpassed and fears that its economic hegemony will not be guaranteed because US knows all kinds of "sweetness" brought about by economic hegemony.

The supremacy strategies and tactics of the United States differ at various stages and in different fields. However, it can be summed up as follows: to lead the world through establishing universal international organizations; to control the global economy under the banner of national self-determination and trade liberalization; to avoid direct colonial rule but to rule the entire world; to maintain its financial dominance by keeping the hegemony via issuing dollars (Li, 2009).

In the international arena, the United States has always acted as the "world policeman." In a sense, the United States played a significant role in establishing and maintaining the international order, although this order is unfair and flawed. Therefore, to perfect the new economic order, it requires more economic discourse power, we must speak in strength! The world economy follows the law of the jungle as well, this rule is so called survival of the fittest.

Of course, we always oppose hegemonies and power politics, but here we are talking about the No.1 in the economic area, and this is different from the political hegemony. It is recognized widely that economic hegemony can bring economic benefits to its own country, especially in formulating and operating the economic system. Whether China's economy will become the world's leader or not, what we need is a natural result excluding all the other abnormal ways. Even in the face of such an enormous temptation, we still must abide by the guidelines for economic development. As for the world leader, we shall think of it like this: "It is my luck if I own it, while it is my fate if I lose it."

Can China be No.1?

After a series of questions have been discussed, another question we want to know is: Can China become No.1? According to the current development situation in China and the international situation, China has some basic conditions to become the No.1, but it is not sufficient. Therefore, we think China can become the No.1, but not now, maybe soon. There will be all kinds of pressure in addition to enjoying a variety of benefits after being the No.1. Therefore, to become the No.1 is not as easy as what you think. The pies will not be fallen from the sky, this principle is well known by the world leader. Certainly, there must be a price to pay to become the No.1, and sometimes the cost is extremely high. The financial crisis in the United States can be regarded as a potential harm caused by its economic hegemon. Only when it has been accumulated heavily will it erupt and its power will exceed the normal economic scope. After becoming the No.1, it will be more difficult to maintain. This is so-called "It is easy to fight for sovereignty over rivers and mountain, but it is difficult to keep it from being robbed again." Think about it carefully and deeply, does China still want to become the No.1?

Napoleon has ever said, "Soldiers who do not want to be generals are not good soldiers." For China, the development of economy should not be disturbed too much by human factors. Whether China can become the No.1 or not, this could not be controlled by one or two.

As we all know that it is not so easy and fast as what we think if China wants to overtake the United States or replace the United States as the world's economic No.1. For now, China still needs to move forward stably under the world economic order led by United States. Only by doing so can China devote all its efforts to development. In recent years, the United States has helped China a little bit on economic development. After all, the United States has maintained a relatively stable space for China. From this point of view, the United States is still quite "authentic".

In the face of the topic "When will China overtake the United States?" the most appropriate attitude should be talking more about the issues and less about catch-up, having more senses of worry and less pride, having more senses to go ahead with reform and innovation and less self-defending. Sometimes, intentionally planted flowers would not blossom, unintentional plated trees would be grown up rapidly. All the Chinese people know this truth very well.

China, as a traditional East Asian country, it is understandable that China wants to regain its position as an enormous power during the peaceful rise of China. However, if it is going to be excluded or suppressed by other countries, the reason is that the other countries are considering whether China will become a king or a hegemon, will China bring peace or war to the world? Perhaps when we return to that part "the peaceful rise of China's economy," we will have a clear and definite answer.

Chapter 2:

It Is at a Price to Be the No.1

There are some very interesting phenomena in both animal world and human world. That is, there will always be a so-called leader intentionally or unintentionally, such as the king of beasts and the class leaders, who become the leaders of large and small groups. Of course, we hope there is no such kind of leaders, no classes and no hierarchies in the world. It is equal between different countries, they can respect and love each other. Unfortunately, this is only a wishful thinking of some countries, it is not possible to reach a consensus. It is necessary to select a leader that have the leading ability for this world that contains hundreds of countries. However, who should be the leader? Which country can take this responsibility? It cannot be decided by one or two countries. To be the leader is not easy, because there will be many countries that would not agree with the leader and may fight against the leader, it is not easy to convince them, it is needed to have a strong hard power and soft power to convince the public. Otherwise, some countries will refuse to accept it, then this kind of leader will not be stable, will be replaced by another country probably. The hard power contains the economic strength, the political power, the military strength, the scientific and technological strength and so on. The hard power can be easily seen and found, however the soft power is different, it cannot be seen or detected so easily, the soft power is mainly referring to the cultural power, brand strength and so on. Nowadays the United Sates is the leader undoubtedly, because the hard power of the United States is unquestionable, in addition, its soft power, such as Hollywood's cultural strength, KFC, McDonald's brand strength and so on. This is also well known by the world people.

In addition to the United States, which country can play the role of the world leader? Or is it possible for China to overtake the United States as the world leader? Is China eligible to be the world leader? No free lunch in the world, the truth or principle is the same when talking about who is suitable to be the world leader. China is now the second largest economic entity in the world. If China is to attack the throne of the world leader, is China ready? Have we ever thought of the difficulties and obstacles we may encounter on this road? And have distinguished between friends and foes? All these kinds of problems will come one after another. Perhaps when we really can answer these questions well, it will be a step closer to the world leader for China.

Although all countries know that it is at a price to be the world leader, however it is very paradoxical that all countries have sharpened their heads to become the world leader. If you do not believe it, let us look at the United States first, he has always advertised himself as the world police. No matter what happened in a certain of country, it seemed that it was relevant to the United States. Is this still not obvious that he wants to be the world leader? And indeed, the United States is indeed the leader in the world today because it is incontrovertible for now. Let us look at Japan, this country has been hiding in the United States this big tree for a long time, recharging himself, this is just an example of sleeping on the brushwood and tasting the gall – to nurse vengeance. Who is willing to be attached to another country for a lifetime? Japan's strategy was to fool the United States into fighting with China first and then to gain the benefits from it lately. Then Japan can fight with Russia and the United States after turning China into his base and then to realize the hegemonic ambitions which had not been realized during its militaristic period. These are the strategies that already been established in Japan for both the Liberal Democratic Party and the Democratic government. Their ambitions are waiting for the opportunity to get rid of the United States, surpass the United States and then become the world leader.

There is another economic entity that can rival the United States, that is the European Union. However, since the European Union is composed of many independent sovereign states, it is still quite difficult to become the world leader in the form of an alliance. The so-called "The spirit is willing, but the flesh is weak." is probably the current state of the European Union, the current European debt crisis is a big headache for the European Union, not to mention the shortcomings of its internal economic system, which are hard to overcome. Not many cases, other countries are without exception, if there is an opportunity to be the world leader, no country is willing to abdicate. So, to put it in a nutshell, China is also bound to join this "grab-head" camp, and for now, China is also quite powerful. After more than 30 years of foreign economic development, China has now made fantastic progress. In the world economy, it is also one of the world's economic engines that can be tied with the United States as it becomes the second-largest economic entity in the world by leaps and bounds from a trivial developing country that was not worth mentioning. It takes the road of surpassing the United States in time eventually.

China want to become the world leader; this dream is reasonable. Like in the race, no one wants to be the last one, everyone wants to beat the opponent. However, the so-called the shopping malls are like the battlefields and the large-scale commercial warfare of the entire world may eventually result in a costly economic competition and even military competition. Therefore, we must ask ourselves: should we become the world leader? Is China ready for the challenge?

Surrounded by a C-ring or O-ring?

The global financial crisis in 2008 pushed China to the center of the international political arena and because China's total economic output surpassed Japan, this aroused the world's attention to the strategy of China. Dai Xu, a famous Chinese military expert, said that China is being surrounded by a C-ring. The C-ring mainly refers to the U.S. encirclement beginning from Japan, passing from its neighboring countries in South China Sea and India, and then to Afghanistan. In the era of the Cold War, the United States encircled China strategically with only the first and second island chains and were basically in a defensive state. However, China showed a strategic offensive to the United States relying on the victory of the war to resisting U.S. aggression and aid

Korea. As time go on, nowadays the United States not only defended its original line of defense, but also extended to the Indian Ocean and South Asia, West Asia and Central Asia in a "C" -shaped (Dai, 2009). The difference between C-ring and O-ring is referring to the northern part of China whether Russia has joined the encirclement or not. Those who think that China is surrounded by O-ring believe accordingly that Russia's attitude towards the United States has tended to ease from its hostility in the past, and agreed to the U.S. siege strategy indirectly. However, from a national interest point of view, Russia is also aware of this truth." If the lips are gone, the teeth will be cold." So, Russia's attitude is not fixed for now, his position is not clear yet. In fact, it is not hard to see that either the C-shaped or the O-shaped encircled encirclement is due to the United States this superpower. As for the rapid development of China in recent years, the United States has taken notice of it and kept it in mind. It has been eyeing the scene all the time and has never relaxed its vigilance.

If it is as What Colonel Dai Xu said, China is surrounded by a C-shaped ring, how has this encircled situation formed? What is the chain of interest between them? Is it possible for China to break through? Let us look at the starting point of this C-ring first, that is, Japan. Japan has always attached itself to the United States, and we all know that Japan wants to use the power of the United States to compete with China. In the meantime, however, the United States also wants to use Japan's strength to stabilize its position in Asia because of its common interests. The commonalities of interests have tied Japan and the United States closely so that the alliance between these two countries can maintain for such a long time. Japan is an important station for the United States to realize the maritime encirclement towards China. The United States has continuously connived Japan's strategic attack. First it transferred Okinawa to the Japanese army and then, together with Japan, prepared to attack the island with only 110 kilometers from Taiwan. Diaoyu Islands this problem, led to the United States onlookers and even flare-ups once again.

August 15th is a memorable day for the Chinese people because the Japanese government surrendered to China on this day of more than 60 years ago. On August 15, 2012, some Hong Kong people were celebrating by landing on the Diaoyu Islands but they were attacked by the Japanese troops, siege and even seizure happened. In the meantime, on August 18, 2012, Japan's "Soul Mission" also arrived in the waters near the Diaoyu Islands, and nine Japanese boarded the Diaoyu Islands. Then Japan attempted to nationalize the Diaoyu Islands, which put this incident to the culmination. What the most ridiculous is that Japanese Prime Minister Yoshihiko Noda said in an interview with U.S. media on September 7, 2012 that the Japanese government was going to nationalize it, the reason is that they wanted to maintain management steadily. We just want to ask them: The Diaoyu Islands is not belonging to you Japan, how do you have the rights to manage it? However, Japan did not listen to us, he continued to do everything they wanted. On the morning of September 10, 2012, the Japanese government held a cabinet meeting and decided to use 20.5 billion Japanese Yens to purchase and nationalize the Diaoyu Islands, North Island and South Island from the so-called landowner.

On September 10, 2012, in order to protest, the government of the People's Republic of China made a statement on the Diaoyu Islands as well as the baseline of the territorial waters of the Diaoyu Islands and its affiliated islands. Also, the various democratic parties issued a joint statement. However, these statements do not seem to make any senses. On September 11, 2012, Japan signed a "sale and purchase agreement" with the so-called land rights holders formally on Diaoyu Islands. On the morning of September 12, Japanese Chief Cabinet Secretary Fujimura said at a press conference that the so-called nationalization registration of land on the three islands of the Diaoyu Islands has been completed and the landowners have officially changed into countries. In this case, many questions came as follows: who are the landowners that occur suddenly? When did the Diaoyu Islands become private? What right does Japan must carve up the inherent territories of the victorious nations as a belligerent country? ... This series of challenging acts is undoubtedly angered the Chinese people and the Chinese government.

It is reported according to the Voice of China Newsletters that from August 21, 2012 to September 26 this period, according to the proposal of the United States Marine Corps, the military exercises were to be held by the Japan Ground Self-Defense Force. The exercise area and the island combat environment are like the Diaoyu Islands, with a similar amphibious combat environment. Whatever the purpose is, the United States and Japan held military exercises at such an opportune moment. Japan's "island-grabbing" rehearsal? Or as Japan said the military exercises are not targeted at any particular country? As China's position, vigilance is something that must be done and defensive measures are indispensable. The rest is the contest of strength.

Let us have a look at the South China Sea countries that have never been so peaceful. The issue of the South China Sea is essentially a dispute over the sovereignty of the South China Sea islands between China and some Southeast Asian countries. Its focus is about the ownership of the Nansha Islands. However, both from a historical point of view and from a legal point of view, China's sovereignty over the South China Sea islands is indisputable. The sovereignty claimed by the Vietnam, the Philippines and the Malaysia is not reasonable and malicious acts that do not respect the facts. In 2011, the United States, Southeast Asia and the ASEAN countries were very busy in their military exercises in the South China Sea. In the name of anti-terrorism, the United States dug China's corner publicly to pull all the countries together which have territorial disputes with China to form an alliance in the South China Sea. On the other hand, in the South China Sea, several countries are desperately trying to develop cutting-edge submarines and long-range warplanes while the United States sit behind the scenes leisurely.

Finally let us look at the end of this C-ring, that is, India, Afghanistan and other countries. These are the United States' land bases for the C-shaped encirclement in China. From the supports provided by Pakistan, Afghanistan, the Indian Ocean base and India and the 18 military bases in Central Asia, the United States tries to reach out to Mongolia and at the same time directly threaten China Xinjiang and Tibet. India and Pakistan are even nuclear-weapon states with frequent exchanges with the United States and even trying to build a military alliance. Regarding India, a rapidly developing country, he has ever suffered from the phobia in China, but he has also drawn lessons from China's development practice. That is, he always regards China's development as a threat to its own country and fear that China will encircle it. Therefore, the United States can find a breakthrough point in such a "win-loss" mentality in India and act as a so-called umbrella.

From a realistic point of view, in a brief period, China will still face the alliance composed of the United States, Europe, Japan, India and some other Asian countries. In the event of a military conflict, these countries may stand with the United States instead of China. They must be vigilant in every country's situation and maximize their own strategic survival space, in addition to paying close attention to the actions of the world leader like the United States. We should adopt a pro-active strategy to find development spaces instead of being surrounded by the U.S. strategy.

At the Chinese Communist 19th CPC National Congress which was just closed, President Xi Jinping made remarks on the major events of the past year, such as holding the first "One Belt One Road" summit on international cooperation, initiating the founding of the Asia Infrastructure Investment Bank, the APEC Informal Meeting, the 20 The summit of leaders of the Group, the Xiamen summit of BRICS leaders, the Xiamen meeting of BRICS leaders, and the summit of AsiaInfo. They proposed that all-round diplomatic work should be conducted in an all-round way to promote the diplomacy with Chinese characteristics comprehensively to form an all-round, multi-level and three-dimensional Diplomatic layout for the development of our country to create a good external environment. We should keep good relations with neighboring countries based on finding and cultivating the common interests between the two countries and expand our friends circle constantly so that we can get the superiority in our national development strategy and expand our strategic living space.

Who is willing to treat China as an ally?

Watching from China's interior, China is really surrounded. That is because, to a certain extent, we have envisioned the surrounding environment as an imaginary enemy, but ignored the strategy to turn enemies into friends. If we watch from the outside, there is no such absolute encirclement. Because these neighboring countries have their own respective interests and troubles, it is still quite difficult for them to form an overall force to oppose China together. Every country has its own thoughts: If China gets captured by the United States, what benefits can our country receive? Will the situation be better than now? Therefore, China is not isolated absolutely. We want to find a country that can become an ally with China, or even if such a possibility exists, we must work hard to realize it. Look at the problem from another perspective, perhaps we can find a different breakthrough point.

We must understand that it is very important to have advanced and powerful military capabilities to become the world leader, but it is even more important to have allies and friends. The reason is that if we face the attacks from multiple countries, we will become so weak no matter how powerful our military strength is. Therefore, given the status of the United States as the world leader, China will probably reach political compromise and consensus with the United States in the future as China is on the way to be the superpower. But it is hard to find reliable strategic partners, the biggest difficulty is how to maintain good relations with the other countries while establishing new friendly relations with the United States. In other words, China must establish good relations with many countries that are friendly with the United States currently. Only when China weaves up a complex network composed of new political relations will it be expected to become the world leader economically without being blocked by other countries. Similarly, only after finding a true strategic allied army will China be able to take over the United States and become the world leader really and truly. To take a step back, even if

China cannot become the world leader, China will not be "returned to its original state" and will regress for several years. Without the allies, it is like an egg hit by a stone. It can only be self-defeating. Therefore, China should consider it thoroughly before making any decisions, who will be willing to become China's ally on earth?

Regarding the ally, maybe Russia is the best candidate, as his position is still not fixed. We cannot underestimate the key role that the Russia can play in the arguments whether China was surrounded by a C-shaped ring or O-shaped ring. It has been for a long time for the friendly relations between China and Russia. In the two big camps named capitalism and socialism, China and Russia fought side by side and enjoyed mutual benefits. Moreover, these two countries have much more cooperation intentions due to the special geographic location between China and Russia. So, what an embarrassment it is for Russia in this C-shaped encirclement caused by the United States? If the United States build a "C-shaped" encirclement around China which is starting from Japan, going through the countries around the South China Sea and India, and then to Afghanistan and Central Asia, in this case, then the United States can build another "C-shaped" encirclement with Russia, which is starting from Central Asia, bypassing the Arctic belt, Ukraine and the Baltic states to Alaska and finally ending in Japan. The "C-shaped" encirclement to Russia, and the "C-shaped" encirclement to China, so now there will be 2 encirclements. As a result, the United States is to build an O-shaped encirclement with China and Russia.

It is an indisputable fact that the China and Russia are strategic partners. The national interests are above all with regards to the international relations although there were some historical disputes between China and Russia. The aggressive external oppression from the United States has brought more and more common interests between China and Russia, and both China and Russia should make it clear. China and Russia have had an unpleasant history and perhaps an unpleasant future. However, the bridge between the past and the future is now. At a grim moment of momentous common danger faced by China and Russia, it is not wise to emphasize the past or to talk about the future blindly.

After all, both will have a bright future if they are working together to overcome the difficulties.

In the northern part of China, we have a partner Russia who seems to be an ally, is there any potential partners in other areas around China? We must treat differently for different countries or different regions. In the face of heavy siege, it is important to figure out who is the potential friend and who is the potential enemy! In the east of China, there is a rival that may break out at any time, that is Japan. Although South Korea is a threat as well in a certain degree, however the South Korea is not as aggressive as Japan. At this moment, it is particularly important to get potential friends to deal with the potential rivals in future. We must make Russia feel that it is better to cooperate with China rather than Japan. Japan has made enemies everywhere under the protection of the United States. He has very small territory, but he is ambitious. Until now, each time Japan requests Russia to return the so-called northern four islands of Japan, it also keeps an open eye on China's green fertile Manchuria, North China, the rich southern China and Taiwan, and Russia's Siberia and the Far East. Both China and Russia should make it very clear that Japan is a potential opponent for China and for Russia.

In the southern part of China, aside from the chaotic South China Sea, China needs to strengthen its relations with ASEAN. What being gratifying is that it seems that the Sino-Burma relations have been changing well smoothly after the general election in Myanmar. Vietnam has already been governed by the pro-China forces. Both Thailand and Cambodia are very friendly to China and they both need the big brother China to regulate and appease them. Cambodia, Laos and Nepal are all in the socialist camp headed by China, which has created a very good friendship alliance with China. India's chauvinism and expansionism have led to its isolation in South Asian countries to a certain degree. However, it is not the case that there is no conflict between China and India. India and China are quite similar, such as the population, the speed of development, the problems that may have been encountered in the development, and so on. Therefore, China and India can make common progress and friendly development. As for China, India should have less fear, but more cooperation. How can we allow two large developing countries in Asia? China should let India understand gradually that his worries are useless and unnecessary.

Regarding the western part of China, it is now in a coexistence state of active and passive. The situation in the west and north of China has gotten better and better since the Shanghai Security Cooperation Organization was established. From the news, we know there are many overseas media analysts said that the United States has lost his superiority in the Middle East after the " Middle East turmoil" because the Egyptian President Hosni Mubarak was fallen from power. The Iranian issue is going to be faced probably by China, Russia and the United States. Obviously, China and Russia will gain the upper hand on their geographical location. While Iran is the last country in the Middle East that has not been conquered by the United States, this means that there will be a huge hidden danger for the Middle East. Undoubtedly this is a good opportunity for China to find new allies.

If all goes well in the next two decades, it is going to be suspected by some people that China may become stronger than any of the neighboring countries but cannot be stronger than the total power composed of these neighboring countries. Not to mention the United States. This is the fact that China will need to face in future. On the one hand, "hide one's capacities and bide one's time," this will not improve China's existing situation. On the other hand, aggressiveness will not only damage China's long-term interests, but also will result in its neighbors get together which will be an opportunity for the United States. Good neighbors are based on fencing, which is to define the boundaries. China needs to establish an open society and to settle its disputes peacefully with its neighbors. Terrorism can be used directly or indirectly if necessary, but it must be used based on the fairness (Ding, 2010). Both hard and soft skills are needed by China, to grow stronger and stronger.

Is China ready to be the world leader?

After analyzing the external environment in China, let us return to China's own problems. If the external environment is in the neutral case we are neither under siege, nor being helped, let us ask ourselves: Are we ready to be the world leader? Is China surrounded by its own predicament to some extent?

During the time China was developed very well, there will always be some discordant voices. Some pessimistic comments on China's economy appear in the world media from time to time, such as China's economy will be like the Japan's economy in the late 1980s, and China is risking blowing the real estate market and raw material market bubble in exchange for Economic development and so on. There is no doubt that there is a high degree of similarity in the economic development between current China and the old Japan in the 1980s, such as: the rapid economic development led by exports, the obvious lack of consumer demand, the appreciation of the domestic currency to attract large inflows of foreign funds, the easing of monetary policy Guarantee sufficient funds, the relative lack of real economy investment opportunities, the stocks prices and housing prices soared while the price for general products are stable, the domestic enterprises expanded overseas.

In the late 1980s, the monetary policy was tightened suddenly and this resulted in the burst of Japan's bubble economy. In contrast, in China, although the government emphasized from time to time that the macroeconomic policies should be of continuity and stability, the structural adjustment and the fine-tuning of policies have been carried out quietly. However, it is not as big as Japan in the 1980s. So, in this context, will China really be like the Japan's economy and plunge into a long-term depression in the future? If not, how will China avoid it(Zhou,2010)? Therefore, even if we will not follow the footsteps of Japan's economy, but there are so many social problems need to be faced, China's preparations for being a world leader are not enough. Let us cite a few examples. We can explain many problems without going into details one by one.

In terms of China's infrastructure, it is still weak. The roads and bridges collapsing accidents that happened recently made people feel it is a big threat to walk on the roads. It is a good thing that our China's economy is being developed rapidly. But we need to ensure the quality, if we only focus on the speed of development without quality guarantee, is not it a stupid mistake like putting the cart before the horse and digging the grave? Poor public facilities and worrying construction quality, such engineering problems also exist in the real estate market, which is the largest contributor to the economy. It is true that the fictitious economy can bring simultaneous growth of the real economy, but which one should be developed first? This is particularly important. Anyone who wants to become the world leader needs to solve this problem first: Is his country's hardware good enough? Because in a country that does not rely on hardware, the high-tech software is to be seemed useless. Fortunately, our country is a socialist country, the government can do a lot of things in infrastructure construction compared with the capitalist countries. However, at the same time, we have a problem need to be faced, that is, the leaders of socialist countries must devote themselves to public duty wholehearted. Otherwise, the corruption caused by their rights will become a huge stone that blocks China from becoming the world leader.

In addition to the serious infrastructure problems, the expenses of taxation in China are also widely criticized. It is asserted that it is the highest in the world and thus China is a well-deserved taxes country. Our tax is high, but the expenses of taxation are more terrible, the government taxes have affected everyone's life. For example, the second half of 2011, for those vegetable farmers, their cabbages cannot be sold out at some places in Shandong province and Hebei province, no one would like to buy the cabbages even if the price was as low as one cent. However, on the vegetable market, the price for cabbage has not been decreased. The cabbage price was 10 cents per kilogram when the vegetable farmers sold it to the first level wholesale market, and then the price was 24 cents per kilogram on the second level wholesale market which is just near the first level wholesale market, but when the consumers bought it from the vegetable markets, the price was 40 cents per kilogram. From 10 cents to 40 cents, there were 30 cents that have been robbed by the government via tax method. In one word, the tax we pay is the highest one in the world.

Therefore, tax evasion has become an unavoidable option for the Chinese people to survive in many areas of China. Some people in the financial industry who have concerned about the economic problems in China have asked us a question: Why the tax revenue in China has soared despite the obvious economic downturn in China? Does such an abnormal phenomenon mean that some of the economic truths are not applicable any more in China? Although we did not know how to answer this question at the time, now let us think of it thoroughly, under the premise that the economic environment has deteriorated, most countries, will reduce their taxes substantially, but China's tax revenue does not seem to be affected by this rule. This is puzzling. Look at the history of China, almost every strong dynasty was extremely focused on cutting taxes on people, but why do not we do the same? We have no doubt about the role of taxation. We can use it for public utilities or for adjusting the gap between the rich and the poor. However, when the general citizens cannot afford the high taxes any more, should the China's policies makers take a good consideration then?

It is undeniable that China has accumulated a great deal of problems in the economic development in the past 30 years. This kind of high growth, which is unsustainable at this stage, can be sustained today because economic problems have been transformed into social and environmental issues. This is like "rob Peter to pay Paul," and the banking industry, the manufacturing industry, the real estate industry and the big state-owned enterprises have passed away many costs. The government has also cut spending on education, health care and pension, and the society, the environment and the population are under enormous pressure. It is always from quantitative change to qualitative change for the development of things. It is not hard to imagine that in China, there must be a social crisis and an environmental crisis before the economic crisis occurs. Unlike the developed countries, China will not cause social problems due to the economic crisis. This is what the most analysts overlooked. Economic growth is still normal, this does not mean that there is no crisis, Moreover, the economy seems good, under the strong intervention by the statistics department. But the crisis is coming soon(Ding,2010). Therefore, what we should do at this stage is not to emphasize economic development blindly, is not to clamor for being the world leader, but to work step by step and solve the various environmental and social problems we are facing now.

The Third World War?

If China surpasses the United States and become the "world leader" in the future, the United States may not "transfer power to China peacefully." This means that in the process of becoming the world leader, is there a war that will happen inevitably? Even if it is alarmist, we should discuss it. Of course, it will always be the case that China will not wage a war on any country. However, we cannot prevent the other countries to wage wars. For example, the United States replaced Britain peacefully in the 19th century and became the world leader. But this is not suitable for China, China will not replace the United States through this way after China is risen peacefully. Because both the political model, religious beliefs and languages in the United States and the United Kingdom are quite similar, but the situation between China and the United States is not the same. Professor Joseph Nye in the Harvard University has pointed out in his article entitled "The rise of China does not mean war," that those who think China and the United States can cooperate peacefully, are considering the rising model of China to be too simple. It is not concluded by the United States or China with regards to the rise of China, because the other countries may not believe it. All countries in the world will "have their own way of thinking of things", so there will be another kind of conjecture about the upcoming outbreak of World War III. Why is China to become the world's strategic focus?

From the history, we know it is an inevitability but not a coincidence that the strategic focus was transferred from one country to another country. Before the middle of the 20th century, the focus of world strategy was concentrated in Europe. The reason was that the major powers vied for the international industrial hegemony, especially the British Empire. It is regarded as its heyday at that time, and the Britain was called "the empire on which the sun never sets," and it was the No.1

colonial power at that time. And then in the following 20 years, the world's strategic focus shifted from Europe to the Middle East. It was the competition between the two superpowers, that is the United States and the Soviet Union, they vied for the international industrial hegemony and petroleum resources, which made the Middle East a strategic focus. By the late 1990s, the focus of the world strategic shifted from the Middle East to the Asia Pacific region. China became a focus center. Now, why did the focus of world strategy shift like this? This is because the world economic structure has changed. Economic foundation determines the superstructure, the economy has always been the core and cornerstone of politics. Before and after World War II, the focus of the world economy was in Europe. However, after the oil crisis and the international currency crisis in the 1970s and 1980s, the economy development of western countries was paused for some time.

At the same time, the economy of Japan has been developing rapidly, and then China's economy grew even faster. These comprehensive forces not only affect the economic development in the Asia-Pacific region, but also become the locomotive of world economic development, which will change the global strategic structure inevitably. The United States and Europe will be worried inevitably that if things continue to go this way, the world will be ruled by the Asian countries instead of the Western countries. As a result, unexpectedly, the United States and the entire West have shifted their strategic focus to the Asia-Pacific region and are ready to use various measures to suppress the development momentum in Asia. That is why the United States forced the appreciation of the Japan Yen, that is why the "Plaza Accord," has been issued, that is why the Japanese economy was stagnant. And that is why Soros created a financial crisis in Southeast Asia.

Now, the historical scene seems to be repeating itself. The United States has kept its huge foreign exchange in China and Japan in its own hands, through some secret ways. As Japan has been willing to be controlled fully by the United States, the U.S. strategists have concentrated their wisdom and turned to pondering and torturing China (Dai,2009). From this, if the Third World War really happens it will be a "full-scale drama" jointly directed by the capitalist countries headed by the United States. Look at the fact that the United States intercepts resources purchased by China, robs China's wealth via his deformed real estate industry, and at the same time prepares to take advantage of the dollar trap to swallow up the achievements of China's 30 years developments in one fell swoop. They all know now that they just vomit blood while anesthetizing like a leech locust. China might take the initiative to participate in this hypothetical World War III, when China recognizes the debt trap of the United States and when the power of the people is strong enough, until then the war is probably to break out.

In fact, whether the war break out or not, this is more important than whether the economy of the country is strong enough to threaten the security of the world. What the most important is whether China and the United States can adopt a calm and rational attitude to accept this economic competition between the two countries. On the one hand, the United States should not regard China as his enemy; on the other hand, China should not be arrogant because of the well-developed economy. From the objective point of view, the power comparison between countries is relative, and the shift in economic growth is an objective law of economic development. Moreover, although the gross national product is an important benchmark for measuring the overall national strength of a country, however it is not the only measure. After the transposition of the two countries, the United States will still be ahead of China in many other aspects of measuring overall national strength, and it will still be a long way to go for China changing from big but not strong to not only big but also strong(Chen,2012). Although China now is many times more powerful than any other country in the world, however our current strength is still self-defensive and will not pose a threat to other countries. Even if China really gets stronger one day, China's non-hegemony strategy will not allow China to launch a war on any country, which is the good virtue that our ancestors have always adhered to.

Can China really become the world leader?

As mentioned before, whether China can become the world leader or not, it is far from enough to rely on the economic power solely. What else do we need apart from the economic strength, military strength, and the technological strength? Looking back two hundred years ago, China maintained its social status with a powerful system of centralization of power and maintained a crooked body that did not get on its knees. Today, two hundred years later, the international situation has changed rapidly. Even if we have the economic superiority, we still need to build a strong economic body to support it, and really show the demeanor of leaders in the international community. Is China compatible with the international community's political system and social organization model? If not, then why do we believe that China can become the world leader? Obviously, it is not enough to just rely on the economic strength.

The problem is always an issue and cannot be evaded. Therefore, we must emphasize again and again that the current China, under some circumstances, is facing tremendous pressure and there are many problems that need to be solved urgently. From various aspects, we can see different developments and challenges. In terms of transportation, urban development, environmental governance, abuse of power and urban-rural relations, it can be said that China now faces many development challenges. The crux of the issue is whether all the issues involved can be solved in an orderly manner while maintaining the country's peace and stability and maintaining the existing vitality of development. If the answer is positive, then we can swagger proudly toward the world leader position.

In the big family of the world, the interests and friends are always conserved. Where there are interests, there are cooperation; where there are differences, there are opponents. For example, the South China Sea arbitration case in July 2016 broke the South China Sea's stability due to the interests seeking in the South China Sea made by the United States and Japan. And China did not agree with the result of the South China Sea Arbitration, China would not accept it, would not partake it, would not recognize it and would not execute it. The essence of the South China

Sea arbitration case is the interests between China and the Philippines. China has always insisted on the principle of sovereignty belongs to me, shelving controversy and developing together on the historical legacy of the South China Sea dispute. China is willing to resolve the disputes with the Philippines and work together for developments, in line with the principle of safeguarding stability in the South China Sea, without prejudice to the relations between China and the Philippines, considering from the overall situation.

In October 2016, Philippine President Duterte visited China and President Xi Jinping said, it is quite necessary to improve the bilateral relations, to cooperate in various fields and to solve the international and regional issues of common interest, these two leaders of each countries exchanged their ideas deeply. Do not act like "zero-sum game", but to establish good partnerships and mutual trust with neighboring countries such as the Philippines, this is also very important for the strategic layout, national defense and security. In addition, we must guard against the potential rivals. For potential partners, we also need to prevent from being destroyed by some countries with ulterior motives. For example, the country Russia, his position is still not clear, maybe soon, many countries such as the United States, Japan, Australia, Vietnam, the Philippines and India will form a possible alliance with Russia to restrain China. Even the North Korea, as a socialist country, may not always keep the good relations with China, may not treat China as his good brother all the time.

As for the Europe, it is quite far from China. If China can establish a good relationship with some countries during the tough times in Europe, such as the current European debt crisis, these countries may be friendly to China in the future, maybe they will remain neutral in the military. It is quite clear for the relations between South Korea and China. The more democracy in China the better bilateral relations will be. If one day the North Korea, Russia, Mongolia and Myanmar are all pulled over by the United States. At that time, China will face even more complicated problems. Of course, this is something that all the Chinese would not want to see. Whether he is a friend or an enemy, he told us that it is quite difficult for China to be the world leader and the price China is going to pay may be surprising. Because, a tall tree catches the wind, a person in a prominent position is liable to be attacked. It is hard to guarantee that it will not lead to a joint strangulation from the other countries.

Of course, we do not have to destroy ourselves and to grow the spirit of others. It is well known that China has made great achievements, and the methods are always more than the difficulties. The Chinese people are very diligent and brave, if China can do her duty well, it is not necessary at all to debate whether China will be the world leader or how much does China must pay for this.

Chapter 3:

Will the Grudges between China and the World be Reconciled?

There are too many grievances and grudges between China and the world. Of course, the world here does not refer to a single country, but refers to every country that has "disputes" with China. According to the Chinese leadership, China will not oppose to the entire world, nor will she have the capacity to act so. In the international community, the strength of "unity" between nations is extremely powerful, so various alliances have been existing all the time. Some people have said that if it were not for the eight-nation allied forces to fight with China jointly in the same year, it would be very hard for any certain single country to fight with China alone. It is unpredictable that China would not become a semi-colonial country at that time.

The development context between China and the world can be divided into several stages roughly: opening, closing and reopening. Before the Ming and Qing dynasties, the exchanges between China and the world were still frequent. From the Qin Dynasty to the Ming Dynasty, the feudal rule was carried out all the time and it was self-sufficient in the economy, but China was leading the world in terms of the economy and culture at that time, coupled with the enlightened policies that were carried out by the feudal ruling class, China made great accomplishments in building her relations foreign countries. Take the prosperity of the Tang Dynasty as an example, at that time, the external traffic was developed very well. The land was centered on Chang'an (Xi'an today). There were lines in the east, the south, and the north, and the western route was the famous "Silk Road." The sea routes extended to Japan and some of the South Asian countries, and lately, moreover, the sea routes even extended to Egypt and East Africa (Zhou, 2000). Under the precondition of convenient transportation, the exchanges between China and foreign countries were also very frequent. In the political world, countries in the world learned the suitable official systems from China and visited China frequently. Economic exchanges were not as comprehensive and frequent as they are now. However, the cultural exchanges involved a wide range of areas, such as the monk Xuanzang's fetching Buddhism Books from India, which opened a window for cultural exchanges between China and India, at same time Japan sent their young men and women to learn the languages and cultures in China (Tian and Dai, 2014).

Therefore, the Tang Dynasty was regarded as the political center, economic center and cultural center in Asia, which had a very high reputation at that time. Many countries' envoys, merchants, scholars, monks kept coming to visit China, traded in China and studied in China. A foreign historian has ever noted: Compared with any other era in Chinese history before the 20th century, the Chinese in the early and middle Tang dynasties were the most confident and receptive to different new things, perhaps it was because China established relations with many Asian countries due to the religions that came from the foreign countries; perhaps it was because many of the clan's giants were barbarian descendants at that time; perhaps it was because China has a strong military force to guard the Silk Road and ensure the smooth flow of business travel. In short, the Chinese in that period were very willing to open themselves up to the world and hoped to get excellent valuables from other countries. All these illustrated that China has already built relations with foreign countries long time ago (He, 2014).

When things go back to the bottom there would be unexpected discoveries. For example, opening to the outside world, many people think that this is the original creation of the Third Plenary Session of the 11th Central Committee of the Communist Party of China. However, when looking back, it turns out that China has had this sprout long ago. Shi Jingqian, a famous sinologist in the United States, addressed in his interview with Time Weekly: “When I taught Chinese language, Chinese history and Chinese culture in the West, I found that there was a flaw in

Chinese textbooks, when they mention the modern China History, they always started with the humiliation and aggression suffered by China in the 19th century. When I began to teach Chinese history 40 years ago, I found it very unreasonable. If we want to learn the history of China better, we should start from the China in 17th century, because China was showing a more confident attitude in the world at that time (Zhang, 2011)." Therefore, when studying the grievances between China and the world, it is necessary to mention this period that from the closed-door state to the opening to the outside world. In addition, it should also be mentioned that the historical process from the opening to the closed-door state. Only in this way can people have a complete historical picture of China and the world.

There are many historical reasons for the closed-door state in modern Chinese history. Firstly, the decline of the feudal system and the decadent ruling class, which are also mentioned by many historians or historical textbooks frequently. Secondly, the gap between the economy of its own country (small-scale peasant economy) and the world capitalist economy. During the Ming and Qing Dynasties, capitalism in the world began to sprout due to the rapid development of productive forces. Because the economic foundation determines the superstructure, this sprout also threatened China's original feudal rule. The ruling class was afraid that its own opposition classes would collude with the outside world. At the same time, the world's major capitalist countries started to expand abroad frantically and started the primitive accumulation of capital. As a result, the closed-door policy was the only best policy at that time (Wang and Zhu, 2017).

From the "closed door state" to "open to the outside world"

The historical origins of the closed-door state in modern Chinese history could be traced back to the sea ban policy in the early Ming Dynasty. The people should not go to sea and trade with foreigners arbitrarily, the coastal ports were blocked, and even the sea-going vessels would be destroyed to cut off the trade with the outside world completely (Shang, 2007). The direct reason for the sea ban policy in the early

Ming Dynasty or the policy of "closed-door policy" in the early Qing Dynasty, of course, was to safeguard the domestic domination and prevent invasion. The fundamental reason was still due to China's natural and economic conditions. At that time, China's economy was self-sufficiency, so the foreign trade was almost not required. The sea ban policy of the early Ming dynasty also caused serious problems, which in turn hindered the development of overseas markets and the development of the capitalist sprout and suppressed the primitive accumulation of capital, which made China lag the other major capitalist countries in the world.

Compared with the closed-door policy, the sea ban policy was still light. It only prohibited private offshore trades, it allowed the officials to go to sea to declare the authority of the Ming Empire, for example, the well-known Zheng He's Voyages. The foreign businessmen were also welcomed to China to trade with the Chinese, but the overseas trade must be under the auspices of the official, this is so-called "tribute to trade" (Xue, 2011). In the early Qing Dynasty, it banned overseas trade in an all-round way and practiced "closed-door policy." So why did China's **foreign policy** become more stringent in the Qing Dynasty? The direct reason is to curb the people's struggle for resistance in the southeastern coastal areas and to prevent the Chinese from colluding with the outside world to form a powerful anti-Qing power. At the same time, to prevent the attacks from the Western colonialists the Qing rulers carried out national defense by using the policy of "closing their doors to their country." However, in our opinion, the most fundamental reason is the poor economy. In the traditional agrarian society that relied on self-sufficiency, the feudal rulers were self-satisfied, China lagged the other countries in the world and excluded all foreign things blindly.

During the Qing dynasty, the sea ban policy had been escalated into the closed-door policy. It was positive for the closed-door policy to prevent foreign aggression and protect the natural economy. However, the result of "self-defense" had hindered the economic and cultural exchanges between China and foreign countries. Also, it hindered the embryonic development of capitalism, the science developments and the social technologies were hindered as well, which resulted in China's lagging far behind the West in modern times (Deng, 2013). Since the Opium War (1848), under the intimidation of the imperialist gunboat, the ports along the eastern coast of China were forced to open through the unequal treaties, namely "open door". Now, the backward and decadent feudal system was unable to resist the advanced capitalist system, coupled with the corruption and compromise of the Qing government. China's door was then forced to open to the outside world. However, it must be emphasized that this type of opening-up is forcibly open, which differs from the current reform and opening. It is a humiliating and inequitable opening to the outside world, and it has brought tremendous disasters to the Chinese people. Starting from the opening of the treaty ports, China was forced to become involved in the capitalist world market and became an appendage of capitalism gradually. As a result, China's natural economy began to collapse, which resulted in the historical change in the modern history of China from "closed-door state" to "opening to the outside world."

From modern China to the founding of the People's Republic of China in 1949, the Chinese people had been bullied by foreign powers and were suffering from the internal trouble constantly. After the founding of New China, the founding leaders faced a catastrophic situation in which not only was the internal society disheveled, but also the remnants of hostility remained stubbornly opposed and vandalized. Therefore, for a prolonged period, China could not open to the outside world fully. Later, Mao Zedong suggested that China needs to clean the house and then invite guests. With the gradual improvement of the national economy, China seized every opportunity to start its diplomatic activities with the United States, especially with the Soviet Union. Because the socialist camp was led by the Soviet Union and could compete with the United States at that time (Zeng, 2010). After the Second World War, the two opposing camps of socialism and capitalism have been formed in the world. As a socialist country, China is naturally standing on the Soviet side. However, this kind of opening that relied on others will not last too long. Therefore, the following rupture of Sino-Soviet relations caused some difficult outcomes for China.

It was not until 1978 that the Third Plenary Session of the Eleventh Central Committee of the CPC realized that China took the initiative to open to the outside world truly. Based on independence and self-reliance, following the principle of equality and mutual benefit and mutual trust, China should work with other countries in the world in developing economic cooperation and technology communication (Xu, 2011). This benign opening is a major strategic decision to speed up the socialist modernization and a starting point for setting up a new era of socialist modernization featuring Chinese characteristics. Since the reform and opening, the Chinese economy has then been developed rapidly. China's economy has taken a tremendous stride toward the world and has integrated itself into the economic globalization. Since China adopted the strategy of reform and opening, its achievements have drawn worldwide attention. However, the Chinese pay more attention to the independence of the country. Therefore, opening to the outside world in China is to be under the premise of maintaining its independence in all fields of politics and economy. It is different from the passive and invading opening to the outside world; this point should be emphasized in any means.

"Laughter" and "tears" of economic globalization

Under the international environment in which peace and development become the theme of the times increasingly, all the countries in the world regard opening to the outside world as one of the important ways for their own development. A country cannot have all the world's advanced technologies and management experience and all resources, but must make up for its deficiencies through opening to the outside world (Lian, 2000). However, the taste of life is never only "sweet" without "bitterness", nor is it only "laughing" without "tears." Economic globalization is just like a taste of life, one knows the taste oneself when living in it.

Economic globalization is a basic trend of economic and social development in the world today and one of the key features of the contemporary world economy. In the World Economic Outlook published in May 1997, the International Monetary Fund put forward the definition of economic globalization: Economic globalization refers to the increase in the scale and form of transnational goods and services transactions and international capital flows, the rapid and widespread dissemination of technology have increased the interdependence of the economies of all countries in the world (Xu,2006). In view of this, economic globalization has made the world a global village. As the process of world economic globalization is still at an initial stage, its impact on the economies of various countries and the world is unpredictable. However, it is very clear that economic globalization is a "double-edged sword." The benevolent sees the benevolent, the wise see the wisdom, and some economists believe that economic globalization is a favorable progress that can make China becomes richer. However, other economists are skeptical. They point out that if the economic globalization is good, why is the international economy so confused (Chen, 2010)? It is easy to see that there have been many related studies on the pros and cons of economic globalization and it is not necessary to repeat them one by one. Moreover, it needs to be specially explained that what being discussed about here is the relationship between China and the world. Therefore, it focuses on the "laughter" and "tears" that economic globalization brings to China's economy.

Economic globalization is a "double-edged sword" for every country. This is especially true for China. Therefore, economic globalization has provided China with an opportunity to meet the challenges it possesses (Zhou, 2016). In terms of economic development in China, the "benefits" brought by globalization are mainly manifested in the following aspects: Firstly, it is good for China to give full play to China's comparative advantages and to enhance its international competitiveness. Globalization perfected and consolidated a unified world market, it enabled the free flow and optimization of production factors in the world and improved the efficiency of resource allocation. China has comparative advantages in labor forces, resources and market advantages in globalization. Moreover, the comparative advantage of a country is not permanent. Some disadvantages may also be converted positively through exchange and study, and then become advantages. With the progress of economic globalization, China is in the process of studying and accumulating, and is also forcing China's labor-intensive products to shift to capital-intensive or even technology-intensive products.

Secondly, the technological proliferation and increase of economies brought by economic globalization and the readjustment of the industrial structure in developed countries are conducive to the improvement of the general manufacturing industry in China. The rapid economic development in the world and the low interest rate policy in developed countries are conducive to attracting foreign investment by the favorable conditions to speed up the economic developments in China (Li, 2005). That is, using foreign investment, the structure of China's exports can be optimized.

Thirdly, globalization has brought the economic relations among countries closer and closer and has made their interdependence be increased highly, it formed a community of interests like "I have you and you have me", and increased humanity's global awareness, cooperation and dialogue, peace and development, which have become the main topic of the times (Yan, 2012). As a result, China's issue will no longer be a mere issue for China. For instance, the issue of environment and trade frictions have become global problems. If they are not resolved, they will directly affect the further development of globalization. Therefore, globalization has also forced the developed countries to consider the problems that China faces and work together to solve them.

Economic globalization is directly promoted by the developed countries. The rules of the game are also governed by the developed countries. As such, the developing countries are the biggest victims of the globalization undoubtedly. China, as the largest developing country was harmed obviously. In the aspect of China's economic development, the "disadvantages" brought by globalization are mainly manifested in the following aspects:

Firstly, due to the various levels of economic and technological development in various countries in the world, it is impossible for them to have equal status and interests in the economic globalization, this is the so-called "arms twist thigh," China is still subject to the developed countries to a certain extent. For example, the developed countries can make use of the cheap local labor and natural resources in China to obtain maximum profits, and occupy the market rapidly by their own advantages and economic strength. In such fierce market competition as jungle and survival of the fittest, China must be at a disadvantage in many aspects.

Secondly, in the field of international direct investments, quite many studies show that the developed countries use economic globalization to transfer their heavily-polluting industries to China through multinational corporations because China's environmental regulations are not as strict as the Western ones. As a result, China is being asked to fulfill more environmental responsibilities under the pressure of all countries in the world. The issue concerning the world environment has become a major topic of the World Economic Forum. The western countries always shirk their responsibilities via diverse ways, and they hope that China will bear more responsibilities and thus there exist all kinds of "China's responsibility theory."

Thirdly, as to the third advantage that was mentioned above, if being viewed from another perspective, will become a disadvantage undoubtedly. Under the slogan of "You have me, I have you," in the western medias, there is also a hidden crisis that may break out at any time. Because with the increase of the interdependence between countries, all countries in the world have formed a chain of "one won then all won, one lost then all lost." Taking the global fiscal crisis that broke out in the United States in 2008 as an example, almost every country was affected by that crisis, which reduced the security of its economy. In addition to the above three points, one more point need to be kept in mind is that economic globalization does not represent "sovereign integration" and the national interests of the country are still above all (Li, 2016). In the context of economic globalization, western countries have propagandized that sovereignty has been weakened and the concept of sovereignty has become obsolete. Therefore, it is necessary to make a concrete analysis of these arguments and keep a clear brain always.

Must admit, but also should be wary of that in the economic globalization, due to different strengths, developed countries and multinational corporations will benefit the most, while developing countries benefit very little. Therefore, the gap between developing countries and developed countries will widen further. Some of the least developed countries will be excluded from economic globalization and become marginalized and even become the modern technology colony of developed countries and multinational corporations. However, it is irreversible whether it brings "tears" or "laughs" from globalization. As a developing country, China can only find ways to adapt to it and to work with most countries to establish a fair and orderly new world economic order. The facts of the economic development in the world are clear enough to prove that any country if it has the right development strategy it can succeed in the economic globalization. Why is China doing nothing?

The continuous trade friction

As China continues to expand its opening up to the outside world and integrate itself into the global economic environment continuously, the contradictions are emerging one after another. China's market economy has not been recognized by the United States and the Europe Union due to frequent occurrence of trade protectionism, trade friction, exchange rate issues and punitive tariffs. After China joined the World Trade Organization, cooperation and friction have become the main topics of China and the world. Moreover, the trade friction that occur in recent years is alarming.

Taking year 2012 as an example, according to the statistics of the Chinese Ministry of Commerce, 77 trade remedy investigations hit China in 2012, involving 27.7 billion U.S. dollars, up 11.6% and 369% respectively over the same period of last year. In addition, some scholars think that 2012 was the year when the United States and Europe had the biggest trade friction with China. The United States and Europe have taken "double countermeasures" against China's PV industry successively, almost destroying the industry completely. The above-mentioned "double countermeasures" is an investigation of the anti-dumping and anti-subsidy investigations conducted by the United States. It is therefore called "double reaction." On the one hand, the United States imposed high punitive tariffs leading to a drastic drop in the scale of exports by 60%. On the other hand, it is a dying catastrophe caused by the pending EU anti-dumping investigations. China's PV industry has come to a "crossroads."

If the "double reaction" is established, dominoes will be overruled one by one, all industries in the photovoltaic industry chain will be hit hard. The EU's photovoltaic installed capacity accounts for about 70% of the world's total and the United States accounts for nearly 10%. If both markets close their doors to China, the Chinese PV enterprises will suffer a fatal blow (Chen,2012). Certainly, Chinese enterprises and relevant departments cannot wait on their death, they can start with the trade dumping in the United States and Europe to see whether they have violated the anti-embezzlement policies of the WTO in the relevant industries, or start with the differences in their market standards and international standards, appeal "double reaction." Only in this way can the U.S. and Europe be reasonably required to give fair treatment to Chinese products.

The trade frictions suffered in 2012, of course, were far more than the above example, that was only a big trade friction. At the China's Foreign Trade Situation Report held on March 23, 2012, the Vice Minister of Commerce Zhong Shan pointed out that China suffered eight trade frictions in the first three months of the year, involving a total amount of 2.28 billion U.S. dollars, compared with the amount in the previous year, it had been increased 80%, China had been the country suffering the most trade frictions during the past 17 years. From late June to now, the "Warning Alert" section on the official website of the Chinese Ministry of Commerce, has been updating the information of foreign trade remedy investigations against China frequently. In addition to the EU's investigation into China's wireless communications equipment and photovoltaic industry, there are also a series of anti-dumping investigations launched by the United States, Brazil and other countries on China's exports of motorcycle tires, seamless steel tubes and passenger car tires. According to the statistics released by the Ministry of Commerce in July, China suffered a total of 40 trade relief investigations, anti-dumping, anti-subsidy and special safeguard measures from 18 countries and regions in the first half of 2012, compared with the same period of last year, it has been increased 38%, and 3.7 billion U.S. dollars involved, 76% increase compared with the last year. Classified according to the filing countries, the developing countries such as Brazil and India accounted for 70% of the total number of cases filed. Classified according to the amount involved, the developed countries such as Europe and the United States initiated surveys against China, their amount occupied 60% of the total.

In 2016, China suffered 119 trade remedy investigations in total initiated by 27 countries (including 91 anti-dumping cases, 19 anti-subsidy cases and 9 safeguard measures) The total amount involved was 14.34 billion U.S. dollars. The number of cases and the amount involved increased by 36.8% and 76% respectively from a year earlier. Nearly half of the trade remedy cases are targeted at Chinese steel products, while the rest are mainly concentrated in the chemical and light industry sectors. In the first 11 months of 2016, China's exports were 12.47 trillion yuan, a decrease of 1.8%. However, the trade friction rose from 98 to 119 (Ma, 2017). overall, the trade frictions encountered in 2016 in China were characterized by the politicization. It is not known whether China is accustomed to it, or is it common in the western countries. The trade frictions are one after another, and the two sides of the dispute hold their own opinions. In this regard, it is really hoped that the international organizations can have a uniform standard, or at least not so controversial. However, how can the international community give priority to China’s interests in the game rules of the international community? Therefore, the rapid development of China's economy is bound to suffer the "courtesy" that other countries have not suffered. The

Chinese cannot just accept challenges passively, but also must take the initiative to deal with them.

The Chinese cannot help wondering why there is so much friction between China and foreign countries? In fact, there are many reasons that affect the economic and trade relations between China and the rest of the world. Apart from some purely economic system factors such as trade protectionism, differences in technology and standards, imperfections in the WTO system, etc., the cultural and ideological differences is also one of the reasons, of course, the political needs are also the cause of economic disputes, just like the relationship between the United States and China. The United States is China's largest trading partner, while the United States is also the country that has initiated the largest trade friction with China. This cannot be said to be a mere coincidence. Today, China has become the second largest economic entity in the world, how can the United States, the world's largest economic entity, be unprepared and not vigilant?

The Chinese people fully aware that successive trade frictions were unavoidable phenomenon during the rapid development of China, in the medium and long term, it will become the normal state with the development of China's trade. China is still in a transitional period of integration into the world. China itself is also in a painful period of industrial restructuring, the friction is unavoidable (Yang and Bao, 2017). Both China and the world need to learn from cooperation and understand from friction. Theoretically, the entire world should understand that a stable and rapid economic development in China will be conducive to the development of the world. China is not only belonging to the Chinese but also belonging to the world. Nevertheless, how can this theoretical explanation be understood and accepted by all the countries in the world, especially the current world leader the United States?

China and the world: Depend on each other

The second decade of 21th century has already half over, China was developed rapidly in the first 17 years of this century. The level of economic development has been continuously improved. The political system has been continuously improved as well. The overall national strength has risen stably (Cha, 2015). The Chinese are moving forward towards the goal of Building a Well-off Society. Looking around the world, China itself is progressing, while its position in the world has not been raised to what we expect. The 2008 Beijing Olympic Games and the 2010 Shanghai World Expo should be a good opportunity for us to show the world the achievements of China's economic and social development since the reform and opening. We hope that China will be heard more and more in the world and hope that its political, economic and cultural influence on the world will continue to expand. China must become a world leader, especially in the economic field. China's every move may have an impact on the world economy. It is also hoped that the image of a responsible big country can penetrate the hearts of the people in the world gradually. China, who is to be the No.1 in the world, is not only being changed by the world, but also changing the world.

However, it should not think this kind of discussion regarding who changed who or who influenced who, has any real meaning to anyone. In the international exchanges, it is incredible to think that one party is changed by the other party solely. Therefore, the inextricable relations between China and the rest of the world cannot be explained by mere mapping on one single line. From 2001 to 2010, China's exports rose from US $ 266,098 million to US $ 1,577,789 million, an increase of 493% with an average annual increase of 21.9%. While the export trade expanded unprecedentedly, the China's imports was increased as well. The import growth rate is also leading the world. From 2010 to 2015, China's exports to the world was increased from 10.3% to 13.7% and the imports was increased from 9.1% to 10.1%. The global share of service exports increased from 3.9% to 5.9%. Especially in 2016, China maintained its strong market demand in the downturn of the world economy. From January to November, China's imports of iron ore and concentrates, copper ore and its concentrates and crude oil increased by 9.2%, 30.5% and 14.0% respectively, while imports of integrated circuits increased by 9.3%. Imports of pharmaceuticals and automobiles, the import of spare parts increased by 9.1% and 8.3% respectively. From

January to October 2017, the import of service trade in China increased by 23.7%. China's substantial growth in imports of international commodities and major industrial products has effectively improved the international supply and demand. It has not only increased the economic growth of resource and energy exporting countries, but has also played an indispensable role in the gradual recovery for the economy of developed industrial countries. Today, China is not only the world's number one export country, but also the second largest importer in the world (Mei, 2011). All in all, the relationship between China and the rest of the world is essentially like a "win-win" mode, and neither side should reject the development of this benign relationship.

China is in the process of modernization. China has rich resources and many successful experiences. However, the internal and external conflicts for China still exist and she needs to face these. All kinds of trade frictions mentioned above and the drawbacks of economic globalization are all worth mentioning. All these are inevitable in the process of development and the Chinese people must face it with confidence. It is hoped that in these conflicts and frictions, everyone should uphold the principle of "one world, one dream," instead of thinking of independence. World peace and development are the blessings for everyone in all countries. Those hegemonies and power politics are doomed to be cast aside and impossible to survive. No matter how hard the future is, China, like the rest of the world, will not be isolated from the rest of the world.

At present, many people, whether they are domestic economists or international economic workers, are optimistic about the development of China and the world. For example, the former Vice President of the World Bank, Lin Yifu, he believes that the new world economic pattern is undergoing qualitative changes. China is playing a huge role in the international fiscal crisis. In the past 30 years or so, with sustained and rapid economic growth in China, it is still possible to maintain its high growth rate in the future and become a new force that will change the pattern of the world economy. The Former World Trade Organization Director-General Mike Moore once said that the WTO without China is not a worldwide trade organization. Yumkhella, the director general of the United Nations Industrial Development Organization, said that China's being added to the WTO benefits not only China itself, but also benefits the developed countries, emerging industrial nations and some of the least developed countries in Africa. After 10 years, China won, the world also won (Guo, 2011). Yes, China won and the world won. However, it is also hoped to see another scenario where the world has won and China has won, despite all the efforts we must make.

Those cooperation or friction we mentioned, they cannot change the close economic relations between China and the world, of course, there will lurk a lot of crises, the close cooperation coexistence with the crisis, this is the specific portrayal of the current and future relations between China and the rest of the world. It is also known that only by opening up can China develop and only by sharing can the world win together.

The future of China and the world

Everything should focus on the future to grasp the reality. From 2008 to 2010, the worldwide fiscal crisis originated in the United States accelerated the economic downturn of the West, meanwhile, it is beneficial to the development of China's economy. Because China transformed this global crisis into a crucial and important opportunity for accelerating its own economic development. Chinese enterprises made heroic efforts to develop themselves through their own styles, methods, engineers and senior managements, workers and machinery and equipment. Price water house Coopers (PwC) report shows that China is expected to overtake the United States in 2018, mainly due to the fiscal crisis - it accelerated the transfer of power centers to emerging countries. Goldman Sachs predicts that by 2030, the Chinese stock market will suppress the United States and become the world's first stock market. China will become the world's largest economic entity. China will have global power and influence on five continents. By that time, China will no longer be just China but a powerful China. It will enjoy international prestige, will have modern armed forces and a Moon base (Picarl, 2012). Those predictions, of course, should not be exaggerated, Chinese people may not fully believe it. However, the influences of China to the world is increasing gradually, which is an undisputed topic. However, Chinese people still have some worries about whether China can be recognized by all the countries in the world.

After removing the beautiful exaggerated words, let us imagine the future of China and the world objectively. The world began to examine the issues of real economy and fictitious economy due to the impact from the subprime mortgage crisis in the United States. Let the real economy be developed a little faster, and the fictitious economy, a little bit slower, this was the voice of the public. Due to the subsequent impact of the crisis, the Greece and some other EU countries began to plunge into the sovereign debt crisis, which is now called European Debt Crisis. As one can imagine, the United States and the EU in the future will face a very difficult situation. In the coming decade or so, the major developed countries may enter a period of strategic contraction. At the same time, however, China has enormous potential for development. It is also quite possible to take advantage of such a strategic opportunity to narrow the gap with developed countries in all aspects of economic and social development. Nonetheless, the first problem to be solved is the issues from the new economic growth (Tian and Dai 2014).

It is widely known that before the fiscal crisis, most of the impetus for China's economic development came from import and export, and for a long time China's foreign trade had been favorable balance. However, the external environment China is facing now is very terrible. To reverse this situation, it is necessary to find a new impetus for economic growth in China. The Chinese leaders have proposed to promote the economic growth via stimulating the domestic demand. Therefore, we can predict that in the post-financial crisis era, China will reduce its dependence on external demand in its future economic development. This is not to say that China should be isolated from the rest of the world but should reduce its dependence on the outside world. In addition, China is also likely to be a situation of import and export deficits. This is not a bad phenomenon but a very favorable situation because the future trade deficit can just be offset by the huge trade surplus and thus the large amount of foreign exchange will not be idle.

There are a lot of recent problems with great uncertainty in today's dilemma world. From the closed-door state to the opening to outside world, from the semi-colonial semi-feudal society to an independent China, during this period, China met too many difficulties. People say it is wonderful in the outside world, but it is helpless as well. The Chinese people have seen too much frustration in the past, and today they have the strength and confidence finally, they have the courage to meet with the outside world, and the ability to digest it, they are respected based on the equal footing, they can tell what is beneficial to them and what may hurt them. In the process of continuous integrating with the world big family, the Chinese have not lost themselves. From the initial "introduction" to the present "going global", the Chinese nation has been adding bricks to its own development with its unique charm, and has been making itself stronger and stronger constantly with the help of external forces (Sun, 2015). The road to opening is not smooth, the Chinese people must make double efforts to realize their goal. The Chinese people do not have to always remember the past, nor indulge in the present. What they must do is to look forward to the future in the longer term.

Neither any country nor any nation can deny that China's peaceful development is a resource and will benefit the world peace and world economic prosperity greatly. On the contrary, if China's economy, politics and society are in turmoil and recession, 1.4 billion people in the world will be suffered. No one wants to see the sufferings. China's development in the future can contribute more lights and warms to the world. Just like the fiscal crisis and the debt crisis in Europe, China is embodying the image of an enormous power. Moreover, if China wants to achieve a great rejuvenation, the Chinese people need to pay great attention to any important opportunity whether it is good or bad, why shall they be afraid of it if they are ready?

China's global strategy views

The Chinese nation has been a nation that loves peace and does not seek expansion since the ancient times. It is therefore a nation that is not aggressive and ambitious. Such a national spirit and cultural tradition have been maintained till now. Under the influence of this national spirit and cultural tradition, the strategies that the historical rulers adopted were focused on how to improve the efficiency of internal rule, and focused on how to consolidate the dominant position. In the field of foreign affairs, they insisted in building high walls to prevent themselves from being attacked by the foreigners. This kind of strategy called "defensive foreign affairs" has become the main idea of the recent China's policies makers, it is termed as defense doctrine (Tian and Dai, 2012).

In the period of human being's lack of effective solution to the long distance and rapid transportation of troops and the fact that human beings have not yet developed strategic long-range attack weapons, defense doctrine was an effective strategic choice for the Chinese nation. However, with the development of social production and science and technology, it is no longer a myth that a country sends troops thousands of miles away within a few minutes, and a deadly attack on the enemy by an army can be operated thousands of miles away. The Gulf War in 1991, the Iraq War in 2003 and 2010 and the Libyan War in 2011 are the best explanations. From a global perspective, when facing this new means of war and armaments, simple defense can hardly be said to be useful. Therefore the "defense doctrine" is not working any more. In other words, any form of defense in contemporary warfare is passive and will result in the failure finally. Precisely because of this, it is a crucial moment for China to abandon this kind of "defense doctrine" and to establish a positive national defense strategy.

When talking about China's establishing the national defense strategy, it does not mean that China must attack the enemy troops first. Instead, China can start attacking the enemy base camps as soon as she is attacked by the enemy, then China can deal a deadly blow to them and annihilate their further strategic offensive until the enemy stops. The

Chinese military leadership call this strategy as "positive national defense strategy." The premise for implementing a positive national defense strategy is to establish a correct global strategy first. In the 1960s, Mao Zedong called on people all over the world to unite and fight against the domination by one or two superpowers. This is a global strategy for China during that period. It enabled China to defeat the external attacks and to defend its national interests and national territorial integrity successfully. After the 1980s, major changes have taken place in the international situation. China abandoned its original global strategy and replaced it with a new international strategy (which in the current authors' view is not a truly global strategy) oriented by seeking the greatest economic benefits. Nowadays the international situation has been changed a lot, due to the unilateralism adopted by the United States, the dark clouds of the Taiwan Strait war have been shrouded in the air through which the hostile forces wanted to make China be an inferior position. Therefore, it is required that China must choose and determine its own global strategy promptly (Lu, 2016).

Mencius was one of the ancient Chinese sages, he said: I am trapped in my heart, I am thinking of what I want to do, then I am going to do...thus I know people survive in disasters and perish in comfort (Mencius, ancient China). On the one hand, China should exercise its utmost patience and sincerity to implement the peaceful unification of the motherland, on the other hand, Chinese people must destroy the plotting to divide the motherland with their own global strategy. China's global strategic layout should be implemented step by step and hierarchically, and should include the following points: public opinion strategy, equipment strategy, base strategy, regional (national) strategy, space strategy, maritime strategy, strategic mobilization and strategic direction, and the strategy for Taiwan, all the above points can be summarized as follows （Tian and Dai, 2014）:

- Propagandize China's thought of peaceful development. China should publicize to the entire world the China's national policy of no seeking hegemony, oppose the "China Threat Theory" created by hostile forces, so that the international community will understand China's peaceful development policy. China must do a good job on the American people in public opinion, resist and expose the dehumanization of China by the ultra-right forces in the United States, and reduce the "fanned hatred" and misunderstanding that the Americans have. At the same time, China should keep good relations with her European friends, maintain the friendly relations with the African people, make new friends in South America, and resume the friendly exchanges with Japan positively, if necessary, China can make good friends via modern medias, internet and televisions in a certain period.

- Accelerate the development of national defense industry. Faced with the threat posed using ballistic missile defense systems, aircraft carrier battle groups and space-based laser weapons by international hostile forces, China must oppose it and speed up the development of the national defense industry with a focus on the development of long-range and offensive nuclear and air weapons. So, it is necessary to resume heavy industry that had been vandalized because of the agitation of the market, the development of the national defense industry will drive the development of other national economic sectors. This has been illustrated by the U.S. economic history. China should increase investment in the production of productive materials, especially investment in research and education, seize the high ground of information technology and win the high-tech war in the future.

- Do an excellent job building a strategic base. Build many suitable strategic bases for implementing an active defensive strategy. We should consider building a strategic base in mainland China and must choose a correct place for the base scientifically. When possible, consideration should also be given to establishing a strategic base for China outside the country. Being gentle and generous in the international struggle like Confucianism will not work.

- Amending the previous non-aligned diplomatic line. The current international situation is quite different from that of the 1960s. China should re-examine the international non-aligned diplomatic theory, it cannot be continued mechanically. China should deepen and perfect the "Shanghai Cooperation Organization," and form a strategic alliance with all neighboring countries. Especially, enhance the scientific and technological cooperation with Russia in the defense industry to reduce the national defense pressure cost. China should intensify exchanges with other countries and nations in the world to reduce the resistance when China is forced to implement its unification by non-peaceful means, actually in order to reduce the offensive costs. It is the same in the economic and trade areas, it is necessary to reduce the dependence on one or two countries a little bit, such as the United States, strengthen economic and trade ties with Europe, especially the European Union, reduce foreign exchange reserves in the form of the U.S. dollars and promote the development of science and technology in China with the existing foreign exchange reserves, that is to say, buy the foreign technologies and equipment with those unused foreign exchange reserves.

- Start the space strategic deployment. Information technology and digital technologies have made space a competitive site, the United States and Russia have established their own space forces, so China should establish one as soon as possible. At the same time, it is necessary to speed up the development of the civilian space industry based on the marginalization of space forces, which will not only increase the combat effectiveness of the Chinese army, but also boost the economy of the country.

- Implement the maritime strategy in two levels. The first level is the strategy of cross-harboring 200,000 to 500,000 sails in the Taiwan Strait and defeating the aggressors by the People's War. The second level is the strategy of offshore combating, the ships for ocean-going attacks should be designed in smaller size, fast speed, strong fire and less load. In this way, it will be possible to avoid imitating the old ones designed by other countries in the construction of aircraft carriers because, which will not be able to win at all in the actual battle.

- Establish a strategic mobilization system effectively. The China's peace environment has lasted for more than 20 years. However, the peaceful singing and dancing inside the country cannot eliminate the military threats outside the country. As such, it is necessary to publicize the sense of urgency, get ready for military preparations and establish a national strategic mobilization system. Strategic mobilization should be carried out in the form of strategic reserve at the current stage. Economic development should still be the main content. The methods for implementing it depend on the strategic command arrangements. The strategic commands are mainly focused on the Supreme Commander's wisdom and courage, but also include the composition, the exercise and development of the strategic staff.

- Strengthen the Taiwan's strategy. The Taiwan issue is the most crucial factor that restricts China's all-round development. As the world knows, the United States has always regarded Taiwan as a never-ending huge aircraft carrier in the interests of the Asia Pacific region. Therefore, the United States does not want the mainland to achieve reunification with Taiwan. Taiwan is now much more important than ever to the United States for her global strategic interests. It has become the trump card for the United States to clamp down on China. However, China's sacred territory will never tolerate invasion by foreign forces, only when China completes the reunification can the national rejuvenation be realized. On the one hand, China will never change her attitude toward Taiwan's independence and will make Taiwan's independence unpopular on the Taiwan island. On the other hand, China must deal with the Taiwan issue more pragmatically, support Taiwan's reunification forces and increase the economic and trade contacts with Taiwan, and let Taiwanese people realize that the motherland is the source of Taiwan's well-being. After the above preparations are completed, the Taiwan issue will no longer be a problem. At the same time, the blue-green camp in Taiwan has changed a lot since the communist party and the Kuomintang started their third cooperation. Since Ma Ying-jeou was elected as the leader of Taiwan in 2008, the cross-Strait relations have been heating up and the conflicts have become less than before. The Kuomintang gained historical benefits from its cooperation with the Communist Party and began to escape from gradual decline.

However, since Tsai Ing-wen took office in May 2016, Tsai's "little tricks" have been played constantly and "keeping the status for the

Taiwan Strait" was talked about frequently. Nevertheless, from removing Tsai Sun (Sun Yat-sen) to removing Chiang Kai-shek Kai-shek) he adjusted the class outline of Chinese history into the history of East Asia and other practices, in fact, he was considering to "remove China " in a sneaky way. The Taiwan media's "China Daily" made a statement that the authorities in power want to cut off the blood and historical ties across the Strait through distorted education and cultural policies, which reflect the mentality of promoting the Taiwan's independence and will lead to the political demonstrations across the Strait and the military showdown finally. So, the Taiwan issue must not be taken lightly. It is necessary to step up research and development of national defense high technology to raise the PLA's modern combat capability in an all-round way and prepare for the military struggle. The Chinese people are not afraid to engage in the arms races with Taiwan through which they can destroy the economic foundation of the Taiwan independence forces.

In short, the hostile and sabotaging forces surrounding China are strong and threatening China seriously. China should not adopt any line of appeasement aimed at averting so-called "China threat theory." This is the idea of traitors undoubtedly. On the contrary, China should step up her own national defense construction promptly and destroy the conspiracy that designed secretly. Of course, the specific measures should be more concealed, under the foreseeable premise, the front conflicts with hegemonies should be reduced or avoided so as to ensure that our national defense accelerates its strategy (Wu, 2015). The goal of China's global strategy is to defend its own national security and national interests from being harmed. However, the current hostile forces that can ultimately harm China's national security and national interests have not vanished, they have been assembled publicly. The greater its pace of self-growth is, the more it can cause unease among international hostile forces. Driven by the interests of the national states, unilateralism and hegemony will never withdraw from the stage of history automatically. Therefore, China must be vigilant in peace time and based on the awareness to survive in the world.

China's global strategy is not only referring to fighting bravely but also referring to her wisdom, it's a clever combination of these two. In other words, the victory over hostile forces can be controlled via the global strategy. By then, not only will China's people, rich people and rich countries live and work in peace and contentment, but people all over the world will also enjoy the fruits of the victory. Although unilateralism is rampant in the modern world, it is only a wishful thinking and a short-term phenomenon. The direction of the historical wheel has never been reversed by power. Peace and development are the main topics of the current times. Although the new national-state conflicts of interests mentioned above are covered in a wide range and are not able to be controlled, there are many forces that can be used to balance the hegemonies among them. China is a force that cannot be ignored in the stability of world peace. Because after almost 40 years' reform and opening, China has become the second largest economic entity and trading nation in the world, the largest foreign exchange reserve country and the most important buyer of the national treasury bonds of the United States (Song, 2010). The peaceful rise of China is conducted in a manner consistent with modern civilization. It is to speed up the rejuvenation of the Chinese civilization during the process of innovation and to represent a great civilized nation in the world.

On April 6, 2017, Chinese President Xi Jinping went to the United States for a summit meeting between China and the United States. This is the first time that the two leaders of both countries have met since Trump became the U.S. President. The two leaders had a friendly and long-time meeting. Both sides spoke highly of the historic progress made in the relations between China and the United States and agreed to promote greater development of Sino-U.S. Xi Jinping emphasized that the good relations between China and the United States are not only beneficial to the two countries but also beneficial to the world. There are one thousand reasons to do an excellent job in Sino-U.S. Relations but no reason to ruin the Sino-U.S. Relations. In the past 45 years since the normalization of Sino-U.S. Relations, the relations between the two countries have enjoyed historic progress despite the ups and downs, bringing tremendous practical benefits to the two peoples. Xi Jinping pointed out: Cooperation is the only correct choice between China and the United States. Our two countries can become good partners absolutely and to make full use of the four high-level dialogues and cooperation mechanisms established by the diplomatic security dialogues, comprehensive economic dialogue, law enforcement and cybersecurity dialogue and social and human rights dialogue, to make a big cooperation cake, develop a list of key cooperation for more early harvest (Cheng, 2017).

However, the Chinese people should keep a clear thinking for a long time that in the current period of rapid changes and restructuring of various economic and political forces in the world, during the historic turning point in the continuous deterioration of the living environment of human beings and under the precondition of the national interests, in the difficult recovery of the world economy, foreign hostile forces are always trying to contain China (Wu, 2012). Not only did the United States and Hong Kong's so-called "New Washington Consensus" of 2006 show continued intentions to contain China, but they still did not forget the "Taiwan Relations Law" during Obama's visit to China in 2009, and he even did not forget to mention the Dalai Lama which has nothing to do with U.S. interests at all, was this implying a deterrent? Therefore, China must not sit back and relax, which is a naive thought of self-destruction; China must not attack it in all directions. That is a foolish way of self-destruction. It is very important to understand these two points so that China will not be enslaved to the other countries. Instead, China will concentrate on doing an excellent job of economic construction and economic development, at the same time, China will protect her national interests, homeland security unswervingly in all kinds of ways.

In summary, from the sea ban policy in the early Ming Dynasty to the closed-door state of Qing Dynasty. Although it has a certain degree of self-defense in preventing overseas aggression and protecting the natural economy, however, the result of "self-defense" had hindered the economic and cultural exchanges between China and foreign countries. Also, it hindered the embryonic development of capitalism, the science developments and the social technologies were hindered as well, which resulted in China's lagging far behind the West in modern times. After the Opium War, under the intimidation of the imperialist gunboat, the ports along the eastern coast of China were forced to open through the unequal treaties, namely "open door". It is a humiliating, unequal open.

After the founding of New China, not only the internal society disheveled, but also the remnants of hostility remained stubbornly opposed and vandalized. Therefore, for an extended period, China could not open to the outside world fully. It was not until 1978 that the Third Plenary Session of the Eleventh Central Committee of the CPC realized that China took the initiative to open to the outside world truly. Based on independence and self-reliance, following the principle of equality and mutual benefit and mutual trust, China should work with other countries in the world in developing economic cooperation and technology communication.

Globalization is a basic trend of economic and social development in the world today and one of the key features of the contemporary world economy. It is a "double-edged sword" for every country. This is especially true for China. Therefore, economic globalization has provided China with an opportunity to meet the challenges it possesses. On the one hand, China has made great progress in the use of its own advantages, and on the other hand, China has been experiencing frequent trade conflicts and conflicts. What is the relationship between China and the world? How to make countries in the world understand that a stable and rapid economic development in China will be conducive to the development of the world?

The Chinese nation has been a nation that loves peace and does not seek expansion since the ancient times, but it does not mean that allow to oppress and being bullied. National interests and homeland security are still the bottom line that can't be touched. China adheres to the path of peaceful development, adhering to the principle of “one world, one dream”. China is willing to develop with all the countries of the world.

Chapter 4

A Super Strong Vs. A Group Strong

It cannot be decided by China's own national strength solely whether China can become a world leader and whether she can become a competent leader. China must consider the international situation she is facing as well. So, what is the current international situation? In this regard, China should examine from many areas. As China develops and expands gradually, all countries begin to discuss the latest evolution of the world situation. Is it a super strong or a group of strong? Or return to the bipolar era? This is another "battlefield" for experts and scholars to express their opinions. What role will China play in the development and changes of the world pattern? Is it true that China will act as a world police and share the entire world together with the United States? Maybe the history will give us the answer.

Since the end of World War II, the two major camps of capitalism and socialism led by the United States and the former Soviet Union have ceased to exist after a series of major international events such as the Cold War, the drastic changes in Eastern Europe and the Soviet Union. The world entered the era of a so-called super strong which is referring to the United States. And the ending of the bipolar pattern must start with the 1991 landmark events. On the night of December 25, 1991, the Soviet Union flag decorated with Sickle axes and the red five-pointed star was pulled down on the Red Square in Moscow under the watchful eyes of the world, which is the most distressing thing for the former Soviet Union leaders and for the socialist countries. It announced that the Soviet Union was over as well as the end of the history of Marxism-Leninism. There had been a full 69 years for the Soviet Socialist Union, finally, it came to the end of history, the country Soviet Union is no longer existing today legally.

The world situation turned from the U.S.-Soviet hegemony to one super strong power in the world from then on. Chinese President Hu Jintao made the following statement: The world today is undergoing major changes and adjustments. Peace and development are still the topics of the times. Seeking peace, seeking development and promoting cooperation have become an irresistible trend of the times. The international situation is generally stable but there still exist some unsettled factors. Hegemonism and power politics still exist. Local conflicts come one after another, and the world peace and development are facing many challenges (Hu,2007). This statement made by Hu Jintao reflects the Chinese leaders' judgments completely on the current international situation.

The principle of Marxist philosophy emphasizes that its development and movement are absolute for anything, while quiescence is relative. By the same token, the development and movement in the international situation are also absolute and under constant changes. The international situation remained West dominated and it was headed by the United States. The United States was a super strong power, and several strong powers coexisted at the same time. As the only superpower in the world, the United States was in the center of global power, and Europe, Japan, China, and Russia are behind of him. As a result, one side was the United States, the other side were composed of Europe, Japan, China and Russia. These 2 sides' comparison became the new pattern of international relations. This is what we call the world situation in which there was a super strong power together with multiple powers.

After years, the position of the United States as the overlord of the world has been seriously threatened by the deepening of economic globalization and the rise of other countries in the world. Under a series of economic crises and the pressures from the rise of big powers, it became a hot topic widely discussed by people whether the United States can maintain her hegemony position above all and stabilize the other power countries. Some people think that the world today is still the unipolar era in which the United States dominate. They admit that the

United States is a super strong power, while denying the decline of the United States, they believe that the era of one super power coexisting with multiple powers has not come to an end. Some other people think that this kind of situation has ended, and there form a group of powers which are rising rapidly. With the enhancement of China's economic strength and the continuous improvement of her overall national strength, and the gradual deepening of the EU integration, the United States is no longer a world leader any more. There will occur a group of strong powers, which can be called multipolar, but not unipolar any more. The world's hegemony is the strength of all countries, but not one of them, which is recognized and supported by the Chinese people, from the understanding of Chinese people.

The background for a super strong and a group strong

The disintegration of the Soviet Union, the end of the Cold War, the disintegration of the bipolar structure and the United States becoming the sole superpower, all these brought many changes in many aspects. On the one hand, the desire of the U.S. government to dominate the world has been inflated further. Therefore, the hegemonist and unilateralist foreign policies have been stepped up. On the other hand, the old balance has been broken and the new balance can hardly be established for a while. Major changes have taken place in the inter-relations between the strong powers, including the hostile countries during the Cold War. Many countries, including the allies of the United States, required that the United States should promote common development and prosperity through dialogue and cooperation with mutual respect, equality and mutual benefit, thus making it more and more difficult for the United States to push for the unilateral expansion.

Since the Cold War ended, the speed and scale of the European reunification and independence and self-improvement has drawn the world's attention. The EU implemented the Maastricht Treaty, expanded and improved the common market, issued the euro, established a currency union, and promoted the common foreign policies and defense plans, then promoted the unified constitutional reform as well as enlarging the European Union and NATO so that Europe would become an important member of the pluralistic world effectively. They made their own voices, put forward their own ideas, built an image of an overall strength.

Let us look at China's action. Since China implemented the reform and opening, she has been advancing along the road of socialism with Chinese characteristics and has enjoyed rapid economic growth. Her achievements in construction have attracted worldwide attention. Her comprehensive national strength has been enhanced significantly, her politics and society have maintained long-term stability, and China's international status has been improved greatly. Although China's national strength still lags far behind that of the developed countries in the West, as the largest developing country in the world, China's peaceful rise and the adherence to her principle and the non-alignment spirit in the international community have made a significant impact on the world pattern.

All these facts show that it is irresistible for the world situation to become multi-polarized, the multipolarization means that there are many "power centers," which are interdependent, cooperative, competitive, mutually influential and mutually constraining. Regarding this kind of trend and the pattern that it forms, we may summarize as "one super strong". It must be known that the number of countries which admit multipolarity and advocate the establishment of a multipolar world is increasing. This phenomenon is undoubtedly a portrayal of the times in which all the strong powers have risen together. It is an inevitable phenomenon to turn from one pole to an era of multipolarization gradually. Under such a global pattern, people's basic consensus is that this constructive process of multipolarity in international relations helps to establish a new order of balance, stability, democracy and non-confrontation, which is in the fundamental interest of all countries (Yu, 2005).

The on-surface development and progress do not indicate that everything satisfy people. The consensus meeting the fundamental interests of most countries objectively does not belong to the United

States. After the world come to the era of "one super strong," the "one super strong" here means the United States, and she tried her best to promote the "unipolar world" under her leadership and did her utmost to discourage the process of multi-polarization. Although the United States has made various efforts for this purpose, occupied a high place as the world leader and acted as the world police, however the world pattern of multi-polarization in political economy has become a trend of the times and it cannot be blocked by the United States. Of course, from time to time, there will still be arguments that denying the multipolarization of the world.

Some people still think that the world pattern is still the unipolar pattern headed by the United States. The United States will not be able to vacillate her position as a world leader in the world domination. The main reason for this argument may be due to these two considerations: Firstly, to confuse the fact that the United States is the sole superpower in the current world with the unipolar world; secondly, to compare the world's multipolarization with the multi-polar world, in fact, the multipolar world has not been formed yet, but we cannot deny the multipolarization which already exists undoubtedly. Is it a super strong or a group of strong on earth? If you want to have a clear understanding with regards to the current world situation, you had better rationalize the relations among the strong powers in the world.

Evolving to "a group of strong"

The "a super strong" international relations has been formed since the early 1990s and has undergone more than a decade of development and evolution, it formed an obvious multi-polarization pattern which we are seeing today. During this period, the following two features have been showed:

Number one, the single-polarization and multi-polarization have been coexisting, and will continue to fight. As an integrated international relations pattern, the pattern of "one super strong" has the tendency of evolution: single-polarization and multi-polarization. On the one hand, as the sole superpower, the United States promotes unilateralism strongly and attempts to establish the unipolar world headed by the United States. On the other hand, under the impetus of economic globalization, the China's rise, the European integration, the Japan's seeking political and military power, and the slow recovery of the Russian economy, all these show that the multipolarization is about to come, and pose a huge challenge to the unipolarity pursued by the United States. Therefore, the result is that the United States will not be able to dominate the entire world and the trend of multipolarization in the world will continue. The coexistence of single-polarization and multipolarization will keep unchanged for a long time.

Number two, the formation of unipolar pluralism. The multipolar world pattern today inherits the duality from the old bipolar pattern. In the bipolar structure, the two sides opposing the international strategic forces are the United States and the Soviet Union. However, the dualistic confrontation in today's multi-dimensional world has become the "one super" United States and the "multi-strong" - the EU, China and Russia, India and many other world powers, it has become a diversified world landscape. Although under the condition of economic globalization, the confrontation between "one super and multi-strong" is not as intense as the Cold War between the United States and the Soviet Union. However, the relationship among the multi-strong and the relationship between "one super" and "multi-strong" are becoming more and more complicated. The scope and situation of the competitors are also becoming more extensive and complicated. After entering the twenty-first century, the pattern of "A super strong" after Cold War was changed gradually, which was shown in the following three aspects:

Firstly, the emerging market economy was occurring. With the historic opportunity of globalization, some emerging market economy countries such as China, India, Russia and Brazil pushed forward their internal reforms and made fantastic achievements. Their international status and influence were also increasing. All these achievements were impacting the United States' world leader position. The achievements made by these mentioned countries led to the decline of the dominance by the western world headed by the United States. The most obvious manifestation of this is the evolution from the G8 meeting to the "G20" meeting. This shows that many global political, economic, trade and environmental issues will no longer be solved in the G8 system. Therefore, these emerging economies must be invited to participate in the decision-making process. This phenomenon shows that it is now over for the developed countries to dominate the international system and international issues.

Secondly, the contradictions between the western countries headed by the United States and the Russia have been increased. The geopolitical confrontation between the United States and Russia and the security contradiction between these two countries, have existed for a long time. A lot of them are the continuation from the contradictions between the United States and the Soviet Union during the Cold War. The conflicts between the United States and the Islamic world are due to the differences of culture, beliefs and values between them. The new trend now is that it is possible for Russia to combine with Islamic extremists to fight against the United States. If this combination occurs, it will inevitably lead to further contradictions between the United States and the outside world, and the international environment will be even worse.

Thirdly, some slight changes have taken place in the internal relations of the western allies led by the United States, showing the trend of reverse evolution. The world leader position for the United States is benefited from these two: strong national strength and stable alliance system. Europe is the most important part of the U.S. alliance system and NATO is the most important mechanism. After the Cold War, due to the disintegration of the external common opponent-the Soviet Union, the Europe's desire for cooperating with U.S. has been declining, and the differences in the major threat perceptions has been growing. Especially, after the Iraq war, the conflicts between the United States and what Bush called "Old Europe" was even more acute. In addition, with the progress of European integration, the EU has become the leading force in European politics, economy, diplomacy and security and has gained more independence from the United States.

The EU is facing a crisis caused by the debt crisis. Therefore, the European countries will mainly focus on resolving and strengthening EU internal solidarity in their own affairs and will not be able to bear too much responsibility for NATO, which is contrary to the United States. In addition, the economic and trade conflicts between the United States and Europe have increased. The rise of the euro has hit the cornerstone of U.S. hegemony-the dollar hegemony, and has an impact on U.S. interests. Although those countries that use euro as their currency are facing a serious debt crisis, the euro as the world currency still has a greater deterrent to the dollar's hegemony.

The world pattern of current times

From the above, we can see that the relations between big powers are an important reflection of how the world situation has formed, the changes in the relations among big powers today reflect the formation of the world's political and economic pattern. The characteristics of world powers relations are as follows: Firstly, peace and development are still the main topics for our current times. All countries in the world, whether it is a large country or a small one, almost all of them regard economic development as the primary goal and they enhance their comprehensive competitiveness through various methods. Development is the absolute principle. Therefore, all countries follow the principle of peaceful coexistence and mutual benefit for common development and seek development through competition. Secondly, the relations among big powers have very important strategic significance, considering its long-term, comprehensive and complex relations. "Strategic relations" and "partnership" without the alliance are the new things during the multi-polarization after the Cold War and become a unique transitional phenomenon in the reconstruction of a new international economic and political order. Thirdly, the economic factor is the primary and decisive factor in the relations among major powers. The premise for the adjustment of the relations between major powers is to seek, coordinate and balance each other's economic interests. Diplomacy based on economic integration and economic complementarity will benefit both parties. Fourthly, democratization of international politics will become an important goal in the adjustment of the relations among big powers. Opposing cold war mentality, hegemonism and power politics will be an unavoidable long-term task in the adjustment of the relations between major powers (Yu, 2005).

What is the reason for the formation of the world multi-polarization trend? The pattern of "one super strong" international relations is not a static structure, but a dynamic one with the unipolar and multipolar contradictions. Multipolarization is the main trend. Looking at the political and economic situations in the world today, maintaining peace and promoting development have become irreversible trends. The relations among big powers are becoming diversified gradually. Since the American President Obama took over the United States from Bush, the United States has brought the world a global economic crisis, and has brought a furious war to Iraqi and Afghan people and a huge fiscal deficit for the country. In addition, the European debt crisis affected the economy and politics of Europe in varying degrees. In this context, a subtle change happened to the relations among the world powers, the political and economic situation in the world has shifted to multipole gradually. The era of multi-polarization with "a group of strong" is now coming.

It is well known that the things will develop in the opposite direction when they become extreme, and in the case of the United States, it is going to be declined after being prosperous too much. Neo-realism think that the promotion of unilateral hegemony and control of the international system can gain economic benefits, but it also must pay a corresponding price. In the hegemony system, the dominant state will expand all the way until it reaches a balance between the costs and benefits, and once it reaches that equilibrium, the cost for maintaining the international status will be greater than that for its economic growth (Gilpin ,2007). When the economic power is difficult to sustain the expansion costs, the dominant state is forced to halt its expansion." The unipolar structure is the apex of the expansion of the hegemonic state, when reaching this apex, it will not be possible for the United States to grow her resources again, and she will reduce the cost of maintaining expansion and weaken its hegemony." After the Cold War ended, the hegemony of the United States reached her apex. She launched the Kosovo war, the war in Afghanistan, the war in Iraq. During the administration of George W. Bush, the arrogance of her unilateralism and the hegemony policy reached the limit in the world. However, these hegemonist activities also consume the strength of the United States. Unilateralism's unfavorable factors will lead the United States to decline. Wars will only accelerate this process but will not help the United States' hegemony.

Under the conditions of economic globalization, the comparative advantage of the United States in the economic field has been decreasing and the economic forces have begun to spread globally. Since the 1970s, there occurred three transfers in the world's economic forces. That is, the advantages of economic power have shifted from the United States to other major powers, from developed countries to developing countries and from western countries to non-western countries. The first transfer led to the tripartite confrontation of the U.S., Japan and Europe in the capitalist world. The second transfer has enhanced the economic position for the developing countries. This is also a challenge to the United States. At the same time, international organizations formed by developing countries, such as the Non-Aligned Movement, the Organization of Petroleum Exporting Countries and the ASEAN, are consolidating the power of the developing countries and promoting their own development while promoting the multipolarization of the international economic structure. The third transfer has allowed many non-Western countries to gain rapid economic growth and let the U.S. economy be decreased.

After entering the 21st century, the emerging economic countries, for example, the "Diamond 11 Countries" (Bangladesh, Egypt, Indonesia, Mexico, Nigeria, Pakistan, the Philippines, the United Republic of Korea, Turkey, Vietnam),they accelerated the multi-polarization trend of the international economic structure. The emerging countries have formed their own economic development model in accordance with their national conditions. It also broke the single American development model promoted by the "Washington consensus", and the diversification of the development model has become an important part of the multipolarization (Wang, 2009).

In the international political area, most of the countries oppose the unipolar world. China advocates multilateralism in the settlement of international affairs. France claims that his view on a multi-polar world is intensifying. Russia believes that the multi-polar world is "the most sensible and democratic international social system." In addition, many global issues such as environmental problems, non-traditional security and the global financial crisis that emerged during the course of world development cannot be settled by a few large powers or even by one or two superpowers, while it may be solved after promoting the multilateralism. For example, to cope with the current global financial crisis triggered by the United States, the international dialogue mechanism was upgraded from G8 to the G20, this kind of upgrade was a manifestation of the multilateralism development. "Multi-polarization and multilateralism are complementary and mutually reinforcing: the precondition of multi-polarization is that multiple strength centers are based on equal terms, which is in line with the basic principle of multilateralism. Regarding the current multilateralism which is emerged to cope with the financial crisis, it brought opportunities for the multi-polarization development (Liu,2009)."

In addition, the U.S. military strength seems to be too powerless to maintain a unipolar world. The United States owns the most powerful military force in the world. However, the major powers in the world will not obey him if only relying on his advantage of military strength, it cannot make up for the shortcoming in other fields. As a "trump card" for the United States to promote unipolarity, the role of strong military power in influencing international relations has been reduced greatly. The Iraqi war and the war in Afghanistan have highlighted the inadequacies of the U.S. military. The technological superiority of the United States has also been challenged. Robert Gilpin, a famous scholar of international relations and international politics, believes that the transfer of advanced technology from an advanced society to a backward society is undoubtedly an important reason for the power redistribution in the international system. The United States has world-class sciences and technologies that support the economic development. To maintain his technological superiority, the United States adopted an export control policy to limit the proliferation of technology-intensive industries.

However, under the condition of economic globalization, the technologies were already proliferated because of the international cooperation and international labor division. Some countries will form a "backward advantage" after adopting the advanced technologies, which is a challenge to the United States technological superiority. The revival of non-Western civilization, has challenged the hegemony of the Western civilization headed by the United States. After the 1970s, the revival of non-Western civilizations such as Confucianism civilization, Japanese civilization, Indian civilization, Orthodox civilization, Indian civilization and Islamic civilization shows the diversification of world soft power and will break the domination of Western civilization finally. As Huntington once indicated: Power is shifting from the Western civilization to non-Western civilization, and global politics have become multipolar and multi-civilized (Liu, 2009).

As we can see from the above reasons that it is a requirement of times for the world economic pattern to evolve toward multi-polarization, it is in the interest of people in all countries, and it is an inevitable outcome under the background of economic globalization. Economic globalization has enabled all kinds of production factors to be optimized and configured globally, promoted the rapid development of the global economy and even promoted the formation of a multipolar world. The multipolar pattern has led all forces in the world to form a relationship of mutual developing and mutual restraint, to avoid the outbreak of a new world war, and to a certain extent, curb the further development of hegemonism and power politics, and promote the establishment of a fair and reasonable new international political and economic order, and finally, will bring a new world of peace, stability and prosperity, for all people in the world. In addition, it will also help the developing countries grasp the opportunity to develop themselves, especially for China, who want to seek further development in the complex international relations.

At the same time, we should also know that it will be a long, tortuous and complicated process for the evolution of multipolarization. In this process, the conflicts between unipolar and multi-polar, the struggles between hegemony and non-hegemony, will last for a long time. Competitions contains cooperation and cooperation also contains competition, this is an important feature during the multi-polarization development. In the struggles between the world's multi-polarization and unilateralism, the military power is very important. For the great powers in the world, almost all of them attempted to establish a strong national defense force, and tried to strengthen their military's role in safeguarding and expanding the national interest to occupy a dominant position in the world multipolarization, for the strategic initiative in the 21st century international community. In the increasingly fierce competition for the comprehensive national strength, the status of economy and technology is becoming more and more important. The strong economic and technological strength is the fundamental condition for becoming a world leader. Therefore, all countries give priority to the economic development. It depends on the rapid economic development of the world's major powers and the developing countries whether the world multipolarization can become a reality.

Peace and development are still the topics of current times

For the past and the present, is the world pattern "a super strong" or "a group of strong?" What is the specific status of this pattern? For the past, the answer is clear, for the present, the scholars seem to have no clear and definite answer. Most scholars agree this opinion: the bipolar structure has been dissolved and various forces redistributed. The world has been moving toward multi-polarization. The formation of a new pattern will take a long time. From the historical experience, some scholars described that the unipolar pattern is extremely unstable. From the reality of international politics, they emphasized the transitional and complex nature of the current international situation as well as the uncertainty in the adjustment of international forces. At the same time, they think that the United States' unipolar opinion remains stubborn. However, this statement has some problems, because it only emphasizes the current transition period between the old pattern and the new one, but does not conduct any further analysis on the pattern of the transitional period. Therefore, the remaining question is, how should we accurately conclude the current world pattern? After the war in Kosovo, there have also been some different voices in academia. Some scholars think that the world today is where the unipolar forces of the United States rule the world. Multipolarization is only our wishful thinking. These different understandings result from the qualitative ambiguity of the international pattern. To improve, it requires the follow-up efforts of our relevant scholars.

As you know, the world situation was formed under the control of various forces, there is no such thing as a "vacuum" in the balance of forces, or a "blank" situation in the international pattern. In any period of history or reality, there always existed some contrasts for various forces. It is impossible to have no orientation or no pattern. In other words, if somebody say there is no world pattern at all, he must be lying. Watching from the global international situation, there would be three types of world pattern: unipolar, bipolar and multipolar. If we refer to these three typical patterns as "safflower," we will inevitably ask what the "green leaves" are? There must be still many patterns acted as "transition" between these two, which can be called "green leaves" accordingly. Based on this analysis, it is reasonable to think that the comparative structure of international forces after the Cold War is referring to the United States as the only super strong country and several other "strong countries", that is, the unipolar and multivariate world structure. Unipolarity is the only world power that refers specifically to "the United States," while diversity refers to many regional powers or regional groups such as the EU, Russia, Japan, and China. This unipolar multivariate pattern has both the tendency of unipolarity and the tendency of multi-polarization.

Undoubtedly, the United States occupied a dominant position in the post-Cold-War international pattern and thus he became "a super strong." At the same time, the multipolarization of the international pattern after the cold war was also developing. For the European Union which was a very important pole in the multipolar world, her strategic goal is to restore and establish the status of the former "world center" in Europe, and to continue to speed up the European integration. Russia is also adjusting her foreign policy constantly to restore her status as a former superpower. Although Japan always hides under the umbrella of the United States, she does not forget her mission, her goal of moving toward a political power remains unchanged. She has been increasing her international obligations and responsibilities gradually in the international affairs, participating in various of international peacekeeping operations and she has attempted to become a permanent member of the UN Security Council. China has become active in the international arena increasingly and has maintained her stable growth. Also, China has become an important positive force in the readjustment of major powers and has promoted the multipolarization of the world effectively. And China has always stood for the peace and development, which is the important topics of current times.

Why are the peace and development still the topics of our current times? In addition to the things that the Chinese People have learned in their political textbooks, the Chinese People can regard themselves as the out-of-school scholars or bystanders. The overall situation is that the world needs peace and people call for peace. All those things that were done by hegemonism and power politics are all strongly opposed by people in all countries in the world. Please do not say that those protests are useless, nor should they say that opposition is just a bluff. You must know that people like water and the water can carry boats, and the boats can be capsized by the water as well. Once the people were infuriated, what are the rulers in the eyes of the public? The governments of various countries also dare not ignore this issue, even in the United States, they indoctrinate their own people with the idea of the "American dream" constantly. For what? That is to calm the public anger, calm the people, tell people that the present is temporary, and the future will be bright.

The peaceful development of the world is the common aspiration of all peoples and it is an irresistible historical trend. "People will survive if obeying the trend, or he will die," this is the truth. Local and small-scale turmoil can only be regarded as the small conflicts next to this "mainstream", and it requires the majestic spirit of stepping on the coast for the peaceful development.

The outlook for future of the world

The current multi-polar world is still changing from time to time. The final formation of a multi-polar structure will take a long time. In this process, there are many unfavorable factors that may block the formation and development of a multi-level structure. What will the world pattern be in future? When will it be formed finally? This depends on the gambling stratagem among the major powers in the current world. The unsafe and unstable factors in the current international situation are also the major aspects of disrupting the world structure. These insecurity and instability are mainly manifested in the following areas:

Firstly, the conflicts among the major powers still exist. In 2011, there happened some complicated changes in the international situation. The financial crisis was deepened, the wars happened in some areas and the Asia - Pacific strategic importance was rising. Despite the marked improvement in the relations among big powers in recent years, the friction and conflicts of interests were also increasing, there existed some contradictions between the rise of unilateralism and the strengthening of multilateral cooperation in the international community. In the new year, the relations development among the major powers will be further tested by the Middle East issue, the North Korean nuclear issue, and so on. The relations between China and the United States will also continue to be tested by the Taiwan issue, the Diaoyu Islands issue, the South China Sea and other territorial issues.

Secondly, the prospects for world economic development are not optimistic. At present, the world economy has not been out of the doldrums fully and is still facing serious uncertainties. In 2011, those which were already been out of the doldrums was stilling in the recovering process. Those institutions that had made optimistic forecasts earlier have downgraded their forecasts for the world economic growth recently. In September 2011, the International Monetary Fund estimated that the global output in 2011 will reach 78.85 trillion U.S. dollars by purchasing power parity (PPP), an increase of 4.47 trillion U.S. dollars from the previous year, with a real growth rate of 4.0%, down 0.4 percent from its forecast in April 2011; GDP at market exchange rates will exceed 70.01 trillion U.S. dollars, up US $ 7.10 trillion from the previous year, but the real growth rate will be revised downwards from 3.5% to 3.0%, down 0.5 percent. In December 2010, Goldman Sachs predicted that the world economy will grow by 4.6% in 2011, while in the August 2011 report, Goldman Sachs lowered the figure by 0.5 percentage point to 4.0%. The overall trend of world economic development since 2011 is a downward trend. It has dropped to 2.2% in 2016 and dropped by nearly 1.8 percentage points from 2011. The United Nations estimated that the global economic growth in 2017 will increase from 2.2% to 2.7%, and in 2018 it will be 2.9%. The outlook for global economic development is still not optimistic.

Thirdly, the intense issues in some areas are extremely serious. The Iranian nuclear issue, the North Korea nuclear issue, the North Korean crisis, the internal political contradictions in the former socialist countries in Eastern Europe and the Near East, the Taiwan issue, the issue of the Diaoyu Islands, the issue of the South China Sea and so on.

So, what will the pattern be in the future world? Governed or chaos? We need to seek truth from facts. We must make a reasonable presumption of the future pattern in the world according to the current multi-polarization trend, the power balance among the world powers, and the reasonable prediction of the future world. Regarding the pattern of the future world, different countries have different opinions. Taking these two countries-China and the United States as an example, in March 2012, the United States published a cover article in its "Times," predicting the ten major trends affecting the world in the next 10 years, emphasizing that the 21st century is a United States century, it extended the G2 concept to "axis" for the first time. China is reluctant to accept the U.S. statement. The United States has drawn China into the axis. Of course, China will not admit the self-centered arrogance of the United States. There are still some people think that China will rise gradually, Europe will become more unified, the wars will continue, the United States, Russia, China and the Europe, these four are going to be the biggest four parties in the world.

After all, how the world's political and economic pattern evolves depends on the political and economic strength of various countries. Therefore, how the future world structure develops depends on the political and economic power of all countries in the world today. According to the current economic strength of major powers, the power balance among big powers will ultimately result in a relatively stable multi-polar world structure. Whether the multi-polar world structure will finally come into existence or not and how long it will take to form will depend on the strength of the countries in the world in terms of politics, economy, military affairs and so forth. Therefore, all countries should pay attention to developing their own economic strength, adopt the Marxist theories, the economic foundation determines the superstructure. No matter how the world economic structure changes, we should deal with the ever-changing forms of the world with an unchanged development concept.

Both the past "a super strong" and the current "a group of strong" will eventually form a stable pattern of multipolarization in the world. Peace and development are still the topics of our times. However, these two topics are facing challenges that cannot be ignored. The unjust and unreasonable international political and economic old order has not changed yet. As a result, some local and small-scale wars, tension and turmoil still exist, the North-South gaps are increased further, as a developing country, China will face more challenges from different areas in the world during her rising.

In fact, at present, China has been entering an international friction period. According to relevant scholars, it is estimated that this friction period will last for at least 20 years. This friction is not accidental, but inevitable. It is not tactical but strategical (Zhao, 2012). In view of this, on the one hand, China needs to resolve international hostility through dialogue and exchange. At the same time, China must also adhere to tit-for-tat, halting and daring to struggle on the issues of the national interests. In this regard, Deng Xiaoping, China's second-generation leadership core, did a very good job. He did well in the use of struggle strategies. When Deng Xiaoping talked about "One Country, Two Systems" and the issue of peaceful reunification of Taiwan in October 1984, he said in a clear-cut manner: The use of force must not be easy because China must concentrate on economic construction and solve the overall problem via non-injury methods in the process of reunification.

However, China cannot give up the use of force, China must keep this in mind when using force and this is a strategic consideration for the next generation."(Deng,1993) This perfect strategic concept of Deng Xiaoping has led us to guide our overall diplomatic activities. In the face of the complicated and volatile international situation, China cannot limit the ways to the simple practice of achieving a peaceful rise of the country by dialogue, consultation and cooperation, as it will limit the Chinese people's thoughts and hands and will lose the struggle strategies, thus will also narrow the road to peaceful rise. The world is already full of contradictions and conflicts. China, a "huge creature" with a population of 1.4 billion, whose rise will inevitably bring about a tremendous impact on the existing international system and the world pattern, will surely arouse the suspicion and anxiety of the west and the surrounding countries. In this regard, China emphasize that she should eliminate misunderstandings through consultation and dialogue and promote common development through cooperation. However, in the face of aggressive opponents, China cannot compromise blindly. The Chinese People must protect the national red line and carry out tit-for-tat struggles if necessary. Even the force can be used to promote the dialogue and correct the cooperation.

In the face of the new challenges, all countries in the world should go beyond the traditional concepts, follow the trend of the times, strengthen exchanges and cooperation among the nations, seek common ground while reserving differences, coordinate and cooperate each other closely. China should push forward the world multipolarization and the democratization of international relations actively, strive to establish a new international economic order that meets the requirements of each country, reform the irrational international financial and trade system and guarantee the equal development of all countries, especially the developing countries. China should respect the diversity of the developments and civilizations in various countries, and all kind of civilizations, all kinds of development paths should coexist to make up for their deficiencies in the competition and make progress together in seeking common ground while reserving differences. To establish a just and reasonable new international political and economic order, let us make active efforts to achieve a lasting peace and universal prosperity in the world.

Chapter 5:

What China will Do When Becomes No.1 in the World?

It became a hot topic that was widely discussed both inside and outside China. Optimistic opinion views China's economy will surpass the United States' in a couple of decades or even within a decade. However, the opposite opinion is somewhat pessimistic. That point of view regards that hidden enormous economic problem will gradually show-up and will be detrimental to China's future economy It will eventually lead to an economic crisis just like what had happened in the United States and Japan. In short, it is at risk of being increasingly polarized in the world regarding the future direction of China. In this polarization debate, the result will be: "The winner is the king and the loser is the invader."

In China, the official economists have optimistic opinion. The authoritative analysis team from the Chinese Academy of Sciences predicts that from 2020 to 2030, China's total economic output will reach the highest in the world. From 2040 to 2050, the per capita GDP will reach the level of the developed countries (Zhi, 2009). At the end of the 21st century, per capita GDP and per capita social development will reach the level of the developed countries. The report's author declared that the 21st century is the century for China to rise rapidly. Of course, there are many media employers who also think that China will eventually surpass the United States and become the world leader. In the eyes of most people in the world, China is indestructible.

During the time when the rest of the world was in deep crisis, China seemed to be undisturbed and even more prosperous. It seems that nothing can stop her rapid progress. Undoubtedly, China will replace the United States which is deeply in debt crisis, and become an indispensable economy in the world. Some top businessmen and powerful decision makers are convinced that China's "national capitalism" model will be a great weapon to deal with the modern global economy in the future. In response, the senior reporter of Time magazine in the United States, Michael Schumann stated: Please think twice (Schuman, 2012). In his opinion, if China does not change her economic development model, the economic crisis will inevitably happen soon. Then, the Chinese people would like to ask the following question: Would china surely become the world leader if she has transformed her economic development model or if she is resolutely and effetely solving the problems that may threat her capability to become the world leader?

If so, let us follow this kind of thinking, and look at the future of this world leader, even if this world leader is temporarily hypothetical. Back to reality, although China has many problems in the process of development, it is good that we have realized the problems and have been constantly exploring them. After all, there is no -precedent to learn from for China's development and the problems that China encountered are unique. The entire world acknowledges that China is not qualified as the world leader yet, but how about the future? Who has imagined China as the world leader? Who is trying to curb China's further development? If China really becomes the world leader as what the "prophets" predicted, what will be the impact to the world? How will the world be readjusted? Will the new international economic order be established in accordance with the wishes of the new leader? How can China be a good leader? Can Chinese persuade people with actual strength? These kinds of real problems will emerge one after another once China becomes the world's new leader.

Who imagined China as the world leader?

There exist various opinions with regards to whether China can be the world leader now or in future and when will China surpass the United States and become the world leader? There are different predictions with their own logic, but please note that everyone is discussing when China will surpass the United States and become the world leader, but no one is discussing whether China can overtake the United States to become the world leader or not. They are critically different, as the former question deals with the procedural issue while the latter discusses are referring to the results issues. According to the former, it seems that China's becoming the world leader is inevitable, because the length of time shows only a process, but the result is only one, that is, China will become the world leader. As such, the Chinese People want to know that who imagined China as the world leader. At least for the moment, this prediction is just an imagination.

From an international perspective, the International Monetary Fund released a report in 2011 saying that China would become the world's largest economy in the next five years (Li, 2011). It also mentioned that the share of the United States and China in the world economy will change by 2016. China's share will increase from the current 14% to 18%, while the share of the United States will decrease from 20% to 17.7%, slightly lower than China, ranking the second in the world. Some people have doubts about the IMF's data. They= think that the China's actual economic scale contains "-water (fake numbers)," the scale of China's economy was enlarged on purpose by some individuals. However, even if calculated with actual exchange rate of international currencies, it will not change the fact that the United States will eventually lose her world leader status.

On the Christmas Eve of 2010, a per in the Economist states that China will become the largest economy in the world in 2019 (Lachman, 2011). Almost at the same time the Nobel laureate Fogel made his forecast, he suggests that China's economic output will become the largest in the world by 2020. As for the forecast time of other financial institutions, there is only a slight difference, their predicted time is also around 2020 or so. According to the Japanese media reports, in 2007, the Japanese scholars conducted currency conversions on their GDP in various currencies and reached the conclusion that the China's GDP will overtake the United States by 2020 and become the largest economy in the world. Regarding when China will eventually surpass the US, the

Deutsche Bank gave out the prediction of 2020, Goldman Sachs said 2027, and JP Morgan announced its between 2010 to 2025.

In addition, the economists at the World Bank predicted that China's economy will overtake the United States and the EU in 2030 and then become the world's largest economic market, at that time, China, the United States, the European Union, India and Japan these five countries will promote the world economic growth jointly, this is so called “five dragons” (Guang, 2008). Lin Yifu, the chief economist at the World Bank, suggests that China's economy will overtake the United States by 2025. The Chinese People agree with Lin's judgment that China's economy will not slow down in the next decade. Zhang Weiying, a professor at Guanghua School of Peking University, after comparing the current China with the United States of 100 years ago, he believes that the China today is about the same as the United States 100 years ago and that the relationship between the United States and Britain 100 years ago is like the current relations between the United States and China. At that time, the United States was an emerging market. Britain was an overlord. Americans borrowed money from Britain. Forty years later, the United States replaced Britain and became a world economic power (Zhang, 2009). Zhang Weiying believes that the United States subprime mortgage crisis that broke out in 2007 was an opportunity for China to rise. Because after this crisis, China will likely replace the United States gradually, the most likely possibility is that China will become the world's largest economy in 30 years. Zhang Weiying estimates that the China's GDP will account for 23% of the world by 2040, which is such an inspiring thing for the Chinese People.

In China, in addition to some predictions made by the relevant scholars, some academic organizations have given their own forecasts as well. For example, on April 7, 2011, the Social Sciences Literature Publishing House held a seminar on "The Rise of BRICS and the Global Development and Governance" in Beijing and a press conference on the "Blue Book for Emerging Economies" in the same year. They discussed the rules of development and changes in emerging economies and the new trend of global development and governance. The Blue Book on

Emerging Economies, the BRICS Economic and Social Development Report (2011) was formally released at this meeting. In this Blue Book, it predicted that the China's total economic output may surpass the United States and ranks the first in the world by 2020 (Lin and Zhou, 2012). This prediction is like the opinions of the foreign countries scholars.

However, if take a closer look, we can easily find that there are still differences between the predictions by the Chinese and that by non-Chinese. In a nutshell, regarding the prediction when China will become the world leader, the foreign academic scholars were more radical and the time they predicted was relatively short. However, the academic circles in China were relatively conservative and their forecasting time is naturally longer. This is a reasonable result, but fortunately the Chinese people keep a clear head. They insist on that no matter how the outside world imagines China as the world leader, the Chinese People should always keep a clear head, bearing in mind the road at our own feet. China must not lose her way and get confused.

The world pattern will be readjusted

The so-called world pattern is a wide concept that refers to the major political forces in the international arena, each country will consider its own benefits, so the mutual restraint forces will be formed during a certain historical period after contrasting with each other. If we want to make a more detailed category, the world pattern mainly includes the world political pattern, the world economic pattern and the world military pattern.

Let us start with considering the overall world pattern. Because the economic, political and military factors that make up the overall pattern of the world are closely interrelated, the interaction among them is enormous. Judging from the process for forming a global system, the role played by the war is huge, decisive and even destructive. After the First World War, the imperialist powers established the Versailles-Washington System and established the imperialist rule in the world through the Paris Peace Conference and the Washington Conference. The Britain and the France dominated the world, the United States and Japan competed for the Asia-Pacific region (Jin, 2006). After the Second World War, the "Versailles-Washington system" was disintegrated gradually because of the aggression and expansion of fascism, and replaced by the "Yalta System" represented by the United States and the Soviet Union. This became the new post-war world pattern, it was also called "bipolar pattern."

In the late 1980s and early 1990s, the drastic changes in Eastern Europe and the disintegration of the Soviet Union showed the collapse of the Yalta system. Since then, the world has evolved from a bipolar structure to a multi-polarization trend (Lu, 2015). The final formation of this trend will take a long time. In fact, the current world is in a period of transition in which the old pattern has been disintegrated and the new pattern has not yet been formed. In other words, it is a period of struggles between the multi-polarization and the "unipolar world" which refers to the United States. Therefore, we have let the world pattern during this period be vividly called "one super strong." It is not hard to see that the United States is a key role in the evolution of these world patterns. So, if China replaces the United States and becomes the world leader, does it mean that China will play a decisive role in the future world pattern? With the improvement of China's overall national strength, the strategic balance role China will play in world affairs will become more and more important. Therefore, it is no doubt that it will be very difficult to achieve coordination and stability without China's participation in settling some international affairs. (Tang, 2009)

In the post-Cold War era, particularly in the past 10 years, emerging powers such as China, India, Brazil and Russia have rapidly gained economic power, and the rising of emerging markets is a prominent phenomenon in the world economy. When these emerging powers achieved the rapid growth of their own economies, the impact on the world economy and their contributions for the world economy have also been increasing. According to the statistics from Goldman Sachs, from 2000 to 2008, the "BRICs" formed by China, India and Russia and Brazil have contributed 30% of the world's economic growth. Ten years ago, it was only 16%. Goldman Sachs also predicted that it is possible for China to overtake the United States and become the world's largest economy by 2027. The total amount of the "BRICs" economies may keep pace with the "G-7" by 2032 (Wei, 2011). It is foreseeable that the rise of emerging powers such as China, India and Brazil is ending the short-lived "unipolar times" gradually. As a result, the confrontation between China and the United States will not be that serious any more, and there will occur a multi-polar system. The United States is likely to remain the strongest country, but her overall leadership has been weakened - and it is still being further reduced (Walter, 2011). Therefore, the future pattern of the world will no longer be dominated by the United States. After becoming the world leader, China will bring a new pattern to the world. On the diplomatic principle that China will never seek hegemony, it will be possible to form a multi-polar world.

Even though China herself has always stressed that the rise of China is peaceful and does not harm the interests of other countries. However, the other countries in the world have all kinds of speculations about China. In all kinds of professional reports, it is not uncommon for China to become a superpower. Professor Fogel from the University of Chicago published an article in Foreign Policy Magazine in 2011, he imagined a new world pattern dominated by China: By 2040, China will become the only super economic power and the United States will be far behind China, China's total economic output will reach 123 trillion U.S. dollars. China's per capita national income will reach 85,000 U.S. dollars, twice the expected per capita income of the EU by that time. In other words, the general people in China's metropolitan area will be much richer as the general French people at that time. Robert Heplode, the former chief operating officer at Microsoft, has lashed out at the end of the Wall Street Journal column: Washington politicians and American voters need to realize they are being defeated and they need to make major changes to get America back on the right track wake up, the United States!

The BBC notices that there are 13 countries that consider China's economic development a good thing, this is more than those with negative attitudes. However, most countries are worried about China's growing military power. Take Britain as an example, more than half of the respondents praised China's economic development. However, up to 70% of people think that the continuous military power development of China is not a good thing. As everyone knows, these countries that think China will become a brutal killing nation put their own "belligerence" on China. From a historical point of view, China has never positively invaded any other countries. Even in the most glorious historical period, China could be described as infinitely beautiful at that time, but never desired to extend the "dagger" to other weaker countries. Therefore, the Chinese nation can be said a peace-loving nation. However, peace-loving does not mean that the Chinese People are afraid of war, when facing the foreign aggressors and when the core interests of Chinese nation are violated, the Chinese People not only do not fear the war, but also win the war. China is a powerful nation with more than 5,000 years of civilization, can she allow her national interests to be violated by others? Definitely not! Whether China can become the world leader or not, China will have enough power to protect herself. "If they do not invade us we will not invade them either, if they invade us, we will do the same to them," China will not take the initiative to aggression, but China will never have been bullied passively. This is the firm stand of China in her way to the world leader position. (Deng, 1937)

Apart from the real changes such as politics, economy, and military affairs, the ideological changes are imperceptible. For all things in the universe, nothing is as stubbornness as the old minds; nothing in the universe can be as enchanting as it is to go beyond the outdated ideas. After China becomes the world leader, the new world pattern will include the ideas, this new element. Even if it is not a convention, even if there is no explicit provision. However, China's adherence will make the world recognize it as an indispensable and important part of the world system elements. From the China's perspective, it is currently under the peace and development stage, the country should keep holding to its core interest and meanwhile not be ignorant of hostile forces and external interferences to disrupt is progress. It is a difficult exploration for

China to take the new road to realize the national rise. The Chinese People need strong confidence and sufficient force (Yang, 2011).

The concept of superpower will change

What is the superpower? There is no standard answer for this concept so far. Different people have different opinions. However, we can simply define the superpower as the most powerful and aggressive one in the world and consider it as the world police. The 20th century is a century of the United States, in this century, the United States was the world's largest economy and the richest country in the world, of course the people living in the richest country were the richest people. Maybe this is the understanding about the concept of superpower before China becomes the world leader, but if China really becomes the world leader, it would mean that the concept of the superpower would change as well. Because while China rises and becomes a super-economic power, the relations between the rich country and the rich people may not be relevant. From this point of view, China is getting poorer compared with the western countries. For example, China is holding 3 trillion U.S. dollars in foreign exchange reserves, but the per capita income is one tenth of that in the United States. The so-called wealthy and powerful nation seems to be only a slogan after China becomes the world leader (Lachman, 2011).

The above opinion is based on a series of facts. For example, if being measured by GDP, when China's economy was doubled, the total social wage as a percentage of GDP was declining. According to the official statistics released by the National Bureau of Statistics, China's public revenue in 2011 was 10.37 trillion yuan, an increase of 24.8% over the previous year, an increase of 1.76 times for the nominal increase of per capita disposable income of urban residents, and 1.39 times for the nominal increase of per capita net income of rural residents (Wen, 2012). When the wages of most of non-public service employees are not synchronized with the economic growth, China still adopted the policy of paying high salaries to keep a healthy salary system, and continuously giving salaries to civil servants to condone or acquiesce the activities of the state-owned and social enterprises to set their own annual salaries. As a result, the annual salary of Ma Minzhe from PingAn insurance company has been as high as 68 million yuan, and then, each executive working in the state-owned banks want to set their salaries as high as 1 million, some private banks executives even want more than 10 million, such kind of ugly phenomenon occurs in China the highest income of the executives is 80 times more than the general employees (Lin, 2007).

These barbaric systems of distribution by power or by department and position are tantamount to public plunder. It brings a very fundamental problem: the huge gap between the rich and the poor in society. That is, with the constant growth of GDP, the ordinary people in China are almost breathlessness under these huge mountains like the medical care, the education, the old-age pension and housing. However, on the other hand, many government officials, corrupt things, are being exposed from time to time, and the amount involved in corruption and bribery cases is becoming huger and huger, from a few million to tens or even hundreds of millions. Therefore, according to the current abnormal state of China, even if it becomes the world leader, China cannot become the image of the "superpower" recognized by the public. Unless everyone's conception is changed, people think the superpower does not represent the wealth of the people absolutely. All things are changing, so the concept of the public will change or not? Let us wait and see (Marx, 2002).

In addition to its economic impact, as the superpower, we must talk about the politics regards to China. Some people may say that the military affairs also need to be mentioned. However, as for China, the essence of the military is still political, so it does not need to be talked about additionally. Of course, culture is also a crucial factor, but we will not go into details one by one, because in a later part we will talk more about the important influence of culture. Let us return to the topic of politics, the world topic "peace and development" is becoming more and more important due to the economic interaction among various countries. If all countries in the world can accept the fact that China will become the world leader and China can become the world leader with her "peaceful rise," all the countries in the world will need to unite in response to the call of "peaceful rise" of China to establish a global mechanism to protect the world peace and to prevent all kinds of conflicts. However, maybe this ideal pattern will not come true (Xu, 2012).

Although the political power is different from the economic power, these two are closely related. The feelings of the neighboring countries will be the most intense for the political issues caused by China's economic strength. Japan, South Korea and Australia now find that they have diverged from China economically and strategically (Zhang, Wang and Zhao, 2013). These three countries all have very important economic relations with China, and meanwhile hold very close military ties with the United States. Thus, it is inevitable that China and the United States will be linked together in economic and military relations. Politically, as China becomes richer, her influence will also be increased step by step as time go on. This kind of increase will undoubtedly help China to become the world leader. However, whether the current world leader will surrender willingly or not? Perhaps there will be some struggles in the political and economic fields, even in the military fields. If China really becomes the world leader, what may be changed is not only the concept of the superpower, but also some other issues in the ideological area (Zhang, 2011).

Nowadays the United States is still the world leader, many people in many countries bear the good images for the United States, this is mainly derived from the beautiful construction of the "American dream," as people know this dream is achievable, so it also becomes an important reason for the public in many countries to persevere. The freedom and democracy in the United States are the cornerstones of their own people. Every time they face a presidential election, the freedom and democracy must be mentioned and emphasized. China's freedom and democracy have always been criticized by the United States. If China becomes the world leader, will the entire world begin to doubt: are the democracy in the United States better or the socialism with Chinese characteristics much better? Maybe there are many other types of changes except for this type. To put it in a philosophical jargon: "the only constant things in the world are changes."

How to be a good world leader?

Obviously, there are all kinds of predictions about whether China can become the world leader, and it is possible for China to become the world leader, and accordingly, the world pattern will be changed certainly. To be the world leader, China must have the image and posture of being the world leader. In the past three decades, China has exported a large amount of low-price goods on the strength of its low labor cost. China has been the top of the world in multiple aspects, including being the most populous country, the fastest growth economy (Lou, 2009). However, in the next three decades, China will have immense potential for development. Once China becomes the world's largest economy, it is very necessary to make the country richer and powerful, to develop harmoniously and promote world progress. Only in this way can China be respected by the world. In addition, China must also export the excellent cultural value system of the Chinese nation, an innovative mechanism and environment, and a world-class brand full of charisma and high credibility! (Qian, 2007).

To be a world leader, China must let her Chinese culture to be contributed to the development of human society. Since the reform and opening, China has made remarkable achievements in her economic development. However, her splendid culture is not as fruitful as the economy, not to mention becoming the mainstream culture that dominates the world. In general, each country will have a landmark cultural product, such as the United States' Hollywood culture and KFC, McDonald's brand culture; European classical romantic culture and luxury consumer culture; Japan's anime culture and lean culture; South Korea's food culture and "fast fashion" culture. In recent years, these foreign popular cultures spread rapidly in China, just like a virus. However, when talking about China, it seems that China do not have such a landmark cultural product. If this is not a big humiliation, at least it is a very regrettable thing. Although China have all these mentioned above, most of them just hit the "edge ball" (Freud, 2011).

There is a kind of very famous culture in China, that is, the cottage culture. China's ability of copy and paste can be vividly demonstrated in this respect. However, it is not necessary to elaborate on the cottage culture. It is suggested that China should add something of her own apart from studying the foreign cultures, China can consider her own culture, ideology, system, science and technology, but not just copy and paste simply. For example, China's Confucian culture, the rising Chinese Cultural Circle provides a fantastic opportunity for this. The Chinese Cultural Circle is an area that refers to the "Confucian Cultural Circle" which builds a basic society based on Confucian culture (Fukui, 2010). The Japanese scholar Nishijima Sadao pointed out that the constituent elements of the Chinese Cultural Circle are: Taking Chinese characters as the medium of communication, Confucianism as the ideological and ethical foundation, Mahayana Buddhism as the religious belief and so on (Nishijima,1985). This induction is recognized by many scholars. What we want to say is that all the countries in the cultural circle of Chinese characters, including North Korea, South Korea, Japan and Vietnam, have been historically affected by the Chinese culture. China can play a leading role in this (Zhu, 2013).

In this cultural circle of Chinese characters, one can see some similar living culture such as the use of chopsticks, the use of writing brush, and people in this circle enjoy drinking tea, build their houses using tiles, etc. Of course, the cultural circle of Chinese characters that we have listed is only one aspect of the struggle for China's becoming the world leader, the Chinese People look forward to seeing more positive activities. Only when the Chinese civilization becomes the mainstream of world civilization can China become a real leader of the world.

Take a closer look at the world leader today, the United States, she has been able to serve as the world leader for such a long time, most of the reason is that the U.S. dollar is a world currency. Some people are joking that the United States will not be able to withdraw from the stage of history and her world leader position will not be shaken if the U.S.

dollar is still the world currency. Although it is somewhat exaggerated, it is also a part of the facts. So, for China, after becoming the world leader, should she speed up the internationalization process of RMB? It should not be denied that RMB internationalization is an important part of the international financial systems (Zhu and Lin, 2011).

Related to this, an academic report on the International Financial Forum was held in Beijing on September 17, 2012. The major topic of this report was how the world financial system changed after the fiscal crisis (Liu,2012). Some scholars thought that China must pay more attention to the sustainability after internationalization, as the expectations for the RMB internationalization continue to rise. Instead of analyzing how to maintain economic growth, China should now focus on solving the long-term economic development problems. Some people from the financial sector made a clear suggestion at this meeting that China now needs to turn to a real big-power economy. Therefore, the RMB becoming a reserve currency is not only the need of China's economic development but also the needs of the world. China must notice that the macroeconomic policies have an ever-increasing impact on society and therefore it requires more and more detailed macroeconomic decisions. As China increases the possibility of becoming the world leader, the internationalization of the RMB will certainly come true (Yang and Xue, 1994).

Stability is not everything and mutation is needed for development

To become the world leader, it is undoubtedly very important that the harmony and stability of the internal society be established. From the past to the current, the Chinese leaders have always emphasized that China is seeking stability and development (Xu, 2014). No one in such a populous country can imagine how important the stability is for China. However, the stability does not mean everything, it can only be the result or purpose for governing the country and cannot become a means or measure of state governance. If China regards the purpose as a means by mistake, China will regret it and will possibly pass by the opportunity of being the world leader. In fact, it depends on the willing of the Chinese People whether the stability can last long or not. If the ruling philosophy and major principles and policies are consistent with the interests of the people, the society will naturally be stable. The major livelihood problems that have been paying attention to over the years are enough to show that the Chinese leaders are firm in their solving the people's appeals. In the face of external shocks and even aggression, the unity of the Chinese nations can withstand all. The victories in the Anti-Japanese War of eight years are solid evidence.

Let us imagine, if China faces such a foreign war once again, will the Chinese People still have the same courage? Of course, most of the people in China still know the major principle when being faced with a foreign war, but there are some people who "pick fishes in the troubled waters." For example, in response to the Diaoyu Islands issue, some people burned the Japanese food shops, hit the Japanese cars, hit the Japanese car owners, which hurt our Chinese People deeply. In fact, after a brief analysis for this social phenomenon, we know that their direct targets were the Japanese people, but not Chinese people, right? Then why did this happen?

If the Chinese people have sufficient rights to elect and be elected, just like the United States, perhaps China can become stronger. Of course, in China, the systems are relatively approvable, but why were they changed and failed to achiève the desired effects when being carried out? It must be admitted that no system is perfect and flawless, but which is better? The system of multi-party cooperation and political consultation under the leadership of the Communist Party of China has its own advantages, which are likely to be more widely recognized after China becomes the world leader. It is conceivable that China will challenge the democracy and economy in the western countries after considering the current China's strength and the increasing public debt of the United States, the European Union and Japan (Tang, 2011).

Since the United States became the largest economy in the world by the late 19th century, the most powerful economy in the world has always been a democratic country. With the renewed popularity of

Chinese authoritarianism, the slogan freedom works from the western countries will face challenges（Cao, 2016). This change can be summed up in an idiom, that is, the winner is the king and the loser is the invader. In case the economic and political crisis happens in China, the description for China made by the western countries will suddenly be changed. Some people may point out that the "miracle of China" in the past 40 years was only a mirage. The so-called "push the wall down by all people if it is expected to fall" is the eternal rule in the world. Therefore, what China needs to worry about is that once China has a crisis, such authoritarianism will face criticism. Therefore, China can only seek a new pattern of development before becoming the world leader, and take the challenges from both international and domestic various mutations in society, China must combine democracy with dictatorship and put it into practice. Perhaps it can become a new pattern of social development. Of course, this new mode of development for China, especially for the current top designers, is undoubtedly a very difficult choice. For China, a populous country, many things spread quickly from one to another one, and finally, the original meaning will be changed. This is what the Chinese People are worrying about (Sanderson, 2008).

Undoubtedly, China is currently in an important period of strategic opportunities, as well as in the crucial period of reform and opening and the accumulation of social conflicts. In such a special stage, China needs great strategic layout and tactics to grasp both the domestic situation and the international situation and handle the interaction between these two. The Chinese People should remind the decision-makers that they should avoid repeating the strategic blunder of "keeping the domestic stability at any cost" which happened in some feudal dynasties in China's history (Fang,2000). This strategic principle began in the early years of the Northern Song Dynasty. Song Taizong, the founding emperor of the Song Dynasty indicated: If the state has no external worries, there must be internal afflictions. Regarding the external worries, there is nothing serious except the frontier defense which can be prevented. However, it is very terrible if there exist the internal afflictions. He said that the intensification of various contradictions in the country, will inevitably lead to the civil strife, thus endangering the stability of state governing. Therefore, the "Guard internal and ignore external" in the military was the basic principle of the strategic layout in the Northern Song Dynasty (Naughton, 2007).

Although the "Guard internal and ignore external" strategy avoided the separatist regimes of the Northern Song dynasty, it also caused the weakening of the interior and the weakness of the outside of the Northern Song Dynasty. It was under the guidance of such a strategic principle that Song Zhenzong won the war in Danzhou but was willing to sign a peace agreement with the Liao. Like this strategic principle of the Northern Song Dynasty, there were some other existence in the Chinese history. For example, Empress Dowager Cixi paid the foreigners to buy the peace. To maintain the shaking and crumbling rule of the Manchu government, she proposed that "the land should be given to non-domestic servants rather than the domestic slaves."

During the Kuomintang administration, when Japan launched the war of aggression against China, Chiang Kai-shek insisted on destroying the Communist Party first and then resisting Japan regardless the survival of the Chinese nation. Even after the second cooperation between the Kuomintang and the Communist Party, he still remembered the Anti-Communism and even suppressed the Communists under the name of Anti-Japanese War. Objectively speaking, it was very necessary to ensure the stability of the internal power and social solidarity first when dealing with the external issues. However, it was a strategic taboo to ensure the internal stability and to give up the opportunity to defend the national interests externally (Zhao, 2012).

Therefore, in the opinion of the Chinese People, China must also regard the world and work together to cope with international issues, apart from seeking stability in her own development and seeking development through mutation. In the economic field, the global economic governance has become the common aspiration of all countries. At present, in the face of the grim situation such as the European debt crisis, economic slowdown and financial turmoil, all countries are beginning to realize the importance of the global governance. The global economic governance is not simply referring to the exchange of interests, but a process of structuring the new order in the hope of safeguarding the common security of mankind and promoting the common development of mankind (Li, 2015). To achieve the global economic governance, China should give up the thinking of hegemony and the Cold War. We should respect each other, treat each other as equals and strive for equality and mutual benefit, and all nations should have inclusive growth to create a harmonious world (Zeng, 2012). At this level, there is no need at all to select a world leader, every country can be the world leader, every country cannot be the world leader either.

In short，When China becomes the world leader, the voice of the third world will receive more attention because China has even been the common leader of the Third World. In addition, after China becomes the world leader, a new international economic order will be established more rapidly with the re-embracing of the Third World. China has never had the idea of being the world leader. However, when China has such strength, it will certainly belong to China. Of course, a world leader is not a "king of no crown," if China does not continue to work hard to maintain the status of the world leader, it will be fetched by other country easily. China once indeed was the world leader in her history. China hopes that all the progress made in China will be positive to the world and will be beneficial to the world. China also hopes that she can be treated well by all countries in the world and she must also commit herself a sustainable development to contribute to the peace and development of the entire world.

Part II: China Used to be No. 1

Chapter 6

China Used to be the world leader

While talking about whether China can become the world leader or not, people must recognize the fact that China has ever been the world leader before. Although "the hero does not need to mention his courage in the past," to some extent the past glory can prove that China's becoming the world leader is not utopian, but a historical fact that the Chinese People are proud of. Every dog has its day, so it is hard to draw a conclusion whether China can become the world leader once again or not. Maybe it is totally possible, maybe it is impossible.

Indeed, China has ever acted as the world leader, when looking back at the history of the ancient China, the bright civilization of the Chinese nation let all the Chinese People name themselves as the descendants of "Yandi and Huangdi Emperors", which make them feel proud and happy. This pride is not entirely arrogant and self-admirable, but also recognized by the world. It is undeniable that this brilliant ancient civilization is the huge property for the Chinese nation. However, how to carry forward this huge wealth is a real challenge for the Chinese People. Taking the history as a mirror, people can learn about honor and disgrace. What the Chinese People hope for is to take the history as a lesson which can urge China to move forward better and tell the world that the great rejuvenation of the Chinese nation is not a verbal statement without any proof.

From the perspective of world history, human civilization can be divided into two diverse types of civilization, that is, the Eastern civilization and the Western civilization. It is difficult to know at what time there occurred this distinction between Eastern civilization and Western civilization. The widely recognized Western civilization mainly includes the ancient Greek civilization, the ancient Roman civilization, and the Christian civilization. The representative areas for Christian civilization are Aegean Sea, Continental Europe, the United States and some other countries. The Eastern civilization is based on two oldest civilization: Chinese civilization and Indian civilization, the representative regions and countries include China, India, Arabia, Japan, North Korea and Egypt.

Undoubtedly, among these human civilizations, Chinese civilization is the oldest and most historic one. China has long been at the center of oriental civilization and the leader of the Eastern world. Japan, South Korea and so on are the ones who only prostrate themselves in worship to China. An open and inclusive civilization or nation will inevitably bring about a long-term, progressive and energetic spirit and strength. On the contrary, a self-reliant and conservative one will not deserve the status of world leader in any event. Obviously, the transformation of Chinese civilization from "introversion" to "extroversion" and from conservative to open is also an important reason that Chinese civilization can move forward further. Counting the splendid accomplishments of ancient China is a kind of gaining new knowledge by reviewing the past and setting out again from the rich historical achievements.

The "flourishing age" of ancient China

The Chinese people feel proud while studying the world history because they used to be the world leader for thousands of years. China has a long history, a large population and vast territory. China is one of the four ancient civilizations in the world and one of the earliest birthplaces of world civilization. The four major civilizations in the world are the ancient Egyptian civilization, the ancient Indian civilization, the ancient Babylonian civilization and the Chinese civilization. What surprised the world is that the first three major civilizations have been interrupted by warfare among different nations, social changes and natural disasters. Ancient Indians, ancient Egyptians and ancient Babylonians are no longer existing and their civilizations have stopped. Only through archaeological can people feel their charm. However, the civilization of ancient Chinese has continued till now, which has lasted more than five thousand years with considerable years of succession and continues to expand to the surrounding areas, eventually forming a great Chinese culture and a unique landscape in the world civilization (Mo, 2017).

Chinese civilization started from the Three Emperors and Five Sovereigns (in ancient China), and according to legend, Fu Xi is the ancestor of Chinese culture, and the earliest recorded ancient Chinese king. During the early Neolithic Period, he created the Eight Diagrams based on the changes in nature. The Eight Diagrams became the origin of Chinese characters and it ended the history of "records by tying knots." His activities mark the beginning of Chinese civilization. About 2070 BC, the Xia Dynasty established the first country in Chinese history and the first slavery dynasty. China began to enter the slavery society. In the ensuing thousand years, China experienced brilliant Xia, Shang and Zhou dynasties. The two great gifts left by the brilliant Shang dynasty to China and the world today are "Carapace-bone-script" and "Simuwu Tripod."

"Carapace-bone-script" is an ancient Chinese writing and the first type of modern Chinese characters, it is also considered to be the pilot but matured Chinese characters." Simuwu Tripod" is the largest bronze found in the current world. It fully demonstrates the production scale and technical level of the bronze casting industry in the Shang Dynasty, which are amazing. The Zhou Dynasty was a time when the Chinese slavery society gradually collapsed and the feudal society was gradually formed. It was an era of social unrest and national integration. It was also an era of swirling war of ideas and academic contention. It has made a profound influence on the Chinese and even the world history. The most brilliance and prosperity of the Zhou Dynasty lied in the Various Schools of Thought in its later stage. "Contention of a hundred schools of thought" has shaped all aspects of the ideology, culture, political outlook and morality of the entire feudal dynasty for the Chinese and even for today's Chinese, laid the foundation to format national characters of Chinese people. The academic ideology of "Contention of a hundred schools of thought" still deeply influences the posterity.

Confucius and Laozi had not gone away any more after thousands of years as in the present China, Sinology gradually gets popular again.

In 221 BC, the First Qin Emperor successively swept through the six countries opening China's feudal dynasty which lasts for thousands of years. China became the first country in the world to establish a feudalistic society and became the first multinational country in the four ancient civilizations. And the Great Wall, Terracotta Warriors and Horses of Qin Dynasty are still among the world's eight wonders. By the first century AD, China had become one of the most developed countries in the world. Historically, China has had several brilliant periods There are three well recognized times of prosperity which are the flourishing age Western Han Dynasty from the reign of Emperor Wen and Emperor Jing through Emperor Wu to Emperor Zhao and Emperor Xuan, the flourishing age in the Tang Dynasty from the reign of Emperor Taizong to Emperor Xuanzong, as well as the flourishing age in the Qing Dynasty during the reigns of Kangxi, Yongzheng and Qianlong. In these three prosperous times, China eliminated the forces of internal and external threats gaining the mighty power of the military, the unification of the country and the vast territory without a rivalry around it. The society was relatively stable, the economic development was prosperous and its national strength was ahead of the world. Additionally, its cultural prosperity had a huge influence on the surrounding areas.

Emperor Wen of Han and Emperor Jing of Han governed the country with Taoist "inaction" and implemented rest and recuperation policy. They reduced curve and taxes and let people rest. The domestic political environment was stable, if there was no drought or flood damage, people were always self-sufficient and the country's warehouse was full of food. The food in a warehouse called Taicang increased year after year making them rot and inedible. There were millions of monies in the capital and the money was so much that the ropes tied money were broken. This is a very vivid description of the time of Emperor Wen of Han and Emperor Jing of Han (Zhao,2008).

Emperor Xuanzong of Tang adopted a series of positive political and economic measures based on "time of Emperor Taizong", and with the hard work of the vast majority of people, there were further social and economic developments. The Tang Dynasty reached a very high level in all aspects. Its national strength was unprecedentedly strong. The Tang Dynasty became the most developed and most civilized country in the world at that time. It was also the economic, cultural, trade and political center of the world. The capital Chang'an was a cosmopolitan city like today's New York. Domestic traffic extended in all directions, the cities were more prosperous, and the foreign trade continued to grow. Businessmen from Persia and Dashi were pouring in. Mercantile cities such as Chang'an, Luoyang and Guangzhou were filled with businessmen of diverse colors and languages. People wearing costumes of different nationalities came and went, and Chinese feudal society reached its heyday. This is so-called Kaiyuan prosperity(Zhang,2007).

"Kang and Qian Prosperity," referred to the three generations Kangxi, Yongzheng, Qianlong of the Qing Dynasty, from 1662 to 1795 AD, lasted more than 130 years. During this time, they had defeated three separate regimes, recovered Taiwan, and put down rebellions happened in Jungar Banner, Alti-shahr and which raised by Rob Zang Danjin and chieftains in Jinchuan. In terms of the production, they had built irrigation works, stationed forces and opened wasteland for farming. They successively promulgated policies that "men did not need to undergo labor service after they reached a certain age" and "adopting land tax instead of poll tax." The agricultural acreage increased rapidly, reaching 600 billion square meters till Yongzheng more than any dynasty ever (Fu, 2016). In addition, they implemented the policy of adjusting industry and commerce, leading the development of commodity economy, many emerging cities and towns and the overall economic prosperity. Harmony among over 50 nations, political stability, social peace and prosperity made the Qing Dynasty become one of the most powerful empires in the world at that time.

China has enjoyed a leading position in most of the 5,000-year-long history in the world. China has been at the pinnacle of the world's civilization despite the regime changes in the development of ancient Chinese history. And China has made great achievements in economy, politics, military affairs, diplomacy, science, technology, ideology, literature and art. So western historians generally believe that none of the civilizations before modern times had developed more than China (Tao, 2003).

The military strength of the ancient China

China is one of the cradles of the ancient civilization in the world. Indeed, no one nation or country can maintain such a vast and stable territory for the long term like China. Of course, the Chinese territory is not immutable in the history. It has expanded and contracted in different historical periods. But the general trend is same that is to gather and develop in national integration and to consolidate and stabilize in anti-secession and anti-aggression. The Chinese territory, centered on the Central Plains, has expanded continuously from the Central Plains to all around and formed the vast territory of China gradually in the mutual integration of all ethnic groups in history. In the pre-Qin period, the territory ruled by Xia, Shang and Zhou was mainly in the Yellow River and the Yangtze River basin, roughly equivalent to the nine provinces area divided by Dayu. In 221 BC, after unifying the country, the First Qin Emperor dispatched the general Mengtian northward to lead the army to defeat the Huns. The general crossed Hetao area northward along the Yellow River, attacked and arrived to the north of Hetao of Yinshan and south of Gobi desert. After the Qin defeated the Huns, it set the Jiuyuan province at today's Baotou city. Since then, the Hetao area belonged to China forever. After that, the general Mnegtian built the Great Wall based on the Great Wall built in the Yan, Zhao and Qin Dynasty. According to the historical records, the territory of the Qin Dynasty reached east to the sea to South Korea, west to Lintao and Qiangzhong, south to northern Xianghu (in the south of the Tropic of Cancer) and north to east of the Liaohe River including Yinshan Mountains, guarding Yellow River as fortress.

The social system of Han Dynasty was almost the same as the Qin Dynasty, so was the territory. With regards to the territory, the Han Dynasty developed the frontier further based on the territory of the Qin Dynasty. Emperor Wu of the Han Dynasty opened territory and established immortal achievements constantly during all his life, he consolidated the Hetao area, occupied the southern desert, the Hexi Corridor and Qinghai area. Emperor Xuan of the Western Han Dynasty, Emperor Guangwu of the Eastern Han Dynasty and Emperor Ming of the Eastern Han Dynasty also made amazing achievements on territory. Most of today's Xinjiang, and a considerable part of Central Asia were all under the Protectorate of the Western Regions. And the entire Sichuan province, most of Yunnan and Guizhou provinces, the entire Liaoning province, a part of Jiling province and a big part of Inner Mongolia were all under the rule of the Han Dynasty. The total area of the territory was about 10.4 million square kilometers. In the Tang Dynasty, China's territory expanded further. Protectorate General to Pacify the North was set up in northern China with a jurisdiction to the north of Lake Baikal northward. The Shiwei Protectorate General was set up in the northeast and it ruled the outer Xinganling mountains and the Heilongjiang basin. Protectorate General to Pacify Xinjiang was set up in the northwest, whose jurisdiction was extended to today's Aral Sea, east Persia and other regions with a total area of 12.51 million square kilometers.

The largest territory in the history of mankind is not the Roman Empire nor the British Empire nor the Russian Empire, but the Mongol Empire established by the Chinese nation's Mongol hero, Genghis Khan and his descendants, the Yuan Dynasty in Chinese history. During the Yuan Dynasty, the largest territory in China was the most at that time in the world. In 1279, after the establishment of the Yuan Dynasty, Kublai Khan descended the Southern Song Dynasty and unified its area. The territory at that time expanded to south Siberia northward, across Lake Baikal and to the South China Sea southward. The southwest included today's Tibet, Yunnan to today's east Xinjiang, and the territory was to the outer Xinganling northeastward, Sea of Okhotsk, Sea of Japan, including Sakhalin Island. The total area was more than 12 million square kilometers. In 1310 the reign of Emperor Wuzong of Yuan, the Yuan Dynasty and Chagatai Khanate attacked the Wokuo Tai Khanate, and the Yuan Dynasty acquired the eastern part of the Wokuo Tai Khanate successively

whose area was about 14 million square kilometers. In addition, the Yuan Dynasty also has many vassal countries, including Korea, Myanmar, Annan, Champa, Java and the Kinshasa Khanate, Chagatai Khanate, and Iraqi Khanate and other countries. In north, it has Mobei various ministries north of Gobi Desert. In south, it has Southeast Asian countries and in west, there were four major Khanates.

As the last feudal dynasty in China, although most of the history it left to its descendants was humiliation, its territory was still vast and laid the foundation for today's Chinese territory. After the reunification of the Qing Dynasty, the territory of the country started from Tannu Uriankhai area in Mongolia and Siberia to the South China Sea including the Xisha Islands and the Nansha Islands, to the Dawang area in Tibet, Nan kang in Yunnan province, Jiangxinpo area and northern Burma southwestward, to Aral Sea and Pamirs Plateau westward including today's Xinjiang and Balkhash Lake in Central Asia, to Stanovoy Range including Sakhalin and its southeast part included Taiwan and Pescadores northeastward (Zhang, 2016). During the Qin's heyday, the total area was 13 million square kilometers. Of course, the development of the territory in each period is based on a strong military strength. After China has an established territory, it also needs the military capabilities of the Megatron Quartet to resist foreign aggression. In this respect, there are some positive examples of flourishing ages and some negative examples of the fall of the dynasties. Therefore, both successful and unsuccessful experiences show that it is impossible for any country to exist independently in the world's nations without a strong military foundation.

The leading science and technology of the ancient China

China had been leading the world in science and technology before the 16th century (Ming Dynasty). The development of ancient Chinese science and technology includes The Four Great Inventions and their spreading, the astronomical calendar, architecture, medical science, mathematics achievement and renowned scientific and technological works etc. Cultures of Shang Dynasty, Qin and Han Dynasties, Sui and

Tang Dynasties, Song and Yuan Dynasties are the typical examples that ancient Chinese culture made great contribution to the whole world.

Astronomically, the first record of solar eclipse, lunar eclipse and sunspots appeared in Shang Dynasty. Shi Shen, an astronomer, recorded locations of more than eight hundred fixed stars with the use of equatorial coordinates which was edited as Shi's star catalogue by later generations. It is the oldest surviving star catalogue all over the world and one of important reference value to astronomical research. Gan and Shi's Astronomy Book, written by Gan De and Shi Shen in the Warring States period, is the earliest astronomy book on the earth. The first record of the Halley Comet was proved to be written by astronomer of Lu State during Spring and Autumn Period However in the Europe, people did not realize that until 1532 AD. Twelve solar terms calendar created by Shen Kuo appeared in China 800 years earlier than in Europe. Shoushi Calendar edited by Guo Shoujing is quite like the current calendar, but enforced 300 years later.

In Europe, the common usage of equatorial coordinate system started in 16th. The ancient Greece astronomer Hipparchus (about 190 BC-about 125 BC) measured and created the earliest Greek star catalogue. There were two ancient Greece astronomers before Hipparchus who once measured the positions of some fixed stars, but it happened in third century BC anyway, which is much more later than Shi Shen's work. Besides, as far back as third century BC and first century BC, the ancient Greece astronomers had measured to confirm the length of meridian twice, however they did not do their work all by the practical measurement. Sen Yixing, an astronomer, measured the length of meridian by field measurements for the first time in history, creating the method of field measuring to learn the earth for Chinese people, casting out thoroughly the fallacy that when there is one-thousand distance between the north and the south, the shadow of sun in sundial will just move three centimeters. It combined the measurements of latitude with the distance, not only did it create way for the new calendar, but it also established foundation for the later astronomical geodesy.

Mathematics in ancient China mainly focused on calculating and it had made great achievements. Among the achievements, decimal notation, rod calculus and calculation with an abacus were proved to exceed the world at that time and made the mathematics develop forward. In the same period, other ancient civilizations and cultures like ancient Greece lagged in their method of counting because of their emphasis on geometry and their neglect of calculation. They expressed one to ten thousand figures with all the Greek letters. When the letters were not enough, they used the letters " '." The notation used by India were the Greek and Roman notations before the third century A.D. and the real decimal notation was made at the end of the sixth century A.D. Thus it can be seen that the ancient decimal system of notation and counting of China were much earlier and more advanced than other countries. The book *"Zhou Bi Suan Jing"* written in the first Century B.C. introduced Pythagorean Theorem 500 years earlier than the West. The *"Nine Chapter Arithmetic"* written in the Western Han Dynasty had some of the most advanced knowledge in the world at that time. For the first time, the mathematician Liu Hui founded the scientific method of seeking pi in China, laying the foundation for China leading the study of pi in the world for a long time.

In addition, Liu Hui's discourse on volume has connection with the modern volume theory, pointing out that the solution of tetrahedron volume is the key to polytypic volume theory, but the volume cannot be solved by finite segmentation and chess testing. In order to solve this problem, he came up with an important principle which is now known as Liu Hui principle. Modern mathematics guru Gauss and Hilbert discussing about this issue was about the last 100 years (Zou, 2017). Zu Chongzhi in the three Kingdoms Southern and Northern Dynasties was the first one to accurate pi to seven decimal places which was 1100 years earlier than in Europe. The density proposed by Zu Chong was also restored a thousand years after by the German Otto (about 1550-1605) and the Dutch Antoniz (1527-1607).

The *"Nine Chapter Arithmetic"*, written in the first century AD, marks the formation of an ancient Chinese mathematical system and it contains many of the world's first achievements in algebra. It includes the earliest systematic description of the fractional operation in the world, with the surplus algorithm as a surprising creation. The "equation" chapter describes the negative and its addition and subtraction algorithm. Other aspects of its mathematical achievements include the proportion of problems, double method, some calculation of area and volume, solutions of first-order equations, square, cube and general quadratic equation method. The book records the world's most advanced fractional four arithmetic and proportional algorithms. The book also chronicles algorithms for solving various area and volume problems, as well as questions using the Pythagorean Theorem.

The most important achievement in the *"Nine Chapter Arithmetic"* is in algebraic terms, which describes the method of opening the square and opening the cube, and on this basis, there is a numerical solution to the general quadratic equation (the first coefficient is not negative). There is an entire chapter on the solution to the simultaneous equations, which is in line with what is being taught in secondary schools. This was a thousand years earlier than similar algorithms in Europe. In the same chapter, for the first time in the history of mathematics in the world, the concept of negative numbers and the algorithm of addition and subtraction of positive and negative numbers are also recorded. The *"Nine Chapter Arithmetic"* and later what the great mathematician Liu Hui's annotation indicate that since the first century BC, China became the center of mathematics in the world in place of ancient Greece and later laid the foundation of Chinese mathematics 1500 years ahead of the world. Today, with the advent and development of computers, the algorithms and procedural ideas it contains still inspire mathematicians.

In physics, the fifth century BC, the Mohist Cannon described the scale lever principle first. The earliest discussion of pulley mechanics was still in the *"Mohist Canon"*. The book *"Shangshuwei Kaolingyao"* says that "The earth is moving but people do not know. For example, a man sitting in a closed boat, the boat was moving but he does not recognize." In a closed inertial system, no matter what kind of mechanical experiments cannot determine whether the system is still at rest or doing a uniform linear motion. This principle is also called Galileo Relativity Principle.

However, about 1,500 years before Galileo, the Chinese had put forward the oldest statement of this principle. This is one of the greatest theoretical achievements in the history of science in China. Objects immersed in the liquid are floated by the liquid. The earliest account of the principle of buoyancy in China is found in the passage of *"Mohist Canon, Jingxia"*. The passage in the *"Mohist Canon"* includes inaccurate expression of buoyancy principle. However, the entire passage shows that Mohism has understood this relationship. These happened about two hundred years before Archimedes expressing that principle.

Chinese's understanding of the most pronounced appearance of the crystal, the regular geometry of the crystal, and the knowledge of snowflake crystals was at least fifteen centuries earlier than that of Westerners. Around the time of the Era, China discovered that the snowflakes are hexagonal (the *"Taiping Imperial Encyclopaedia"* quoted the *"unauthorized biography of Hanshi")*. In the West, Kepler did not discover this mystery until 1611. There were two methods of artificial magnetization in ancient China basically. One is the method of rubbing a steel needle with a natural magnet, as Shen Kuo said. Another way is to use the earth's magnetic field to make the needle magnetized. This magnetization method was based on experience entirely, but it is an important part of the development of magnetism and geomagnetism, more than four hundred years earlier than the same magnetization method in Europe. Zhang Heng, an outstanding natural scientist in the Eastern Han Dynasty, invented the earth-shaking instrument, the first observatory of earthquakes in the world. Zhang Heng earth-shaking instrument was designed using the principle of inertia. Its basic structure, in line with the principles of physics, can detect the first main direction of the seismic waves. Compared with foreign countries, Zhang Heng earth-shaking instrument appeared earlier than the emergence of similar Western instruments about 1700 years ago.

As for biology and medicine, Chinese ancestors were clever and diligent. As early as primitive society, they began to attach importance to rice and millet. China was the earliest country in the world to grow these two kinds of plants. Asexual grafting technology was also created by

China first. In the Han Dynasty's *"Book of Fan Shengzhi"* there were records of grafting, and after Han, grafting technology developed into grafting between different plants. In the year 304 AD, the "*Southern Herbaceous Plant*" written by Ji Han was the first book containing recording the southern plants and the earliest local plant flora in the world. Two thousand years ago, Chinese medical scientists have summarized the clinical experience of acupuncture systematically. *The Yellow Emperor's Canon of Internal Medicine*, which was written in the Spring and Autumn Period and the Warring States Period, is the earliest and most complete classic medical book combining medical theory and clinical practice in China. Its birth promotes the development of medicine in the motherland from experience accumulation stage to systematic theoretical summary stage.

Huatuo, in the Three Kingdoms period of the Eastern Han Dynasty, was known for his outstanding surgical procedure. He also invented Maze Powder, and succeeded in conducting brilliant and effective abdominal surgery 1,700 years ago. The "Tang Materia Medica", which was promulgated in the Tang Dynasty, was the first pharmacopoeia in the world to be formulated and promulgated by the state, which showed that the state attached immense importance to medicine, 800 years earlier than in Europe. In addition, the concept of immunity has long existed in the history of medicine in China. In the medicine of China, there is a kind of "fighting poison with poison" treatment method. Under the inspiration of this thought, there was a very early record of the treatment like vaccines. According to a true and reliable record, the Vaccination of China was invented in the second half of the 16th century.

Two hundred years later, the British doctor Jenner (1749-1823) succeeded in vaccinated against smallpox in 1796. *Compendium of Materia Medica*, compiled in the sixth year of the Emperor Shenzong of Ming (1578 AD), records 1892 medicines and 11,000 prescriptions of medicines, which are divided into 16 parts. The taxonomic classification of the book already has the initial idea of biological evolution, and the application of comparative anatomy in the classification of animals and plants. This book covers many areas of ancient natural sciences such as animals, plants, chemistry, minerals, geology, agronomy, astronomy, geography and other disciplines. It has a profound influence on future generations and is circulated widely in the world.

The achievements which could most shock the entire Western world and represent China's advanced technology were China's "four inventions." China in the early Western Han Dynasty, already had paper, and then Cai Lun of the East Han Dynasty improved papermaking. In Sui and Tang dynasties, there has been woodblock printing. The *Diamond Sutra* printed in the Tang Dynasty was the world's first engraving printed matter. A civilian called Bi Sheng invented the clay movable type printing, 400 years earlier than Europe, promoting the spread of culture greatly. During the two thousand years from the second century BC to the eighteenth-century AD, the papermaking in China has been at the advanced level in the world. After printing came to Europe, it changed the original situation that only monks could study and receive higher education. This provided an important material condition for the rapid development of science in Europe after the Middle Ages and the emergence of the Renaissance. At the end of the Tang Dynasty, gunpowder began to be used in the military and promoted the development of gunpowder and weapons in Europe, causing the knight class to decline. The compass was used in navigation, advancing the navigation for the oceans and ushered in an era of great geographical discovery.

The Chinese people are not only industrious and wise but also have long been at the forefront of the world in smelting technology. The Xia, Shang, Zhou dynasties are called the "Bronze Age" of China and show the superb bronze smelting techniques of China then. The famous "Simuwu Tripod" and "Five Sheep Statue" are the products of this period. Later, the bronze ware was replaced by iron wares gradually. In the late Western Zhou Dynasty, there were already iron wares and they were promoted in the Warring States Period. Chinese people had a lot of invention and innovation in the field of iron and steel smelting. In the Eastern Han Dynasty, Du Shi invented Shuipai to blast for iron casting with water. Perfusing Steel Method, invented in the Wei, Jin and Southern and

Northern Dynasties is an original invention in the history of China's metallurgy. It is also one of the most outstanding achievements of early steelmaking technology in China (Jiang, 2015). Another notable innovation was the replacement of charcoal with coke in the 11th century. This is very meaningful because Eurocentric insists that this was first achieved by Britons centuries later (Hobson, 2010). Robert Hartwell, in his influential paper, estimates that per capita iron production in China increased six-fold between AD 806 and 1078. In terms of total annual production, the figure was 13,500 tons of iron and would be almost 125,000 tons by 1078. That growth rate was comparable to that of the British in about a century.

Before the 16th century, China's steelmaking technology has long been in a leading position in the world and has been praised universally by all countries. In the first century AD, the Roman naturalist said in his famous book Nature History: "Although there are many kinds of iron, none of them is comparable to the steel from China." The steel-pouring technology was improved continuously after the Song Dynasty by reducing the number of mixing to finish at one time. Before the invention of the crucible-making method, the Perfusing Steel Method was a state-of-the-art. It increased the yield and quality of steel. In Europe, block iron casting was invented around 1000 BC, but pig iron was not available until the 14th century AD. Although the beginning of Chinese block iron casting started as late as the 6th century BC and was about 900 years later than the West, the technology for smelting cast iron was 2,000 years earlier than that in Europe. The invention of Chinese cast iron appeared in the 5th century BC, while Europe lapsed until the 15th century BC. Because the performance of cast iron is much higher than that of bulk iron, the real Iron Age started with the birth of cast iron. The history of social development shows that the advent of cast iron is the main symbol of the improvement of social productivity and social progress. It took only about a century for China to make the transition from bulk iron to foundry iron, while the West took a long journey of nearly 3,000 years. It is unique for China's ancient iron-smelting technology to develop so rapidly in the world. Bernard, a well-known British historian of science, said that this was the only exception to the history of iron foundry in the world.

The developed industries and commerce of the ancient China

Egypt has pyramids, India has Taj Maha, and China in the five thousand years of history has left the world a lot of amazing works, including the Qin’ s Great Wall and the Terracotta Warriors and Sui’ s Grand Canal. The former is created by the wisdom and challenging work of the people in China in more than two thousand years. The historical monument has been hailed as the "eighth wonder of the world." The latter was the artery of the north-south traffic in China before the advent of the railway. In addition to these, ancient Chinese bridges, pagodas and garden architecture are also admired by the world.

Zhaozhou Bridge in the Sui and Tang Dynasties is the oldest existing stone arch bridge in the world. The Winter palace, burned by the British and French troops, is beautiful and magnificent like a fairyland in the world. Suzhou traditional gardens have different forms, making Chinese and foreign tourists enchanted and linger. Ancient Chinese ceramics and lacquerware are also regarded as treasures by other parts of the world. Their refined shapes and paintings have astonished the world. And they are still collected by people today. Ancient Chinese silk, with its lightness and softness, dressed mankind, and was regarded as treasures by the West, and only the aristocrats were entitled to enjoy it as silk was used to open the Silk Road between ancient East and West too.

The ancient China was the long-term world center because of its advanced and powerful economy. As early as the 5th century BC, the feudal economy formed gradually in China. In 221 AD, a unified country based on the world's first feudal economy was established. After that, there appeared three "flourishing age" of the great feudal economy. According to the historical records, during the reign of Emperor Wen of Han and Emperor Jing of Han: There were millions in the capital and the money was so much that the ropes tied money were broken. The food in a warehouse called Taicang increased year by year making them rot and inedible. In the reign of Emperor Wu of Han, the water conservancy and agriculture were more developed. He adopted free business in the salt and iron industry so that the financial strengthened increasingly. In the reign of Emperor Taizong of Tang, the economic started to develop from recovering. Till Emperor Xuanzong of Tang, there was a poem saying that "Even a small county has tens of thousands of families, farmers gain good harvests in successive years, public and private warehouses are full of food, and people have a rich life."

Chang'an in the Tang Dynasty was a metropolis in the world and merchants from all over the world gathered here in the late Tang Dynasty. At that time, the economy of the Tang Dynasty far exceeded that of the Byzantium and Arabia in the same period. Both Han and Tang in history have proved that Han and Tang were the richest countries in Asia and even the world at that time. The establishment of a monetary-based tax system was one of the most important innovations in the Song Dynasty. In the early 12th century, the North Song Dynasty has issued the first banknote in the world at that time - Jiao Zi. This pioneering invention was later imitated by Europeans. However, the widespread use of it in Britain was as late as 1797.

According to historians' calculations, the Song dynasty's GDP accounted for 75% of the world's total economic output at that time, but the population was only 15%. This achievement cannot even be achieved in the United States now. So, no wonder some western scholars nowadays say that the standard of living of a European monarch at that time was not even as good as that of a soldier who guarded the city gate in Bianliang. Marco Polo, a merchant from Venice, the most prosperous city in the West at the time, came to the metropolis of Yuan Dynasty, which absorbed only a few Song civilizations. He was dazzled like seeing a paradise on earth, which can show the prosperity of the Song Dynasty.

During the reign of Emperor Qianlong of Qin, the agriculture, handicraft industry and commodity economy were all flourishing. The revenue level was so high and reached the top in ancient China and the economic scale and aggregate were the biggest ones in the world at that time. China had been the center of world economy until 1800, and its production power and export capacity were both better than that of any other countries.

The economic exchanges of the ancient China

China's ancient economy was developed, its national strength was strong, and its culture was advanced. It had great attraction and influence on the outside world. It carried out extensive international contacts abroad and formed the East Asian cultural circle.

As early as the Qin and Han Dynasty, China had carried out positive diplomacy policies, and the East Asian cultural circle centered in China had a vast influence on regions as far as Europe and Africa. China had close relationship with three Koreas on the southern Korean peninsula and Japan, southward had economic and technical exchanges with Vietnam, westward had communications with Central Asia, Western Asia and South Asia across the Silk Road. China's iron, silk, silkworm reeling, iron casting, Karez and paper making technology (probably in the Tang Dynasty) spread successively to the west. Buddhism was also introduced into China through the silk road. The opening of the silk road is the great event in the world history of communication and it started from Chang'an , across Gansu Corridor, through Jade Gate Pass and Yang Pass, divided into south and north ways and meet at Shule (today's Kashgar in Xinjiang), then crossed the Congling Mountains (today's Pamirs and Karakorum Mountains), and finally reached Dawan (Fergana Basin in Central Asia) and Kangju (Seal River Basin) to the North bank of the Caspian Sea northward, to Shendu (India) southward, to Tiaozhi (The Arabian Peninsula) and Daqin (Eastern Mediterranean) eastward.

After the reign of the Emperor Wu of Han, the Maritime Silk Road was opened. It started from the coastal harbor of Guangdong, arrived at the southern end of the India Peninsula. It has strengthened China's connections with Southeast Asian and South Asian countries and linked up the east and west from the waterway. Anxi did switch trade between the Han and Daqin, and Ban Chao dispatched Gan Ying to Daqin and Gan returned after reaching the Persian Gulf. In 166, the Antoninus Dynasty in Daqin sent ambassadors to visit the Emperor Huan of Han from the waterway, which is the earliest historic record about the direct connection between China and Europe (*Book of Later Han*). In the Southern and Northern Dynasties, a monk named Faxian traveled west to go on a pilgrimage for Buddhist scriptures. After 13 years he came back and then wrote down his experiences as a book named *Biography of Buddhism,* which is important historical data for studying transportation and cultures of China, India, Pakistan and so on.

The economy and culture of Sui and Tang Dynasties were prosperous and attractive to other countries. The Tang Dynasty was open to foreign countries, and the government encouraged foreign businessmen to come to China. The road runs from Changan to the east and reaches North Korea. To the west, the Silk Road reaches many countries such as Tianzhu (all over the Indian Peninsula), Persia (Iran), Dashi (Arabia) and Europe (e.g. Brindisi ie East Rome). The waterway from Dengzhou and Yangzhou could arrive in South Korea and Japan, the one from Guangzhou could the farthest reach the Persian Gulf. Tang and North Korea had communications on business, system, education, species, technology, customs and so on. At that time, Chinese culture affected all the neighboring countries. Japan was one of the representative countries, dispatching people to study Chinese culture. In the fields of writing, costumes, architecture and thought, the famous "Taika Era reforms" in Japan was planned after the Japanese students studying in China returned home. The city of Nara in Japan was modeled after Changan. Japan also promoted the Confucian culture vigorously and the influence it made on Japan can still be found today. There were three highest institutions called "The Imperial College" in the capital Changan with pupils from all over the world, becoming the most significant institutions of higher study in the world.

The Sui and Tang Dynasties and Southeast Asia's Kuomintang (Myanmar) and South Asia's Tianzhu had communications on envoys, technology, religion and so on. Sui and Tang Dynasties had contacts with Central Asia's Persian and Dashi. During the Tang Dynasty, the Chinese learned about the boiling sugar method from Tianzhu, the leechcraft and acrobatics from eastern Rome and the music and dancing style from neighboring countries. A person named Du Huan of the Tang Dynasty had come to Africa. Additionally, according to the records, embassy in East Africa came to China in reign of the Emperor Taizong of Tang.

As early as World Geography discovery of America by Columbus, Zheng He had already departed from China to the Western Ocean in the early Ming Dynasty. Zheng He et al reached farthest the Red Sea coast and the east coast of Africa, strengthening the connection and exchange between China and other countries in the world. It has opened the prelude to the era of great voyage in the world as a symbol of China's embrace of the outside world, and has inscribed China's maritime cause on the milestone of the world's maritime history.

The Chinese like to learn from history and love history very much. The Chinese nation is the most adept one at recording history with the most complete history. During the reign of the Emperor Wu of Han, China's first general history by chronology "*Shi Ji*" was born. Sima Guang, the prime minister of the Northern Song Dynasty compiled China's first chronicle historical record *"Zizhitongjian"*. Additionally, the *Twenty-Four Histories* were linked generations to generations. These historical monographs are momentum magnificent, not only records the history, but are also literary masterpieces, in which "*Shi Ji*" was regarded as "valuable both in historical records and literature." And it makes China become the only one of the four civilizations which has a continuous history.

The Chinese civilization is continuous for more than five thousand years, like the endless stream of the Yellow River. The ancient China led the east of the world with strong national strength and economic and cultural prosperity. The ancient China was the center of East Asia and even the world for a long time, the brilliant history of her is the eternal proud of Chinese people, and it is the basis of China's re-creating brilliance and becoming the world leader once again.

Chapter 7

The Greatness and Limitations of Chinese Culture

When talking China used to be the world leader, it refers to not only the hard power such as military strength, scientific and technological strength, and economic strength, but also refers to the soft power as culture. Moreover, regarding whether China can become the world leader or not, both soft power and hard power play important and irreplaceable roles.

In the long scroll of human history, Chinese culture is one of the most outstanding and striking features undoubtedly. The Chinese People are all filled with pride because China has a splendid civilization history for more than 5000 years. Let us leave aside the "four great inventions" that accelerated the world progress. In terms of literature, the Tang poems, the Song poems and the Yuan music, these are three cultural treasures of China, they played leading roles in the world. There are a lot of very famous poems in China, which Chinese and even foreigners like very much. In the very popular Novel named "The Legend of Zhen Huan," there is a famous sentence: Wish I can find the true love of my life that I would never leave until the end of time. Not only that, the well-known literary writers such as Lu Xun, Guo Moruo, Zhang Ailing, Cao Yu and Ba Jin are all talented people. In recent years, there has been a spate of "Learning Chinese" on a global scale, and the charm of Confucius has also attracted many foreigners. Under the baptism of time, the Chinese culture has become more and more profound. For China, if her culture wants to be continued shining in the new era, the Chinese People need to have a more comprehensive and clear understanding of the Chinese culture first.

Although there is no complete understanding and consensus on the concept of culture in the current world the culture is a product of history to a significant extent, it will be affected by the geography, climate and environment, mode of production, history background and some other factors. The culture is an integral part of people's cognition, belief, art, morality, law and customs, etc (Heng, 2017). Obviously, it was marked with national signals, such as Indian culture, Chinese culture and ancient Egyptian culture. As one of the four ancient civilizations, Chinese culture is not only the oldest, but also the most well-known one in the world because of her gorgeous culture and rich cultural heritage. The Chinese civilization was brewing on the vast and fertile land in the middle and lower reaches of the Yellow River. The Central Plains has become the center of ancient China. Although the Central Plains are now no longer brilliant, the Central Plains were the dreams of those in power at that time. Of course, although the Chinese culture is magnificent, it is difficult for everyone to understand and evaluate Chinese culture differently. Some people think that the Chinese culture ranks the first in the world's culture, while others believe that Chinese culture is outdated and difficult to keep up with the tide of the times. Based on the above two extreme opinions, most "eclectic" people think that it is quite necessary to have a soberer understanding of Chinese culture because of her greatness and limitations.

The greatness of Chinese culture

As the old saying goes, "there are many rivers in the sea." Qin Xiang Li Si wrote in his famous article "some political views to the monarch," Taishan does not allow the soil, so it can become large; rivers and seas do not choose the fine current, so it can be deep. Taishan and the sea achieved their own ambitious with inclusive attitudes, it is the same for the Chinese culture. There are many examples to explain this truth, for example, the development of Buddhism in China is one of them. For Buddhism, a very famous sentence is "Amitabha," which all the Chinese people are familiar with. Chinese Buddhism originated in India and was widely spread in China after its introduction from India. "Journey to the West" is one of the four famous books in China, from this book people can see that it is necessary for China to take a trip to the west, and Master Xuanzang's fetching the real Buddhism books from India is totally real in the history of the Tang dynasty.

In addition, there are "three religions and nine virtues" in Chinese culture, in which "three religions" refers to Confucianism, Buddhism and Taoism. Nine virtues include Confucianism, Taoism, Yin and Yang, legalists, famous artists, Mohists, and peasant families. Although these three religions have different ideologies, they can coexist harmoniously in Chinese history. Confucianism was revered as an orthodox doctrine, and Confucius, Mencius, and others' writings were also considered as the books of saints. Although Taoism was an interdisciplinary subject, it also attracted many fans. The Taoism advocated "to govern by doing nothing," this had a strong guiding significance for the restoration of productive forces after the war. Take the Taoist Zhuang Zi for an example, how many people fell for it from ancient times? The "Happiness Party" in "Tian Long Ba Bu" has its factions and martial arts evolved from "Happy Tour" of Zhuang Zi. Li Shangyin living in the Tang dynasty said in his famous poem "Jin Se" that Zhuangsheng dreamt of butterflies， what he saw in his dream was that Zhuang Zi had become a butterfly. It is said that the Taoist Lao Tzu sit on the back of an old green cow and went straight to the cemetery, and became a "God" finally, people can often see the TaiShangLaoJun from the television, this TaiShangLaoJun is just referring to him, he would never die as he owned the skills to make the elixir. The influence of Confucianism and Taoism on Chinese culture can be seen from this.

Confucianism, as an important part of the entire social ethics and moral system, it maintains the progress of interpersonal relations. Therefore, it can be said that Confucianism provided a good social order to the feudal society. Confucianism places the utmost emphasis on self-cultivation, it focuses on getting along well with the country and governing the country (Zhang, 2016). It pays attention to contributing to the country and society through personal cultivation. In this respect, the Taoists are very different. Taoists pay attention to the personal cultivation and immortality. Apart from the Confucianism and Taoism, Buddhism is also valued widely. People often hear of this sentence: "Buddhism helps and saves all the human beings," this is just referring to the fact that everyone can become a Buddha if he has a kind heart like

Buddha's, "Put down the butcher's sword and then you can become a Buddha as easy as ABC."

However, the Taoists focus on the wisdom of the believers, the powerful characters in the Taoist novels currently prevailing in the market and on the Internet. They all have excellent wisdom, or they were mentored by a very good master, or they have some kinds of elixirs, or they were trained in some certain of deep forests. In such a comparison, Buddhism is somewhat like the China's nine-year compulsory education, one can be practiced if he is willing to do so. Taoism is like a tougher higher education, only a few people will succeed, and Confucianism emphasizes that people can get the peace and liberation of the soul if he studies hard with significant efforts. Confucianism emphasizes reading more books of saints and doing things of saints. Although there are many differences among the Confucianism, Buddhism and Taoism, they all advocate restraining the sensual desires from being controlled and enslaved by the body's instincts. Thus, there exists a lot of Buddhist precepts, and the Confucianism also stressed that everything should "observe the proprieties," the peace of mind is the common pursuit of these three religions.

In addition to the Confucianism, Buddhism and Taoism, there occurred hundreds of other theories in the history of China, which promoted the cultural development of China. During the Spring Autumn Period and the Warring States Period, there occurred a famous book named "Sun Zi Bing Fa," which was known by the entire world at that time. And there also occurred Mohist, which taught the Chinese people that one should be "non-aggression, inaction, and universal love." It was the inclusiveness of Chinese culture that enabled so many philosophical ideas to be put in parallel.

When it comes to Chinese literature, one will think of lots of outstanding works. Chinese literature contains very rich themes, including the natural scenery, human feelings, historical future, and so on. For example, the Three Hundred Tang Poems are well known by all the Chinese People, even these poems were translated into many other languages and were read by the foreigners, and the foreigners love these poems very much. Let us look to a famous Tang Poem: Down the blue mountain in the evening Moonlight was my homeward escort. I saw my path Lie in levels of deep shadow when looking back. I was passing the farm-house of a friend When his children called from a gate of thorn and led me twining through jade bamboos Where green vines caught and held my clothes. I was glad of a chance to rest and glad of a chance to drink with my friend we sang to the tune of the wind in the pines. We finished our songs as the stars went down when I am being drunk and my friend more than happy Between us we forgot the world. As you can see above, it is so beautiful! These beautiful poems show the talents of the ancient Chinese People. Apart from the Tang Poems, there are many Song Poems as well, the Chinese students studied this kind of poems from primary school to junior middle school.

One might say, why do you want so many poems? They cannot fill your stomach, they are totally useless. It is wrong if you think like this, the Chinese culture on cooking which we call Chinese cooking culture or dietary culture is also very famous. The food documentary "A Bite of China" which was broadcast by CCTV in 2012, made the Chinese cooking culture be well known. China has always advocated "Food is essential for people to survive," even the saint Confucius said, "Everyone need food, just like everyone want the sex." Regarding Chinese food, they look pretty, smell fragrant, and taste delicious. After a long period of development, Chinese food has formed eight distinctive cuisine, namely Shandong cuisine, Sichuan cuisine, Guangdong cuisine, Jiangsu cuisine, Zhejiang cuisine, Hunan cuisine, Fujian cuisine and Anhui cuisine, each of these eight cuisines has its own flavor and delicacy.

Shandong cuisine includes Qilu flavor, Jiaoliao flavor, Confucius flavor and so on, such as the "Braised Intestines in Brown Sauce," and the "Eight Fairies fighting Luo Han" are all very delicious food. Sichuan cuisine is one of the most distinctive dishes in China, when cooking it usually includes chili, pepper, bean peas and some other seasonings. "Yu-Shiang Shredded Pork," "Kung Pao Chicken," "Pork Lungs in Chili Sauce," and "Ma Po bean curd," all these belong to Sichuan cuisine. As the second largest cuisine of the palace, Jiangsu cuisine includes Huaiyang, Nanjing and some other flavor, the representative dishes include "Farewell of the Concubine", "Peigong dog meat", "stewed lion head," "Sweet and Sour Spare Ribs," "Taihu hairy crab," and so on. Guangdong cuisine includes the Guangfu flavor, Chaoshan flavor and Hakka flavor, the representative dishes include "Burma shrimp," "crispy suckling pig," "refreshing beef balls," "stuffed Sambo," "Dongjiang salt baked chicken." And because Guangdong is in the coastal and it opened to the outside world very early, Guangdong cuisine has become a representative of the Chinese cuisine abroad. As for Fujian cuisine, the most famous one is "Buddha jumping wall," in addition, Shaxian snacks in Fujian are also very famous (Tian and Li, 2014).

Of course, there are many advocates for Zhejiang cuisine, Hunan cuisine and Anhui cuisine as well, Zhejiang cuisine emphasize light and delicate, Xihu vinegar is one of them. You can imagine what a happy life it is by watching the beauty of the West Lake, and at the same time, enjoying the delicious food. As for Anhui cuisine, there are three kinds of flavor: southern Anhui flavor, riverside flavor and river-Huaihe flavor. The representative dishes include "yellow mountain stewed pigeon," "eight hammers," "old clam Huai Zhu" and so on. These mentioned eight major Chinese cuisines have assorted flavors and enjoy a high reputation in the world, of which all the Chinese People are proud.

The limitations of Chinese culture

Although the Chinese culture is so profound and brilliant, in terms of cultural vision, Chinese culture has its own limitations and shortcomings. Accordingly, the self-criticism and self-reflection need to be made by China.

As one of the important representatives advocating the reform movement of 1898, Liang Qichao once raised some questions in the Xinmin Communique of 1904: "Zheng He's voyage was completed more than 60 years before Columbus discovering the New World, and more than 70 years before DaGama discovering the new route to India, but why could the discovery of Columbus and DaGama make the world look new and create a new era? Why did the Zheng He's feat disappear with the death of Zheng He? There are countless Columbus after the Columbus discovering the New World, and more DaGama-like people embark on sea voyage since DaGama. Why did China have only one

Zheng He without his successor? Is this Zheng He's fault? In addition to these questions raised by Liang Qichao, Joseph Needham also wondered in his book "The History of Science and Technology in China": "If my Chinese friends are as wise as I am, why Galileo, Steven and Newton are all Europeans, but not Chinese or Indians? Why did China gradually lag Europe after the Middle Ages? "(Song, 2009) How to answer these questions? Why did this happen? Most of the reasons are related to the limitations of Chinese culture.

It is well known that the four great inventions of compass, papermaking, printing and gunpowder come from China and have brought tremendous impact to the world. Compass made sailing safer and more efficient. Papermaking promoted the dissemination of cultural knowledge and gunpowder blown up the knights in the West. To sum up, people cannot imagine what it would look like for the world today without these "four great inventions." But what did these four inventions bring to China? Chinese ancestors invented the compass, but just used it for the "feng shui," the compass was widely used in navigation after it was introduced to Europe, this was an important reason for the Columbus discovering the New World and for Dagama discovering the new route to India, so did Magellan and some other naval pioneers. Another great invention gunpowder also had a similar fate, Chinese ancestors used gunpowder to create firecrackers and fireworks, so Chinese traditional festivals such as the Spring Festival, the Lantern Festival are always banging in the sound of firecrackers. Look to the Westerners, they used gunpowder to manufacture artillery, it is quite ironic that China was ever attacked by Western powers after the Western powers studied the gunpowder skills from China and thus China was forced to sign many unequal treaties with the Western powers. The compass kept the invaders from getting lost in the sea, and gunpowder made it easy for their cannons to defeat China's cold weapons. "Backwardness was about to be beaten," the reason was that the Qing government was corrupt and incompetent, but the deeper reason was the limitations of Chinese culture.

Of course, the limitations of Chinese culture did not emerge from the advocacy of individual members such as Confucius and Zhuzi, it was closely related to Chinese cultural foundation. Chinese civilization was originated in the farming civilization. The life of Cowherd and Weaver women was the portrayal at that time. The low productivity and the ignorance made people have a fear of nature. Most of the harvest in a year depended on the thoughts of God. Therefore, the Chinese ancients must deal with the relationships between human beings and nature carefully. For the Chinese ancients, to conform to the nature was the only way to survive. Even the emperor also claimed that he was the son of God. The first sentence in the edicts was usually "To follow the God, the emperor issued the imperial edict..."Just because China has been in an agricultural economy for a long time, it was natural for Chinese culture to respect the nature.

The ancient China had long been the leader of the world. Since the Qin Shi Huang unified China, China has been developing very well. Although some facts have confirmed "the general trend of the world is that it must be divided after an extended period of unification, and it will be unified after a prolonged period of division." In the history of China, such as "Guangwu prosperous era" and "Kaiyuan prosperous era," China were not rich at that time, but the economy, politics and culture were developed very well, China used to be the world leader for a long time. Chinese culture did not show a clear fault, but why did China was ever invaded by Japan? China has Buddhism, Taoism and some other religions, but why is Chinese religious concept weak? Buddhism was originally designed to imprison people's minds and to provide psychological relief to the vast numbers of people suffering from the pain. It did not become the common belief of the entire society. Therefore, what has been done by Chinese people to support their own meaning in life since ancient times? Although the Westerners are individual-based and the Chinese people are group-based. How to explain the phenomenon of "lacking spirit of cooperation" and even "lack of social morality" of Chinese people?

Even though China does not want to admit it, it is a fact that the quality of contemporary Chinese is indeed in urgent need of improvement. Many tourist attractions in China are often left with some handwriting such as "A visit by somebody," "Peter loves Mary forever," etc. Doodle in the cultural relics and monuments has long been nothing unusual. China should not belittle herself improperly, but she should also recognize the actual situation and shortcomings. Although Chinese culture advocates the preservation of the interests of the masses, the Chinese people should be patriotic and united closely. However, the actual situation is that it is not easy to defend the Pure Land of the mind to resist the material temptation with the improvement of material life, and there is no spare time to care about the interests of the country. Therefore, people are becoming like scattered sand gradually. How to improve the public morality of the whole society? It is the mission of Chinese culture to re-establish a reasonable moral system and stop the moral loss.

China could be proud of her splendid culture, but it will be too terrible if she became complacent. After being humiliated by the Opium War, China showed some phenomena of negating traditional culture totally such as overthrowing Confucius, keeping "Mr. De (Ethics)" and "Mr. Sai (Science)." China started to respect the democracy and science of Western countries blindly, which was inappropriate (Xu, 2017). With the development of Chinese culture, although there was no cultural fault phenomenon, however, it was very different from the civilizations of ancient Egypt and ancient India. Some contradictions and defects in Chinese culture have not disappeared as time goes on. On the contrary, these shortcomings in Chinese culture are likely to be deeply originated in the thinking of the Chinese people, which could hardly be eliminated without making heroic efforts.

To inherit the historical culture, China needs to get rid of the rough, distinguish the false and keep the real stuff, it is certainly wrong to reject everything blindly. However, many Chinese people still ignore the Chinese culture and study or imitate the methods of other countries blindly. Many Chinese students do not know who the "Eight Masters living in Tang and Song dynasties" are and even do not know the "New Yuefu Movement." Many Chinese people do not know which poem was the "On the River," referring to. All these mentioned above shows that the popularization of Chinese cultural knowledge is far from enough. Of course, under the popularization of the television media, people know quite a lot about the emperors of the Qing dynasty. Nevertheless, the limitations of Chinese culture should still cause everyone's deep thought. As a part of the Chinese nation, how can Chinese People hold the future development of Chinese culture?

Chinese Vs. Western cultures

In the comparison and communication of central cultures, China has always been open-minded to foreign civilizations and her religious control was not very strict. Most people treat local and foreign religions without any discrimination. Therefore, when "Bodhisattvas" were introduced into China, the Chinese People were willing to accept it with a tolerant attitude. Of course, at the beginning of Buddhism's introduction into China, there were conflicts with Chinese native culture. For example, Chinese culture advocated "filial piety." Many monarchs ruled the country with "filial piety." This was an orthodox Confucianism. It brought about a major influence on the Chinese society today. Buddhism advocates people to be "monks". Of course, the monks here are not simply referring to those who run away from home. In order to gain the living space, Buddhism had to keep a low profile and try its best to cater to the mainstream moral ethics in the society. At the same time, Buddhism also preserved its own characteristics and finally became a "Purdue beings." Although Buddhism has undergone several destructions in China, its vitality was still tenacious, and thus it formed a lot of branches, such as Zen Buddhism, Pure Land Buddhism, Hua Yanzong, Tiantaizong, and created many of their own classic, such as the Zen "Diamond Sutra", "Lankavatara Sutra," "Vimalakirti Sutra," "Hua Yan Zong's Sutra," etc. The most impressed thing to the average readers is a variety of temples, such as the Shaolin Temple, where people studied the "martial arts" if you look to some martial arts novels, televisions or films.

Compared with Western culture, Chinese culture also emphasizes ethics and has a keen sense of community and collective consciousness. The phrase "Not afraid of less but afraid not to unite" is not only correct in the ancient times, but also has some practical significance in modern times. The disparity between the rich and the poor can easily lead to social differentiation (Fan, 2018). In ancient times, there was a person called Chen Sheng, he fought against the Qin Emperor by shouting "The princes would rather live in a peaceful environment." However, the modern China once changed her name to "big pot" and reduced personal enthusiasm. China has taken light of her culture, advocated harmony with nature, and lacked the spirit of scientific inquiry. Therefore, the natural sciences in China have not been fully developed. Confucius led the orthodox Confucianism ceremony, put forward the people to abide by the "three principles," that is, "the king is principle for ministers, the father is principle for sons, the husband is principle for his wife." On the one hand, these ethics and moral education taught people deeply and make many people honest, on the other hand, it also restricts people's freedom and thinking.

In the past dynasties, loyal ministers were common and the women persecuted by the feudal ideology were even more miserable. Like Du Shiniang, she was a courtesan, but she fell in love with a wrong person, she committed suicide after being betrayed by this person. In contrast, Western culture advocates personal arduous work and struggle, for example, the Napoleon who were highly respected. Of course, overemphasizing the personal role not only promoted the overall social productivity, but also made the human relationship become indifferent, at the same time, the competition for personal interests made this materialistic society prevalent with hedonistic values such as hedonism and money worship.

Chinese culture paid more attention to the summary of the macro aspects, while ignoring the original innovation. In the fields of natural sciences and humanities, there were many masterpieces in China, such as Compendium of Materia Medica, Heavenly Creations, Shuijing Explaination and so on. However, the deeper mysteries of the natural world were seldom explored. Instead, it worshiped the beautiful myth of "Chang'e to the Moon" as the ancient Chinese people did not know much about the moon. Although China advocated "to obtain knowledge by investigation of things," it seemed that the Chinese people lacked the true spirit of inquiry in practice. They mainly relied on experiences and ignored sciences. As the Chinese ancestors saw the swallow will fly low and the ants will rush to move before the rain comes, these words were spread one by one, so the descendants knew these experiences accordingly, but almost no one studied the ants or swallows regarding how they could know that it was going to rain. Undoubtedly, some of the China's natural sciences were just empirical summaries. However, the Western culture paid more attention to the study of the relationships between human beings and nature, advocating the transformation of nature and meeting the needs of mankind. Therefore, it is not surprising that natural sciences in the West are more developed.

As mentioned earlier, Chinese culture contained many empirical summaries. Compared with Western cultures, Chinese culture ignored the independent development of science, religion, culture and arts, and paid more attention to the integration of a vast array of scholarships. Proficiency of all the "Eighteen martial arts" was the goal of the ancient China. Although there were many literary peaks in Chinese culture, such as "The Book of Songs" headed by Jian Xia, "The Songs of Chu" represented by Qu Yuan, and a lot of masterpieces Such as Song Poems, Yuan Poems, and some dramas and novels, were very popular at that time. However, since the Nobel Literature Prize was established for so many years, China has never won the prize, which is a problem worth being thought about. Fortunately, people in China have realized the limitations of Chinese civilization gradually and tried their best to make the best use of their abilities through foreign exchanges and comparisons so that the Chinese civilization will become the most brilliant one in the world.

Where is the way for Chinese culture?

After realizing the magnificent momentum of Chinese culture, realizing the limitations of Chinese culture and realizing that Chinese culture should seek long-term development in its exchange of views, as a proud member of the Chinese nation, one should have enough confidence. Culture has its own unique charm and vitality. Some of the core contents of Chinese culture are in line with the theme of the current era and can promote the development of China and the world. The era of peace and development advocated by Chinese culture can be well recognized and accepted by the people in the world. The harmony between human beings and nature, respect for nature and the protection of nature in Chinese culture are in line with sustainable development. It is entirely possible that the concept of development will resonate with people in the world (Sun, 2018). In addition, Chinese culture has a long history, the diversity of cultures makes Chinese culture extraordinary. China has many cultural treasures, such as The Book of Songs, the Tang Sancai, the blue and white porcelain, the Peking Opera and Shadow Play, the Shaolin Temple and the Chinese Kung Fu, etc. The Chinese culture is loved and watched by the world people step by step. That is why China also pays more attention to the excavation and cultivation of her own traditional culture.

As mentioned earlier, China must admit bravely that there are some shortcomings for the Chinese culture, such as being too moderate and tolerant, lacking the adventurous spirit, not performing well and being too conservative, lacking the innovative spirit and so on. China must abandon the dross contents in Chinese traditional culture. Some of the witchcraft and ghosts culture in China should not be trusted any more. The three basic principles and five permanent principles advocated by the Confucian orthodoxy in China are also against the human relations, which is a kind of backward thinking and need to be abandoned certainly.

Of course, it is quite difficult for the Chinese People to give up the traditional ideas, a lot of patient education are required to let these traditional ideas be given up completely. However, China should continue to maintain the good traditions, such as the excellent quality of thrift and demanding work. In the new era, China must do an excellent job in cross-time work of Chinese culture, if she wants to realize the new development of Chinese culture and adapt it to the trend of the times.

Based on reality, can China better look forward to the future. So, what is the practical significance of Chinese culture? Chinese culture is a symbol of China and an important carrier of China's strength. China has a long history of culture, something that China needs to think about is how to give the new vitality to Chinese culture in the new era. The "benevolence, righteousness, courtesy, wisdom and faith" advocated by Chinese Confucianism meet China's basic requirements of self-cultivation and life-saving and should therefore also become a part of the moral standard system advocated by modern China. "The benevolent loves others," so the Chinese should act as the merciful and kind people. "Do not do what we impose on others," the Chinese should not do anything that may harm others. "Be humble and cherish," be polite, abide by the rules and regulations, be a gentleman. Do everything well, take good faith as the foundation of one's life.

In short, as for the attitude on treating Chinese culture, China can neither be complacent nor think that the world will only respect the Chinese culture, of course China cannot be crazy about foreign culture and obsequious to foreigners either. China must inherit and carry forward the culture that is conducive to China's self-cultivation, and abandon those weird or even totally wrong stuff, which are usually the dross contents. China is already aware of the gap between Chinese culture and the culture of the current world leader, and China has been making efforts to narrow the gap. The Chinese people have confidence in Chinese culture. China believes that the Chinese people can make Chinese culture brilliant once again after making significant efforts. As China want to show a beautiful image for the people in the world.

Soft power needs to be developed further

The culture is an inexhaustible motive force for the continuous development of a nation. The further development of China's soft power culture requires the joint efforts of all ethnic groups. China is a multi-ethnic country. As the lyrics said, "56 ethnic groups are just like 56 flowers or 56 brothers and sisters." The ethnic minorities in China are not only parts of the Chinese nation, they are also influenced by the Han culture and have their own colorful culture. Most of the ethnic minorities have immense talent in singing and dancing, and most of the ethnic minorities are generous. Their traditional festivals are as beautiful as their people. For example, the "Songkran Festival" is a traditional festival for Dai people. The Oroqen, Gaoshan, Miao and Zhuang nationalities have their own words and languages. Of course, Mandarin has now become an important language among all these ethnic groups. The development histories of these ethnic groups are not the same, but they are equally influenced by the Chinese culture. As a Chinese, they also love this country. As early as the Spring Autumn Period and the Warring States Period, the integration of all ethnic groups began on a large scale. The population would undergo a large-scale relocation when there was a war. The integration of various ethnic groups would promote the progress of Chinese civilization further. In Chinese history, many ethnic minorities established their own regimes, such as the Yuan and Qing dynasties, and most of the nomadic northern tribesmen fought bravely on horseback. Under the influence of the Han culture, many ethnic minorities have learned the advanced technologies and cultures from the Han people.

Culture seems very weird. It cannot be seen, anthropologists believe that the culture is invisible, but some of the basic elements of culture and many of the representations that stretch from the culture are visible. For example, the architectural style, Chinese architecture and Western architecture have their own cultural styles, cultural essences and cultural connotations. Take the diet as an example, what are the differences between the Chinese food and the Western food? How to distinguish? Why are there so many differences? Almost all Chinese use chopsticks, which is the wisdom of the Chinese nation, but it is not very easy to use the chopsticks well, there are some skills, and therefore so many foreigners that are unable to use the chopsticks as well as Chinese. Can you catch two soybeans at the same time with your chopsticks? Have you tried? But the Westerners use knives and forks instead of the chopsticks. The Chinese people cut the food well before cooking, which is contrary to the Westerners. For another example, when talking about the ethnic cultures, one can find out the costumes of ethnic minorities quickly. Ethnic costumes are also the minority representation and Symbol of National Culture.

China has always stressed that "peace is the most important thing", and "peace" is an important part of Chinese culture. China also stressed that people should be kind and friendly to others, friendliness is conducive to business success, this refers to a form of communication between people. China pays attention to the unity of human beings and nature and the building of a harmonious society. Therefore, China can accept foreign things calmly and even has curiosities about new foreign things (Zheng, 2017). The ability of China's accepting and integrating foreign cultures is probably beyond all foreigners' imagination.

Let us look to the Confucianism in China and Christianity in the western countries the Confucianism in China can tolerate the existence of Christianity, but Christianity cannot tolerate the existence of Confucianism. What is the reason? Confucianism believes that "when someone was born, he was kind definitely," and Christians believe in God, God created the world, and he will help those poor people for sure, if Christians accepted the Confucian goodness theory, they would have to accept the view that "everyone can become a saint through enlightenment and self-cultivation." Therefore, it is unacceptable for Christians to live with Confucianism. Accordingly, the Christian Church was assimilated by Confucianism. This is one of the reasons for the inclusiveness of Chinese culture.

In addition, Chinese culture was not limited to specific aspects. Under the influence of Chinese culture, most of the China ancients paid attention to the concept that "a marriage should base on the equal social ranks between families." However, they often learned from each other, which was more obvious among scholars. The close friendship could be seen everywhere in ancient China, such as the friendship between Li Bai and Du Fu, the friendship between Yuanyang and Bai Juyi, etc. "If three of us are walking together, at least one is good enough to be a teacher of the other two." Since Chinese culture can accommodate and absorb so many new and advanced things, why did China lag western countries in modern times? Why has China ever been invaded by Japan? Why are the Chinese people regarded as "a mess?" China may be able to find some clues from the limitations of Chinese culture, which may also be related to people's lack of confidence in the national culture. Opening to the outside world is not only a global movement of capital, goods and labor force, but also a global circulation of culture through various channels.

The Chinese people would be greatly affected by some strong and aggressive cultural influx, and this would result in the lack of confidence in the national culture. In the 18th CPC National Congress, General Secretary Xi Jinping talked about traditional Chinese culture on many occasions, expressed his approval and respect for traditional culture and the traditional ideological value system, proposed enhancing cultural self-confidence and values self-confidence. President Xi Jinping pointed out in the report of the 19th NPC that it is necessary to strengthen cultural confidence and promote the prosperity of socialist culture. He said there is no great rejuvenation of the Chinese nation without a high degree of cultural confidence and cultural prosperity. The Chinese people must uphold the socialist path with Chinese characteristics, stimulate the creative efforts of the entire nation in cultural innovation, build a strong socialist culture and realize the great "Chinese dream" of the great rejuvenation of the Chinese nation at an early date. Regardless of whether China can become the world leader or not, under the background of such a prosperous global cultural development, China must inherit and carry forward the culture that is conducive to China's self-cultivation, and abandon those weird or even totally wrong stuff, which are usually the dross contents. Only by this way can China become a real cultural world leader (Xia, 2018).

Chapter 8

China's Education System

When it comes to the education in China, people from all walks of life have something to say. The students who have the most say are probably going to complain, "China's exam-oriented education has made us miserable, just look to the heavy schoolbags you will know what a pressure it is that we are having. We do not have enough time to rest at all, we have to study all the time, thus almost all of us are near-sighted after long-term unhealthy eyes using, after we graduate from the university, the embarrassment of not finding a good and suitable job will need to be faced by us." A few years ago, there was a video on the internet which should be able to explain some of the issues. A primary school student cried in tears to the camera, he would not want to go to college, because he could not have time to go back home to take care of his parents whose ages would be almost over 70 at that time, moreover, he did not want to go to the senior middle school and even the junior middle school. Such a young child began to fear the education of all stages of the future, what a shame it is for the education! To study harder, both students and parents become much busier than usual. The most ridiculous thing is that some fathers even conceal some sad news such as the wife's death, to allow children to recuperate in the senior middle school entrance examination, is not this a family mourning? In addition to reading books, many students seem to have nothing else to do. Is this the unfortunate "evolution" of mankind?

However, the parents feel more frustrated. Parents might say, "to some extent, the children's exam is not only an exam of them, but also an exam of the parents, the children's exam needs to be accompanied by the parents, even the college entrance examination needs to be accompanied as well." The Chinese parents sometimes are too vanity and they always like comparisons, even their children's grades will be compared from time to time, parents will feel proud if their children's grades are higher than others. "Look forward to your son into a dragon and look at your daughter to become a Phoenix," although there is nothing wrong, however, as everyone knows, excessive force will eventually lead to the child's alienation and rebellion. People can understand the pain of parents, because they do not have the knowledge themselves, they want their Children to study hard to gain more knowledge. After all, the exam-oriented education is fair to some extent, those families with no background will get a glimmer of hope. For some parents, they own high positions in the society, they feel it will be a shame if their Children are worse than others. No matter what kind of parents they are, all of them love the education warmly and will not be stingy on the education investments, which seems to be fueling the "evil wind" of education industrialization.

On the other hand, the teachers are also affected by it deeply. They might complain, "there are so many pressures need to be faced with, such as the pressure from the school leaders, the pressure from the parents and even the pressure from the students, we are now suffering from these pressures." In fact, the embarrassment of teachers is also possible. On the one hand, they must survive with pitiful salaries, on the other hand they need to grantee the enrolment rate. As such, some teachers will go to another school for more wages undoubtedly. Some of them will even give up the teaching career and go to do something else to make a better living. As you see above, there are so many embarrassments. Of course, all the pressures are not coming from one person, but from the education of this society.

There are always people who are happy and others who are sad. On the one hand, China's education has made people suffered such as the students, parents and teachers, on the other hand, it made all kinds of counseling institutions and remedial schools gain a lot of benefits. Students must study hard in class, once winter vacation or summer vacation comes, they must also go to all kinds of counseling institutions and cram schools. What a pain it is! In fact, most of the teachers in such kind of counseling institutions or cram schools came from colleges and universities, as they were trying to make some extra money.

From the above, one might wonder how that could happen in China. It is due to the problems of China's education system. The current China's education system has not adopted the principles of modern education. The schools remain the main venue for cultivating "eligible successors" for the country. China's education is a "test-oriented education," schools can only encourage single development. Students and parents can only accept uniform judgments, so the grades are extremely important. This kind of "test-oriented education" has hindered the development of young people's personality and creativity (Wei, 2007). It is true that no country has a perfect education system, but China's education embarrassment is more prominent in some respects. In such a country with a long history and a strong cultural heritage, the issues of education is certainly traceable.

The embarrassment on education

When talking China's education system in her history, it is necessary to mention the Chinese imperial examination. It was a very important system for selecting officials in the ancient China. The imperial examination that has a 1300 years history was founded in the Sui dynasty and established in the Tang dynasty, completed in the Song dynasty and extended to Yuan, Ming and Qing dynasties. On the one hand, the imperial examination reflected the principle of fair competition and merit-based admission, it provided the general people with the hope of changing their destiny. Some people with lofty ideals have become the managers or builders of the country through the imperial examination. On the other hand, the imperial examination was also flawed. Many people were going to take the imperial examination to get rich, which resulted in the idea of "official standard." In addition, the imperial examination imprisoned people's thoughts. It devastated the talents and gave a great negative impact on future education. As Mr. Hu Shi said, "People's minds were not independent from the eyes and ears," thus it could only let people become a group of useless and incompetent waste material!"(Hu,1999) Among the methods used in the various examinations today, some systems still look like the imperial examination to some extent, such as taking one's seat according to the number on the ticket, arranging one or two separate teachers to guard the examination and sealing up the examinees' papers after the examination, etc. (Wang,2007). As you can see, the ancient education system not only brought a positive meaning, but also brought the embarrassment to modern education.

The utilitarianism of ancient education was only manifested in the shallow level of gaining wealth, however the modern education appeared in a variant form. The education industrialization is a very hot vocabulary, it reflects the utilitarian education, which is a shame for China. There exists the embarrassment of "compulsory education does not look like real," in the villages as well as the towns, the fairness of education has been questioned. In addition, the phenomenon of indiscriminate charges on education can be seen everywhere, this kind of unethical money-collecting behavior has become a public "secret" in education circles and a "hidden rule" of some key institutions. There was a report which discussed the China's education system a little bit, in this report the writer pointed out that the indiscriminate charges on education in the past 10 years has reached 30 billion U.S dollars according to the conservative estimates by the education experts. One might ask, "When did the school turn into a disguised "toll booth"?

Must admit that the schools are very "timely" to carry out a variety of profit-making projects due to the development of market economy, at the beginning the schools pursued the entrance rate and the employment rate, later they started to pursue economic benefits as well as the entrance rate. In addition to a serious of various costs, the schools also engage in various joint venture projects by using their venues and equipment. Even the teachers have changed their minds gradually and spent most of their time on extra-curricular counseling. Although some schools forbid their teachers explicitly from running amateur training courses during winter and summer vacations to make extra money, however, where there are policies there are countermeasures, some teachers still do what they used to via different methods. For some of the teachers who are very "low-key" and unscrupulous to run remedial classes, school leaders are willing to close one eye at a glance. The parents have no choice but to send their children to the remedial classes, because they thought they "cannot let the children lose at the starting line." In the view of academia today, the industrialization ideas pursued by China's education system reform in recent years have become the root cause of the existing problems of education in China, that is, it will "bring the market relations into an area that should not be introduced," which resulted in the education industrialization(Ji,2006).

Apart from the education utilitarianizing, the thought of "eight-legged essays" in ancient education has poisoned many students. Some people cannot help sighing, "Chinese education has become ill, the most absurd is that they treat decadent education as a traditional model of education. What is the difference between the college entrance examination and the "eight-legged essays"? China's education is just like the feeding education, it is a passive learning, look to the current Chinese students, how much subjective initiative has been played? The dual fermentation of institutional and conceptual issues is the deadliest. Take the graduate entrance exam as an example, many people simply do not have the ability to research, they choose to take the graduate entrance examination just to get a diploma, or to avoid the employment pressure.

In fact, there is another embarrassment in modern education. The Chinese people are now advocating English learning extremely, while the traditional culture is facing a gradual decline. In modern China, the governors adopted the policy of "closing China's doors and locking up the country," they ignored the development of foreign countries totally not mention to learning the foreign languages. However, in current China, the Chinese people treat English as a magic weapon to win the workplace, even though some jobs do not need to use English at all. It is undoubtedly that China are now taking an international route, and economy globalization has also forced the Chinese people to go along with the world. China do not deny that some international talents should have a good command of a world language. However, the need for this world language is reduced greatly for those who want to work only in China.

It will be fine if one does not know the foreign language, it is not so necessary to understand the foreign language well because there are so many translators and interpreters in the world. If everyone can speak fluent foreign languages, will the translators and interpreters lose their jobs? Of course, this is just a joke. What the Chinese people should reflect on is why do they always like to go to extremes so much? Either they did not learn the foreign languages at all, shut their doors and engaged in construction, or all of them started to learn the foreign languages warmly and left the traditional culture aside. Should they also learn and inherit the "golden mean" in a timely manner? Maybe the Chinese people should consider it to avoid many unnecessary embarrassments and censures.

The innocent students

Chinese students have been taught since their childhood to listen carefully in classes and to finish the homework conscientiously after classes. For the students, the education contents are just the ones in their textbooks, the primary criterion for measuring education is exams. Students are busy in classes as well as after classes. The contents in the textbooks are the whole of education. Thus, there occurred the most important feature of exam-oriented education: the score is everything. Therefore, some students often quip: "score, score, score, score is the core, which is not wise at all." To pursue the high scores, some students have become ones with "high scores but low abilities," what the even more frightening thing is that one examination decides the future of a student, in other words, no matter how well he usually behaves in school and how stable his scores usually are, once he plays disorders in the entrance examination, his fate will be changed since then, this means he was "killed by one shot." The academic community in education did realize this issue. There was a proposal that the "headmaster recommendation system" or "average score system" should be implemented.

However, a new problem is to come. In such a country where a network of "relationships" exists, the "scores in normal times" become more operational, and the ensuing problems of corruption will also continue to grow. In this awkward position, students are the weakest ones, they have no choice but to accept it. The Chinese people often say that "we cannot let the children lose at the starting line," which will result in the disappearing color of childhood. "Study has to be started from the baby," although there is an age limitation for children going to primary schools, there are all kinds of private kindergartens. Some parents who do not have time to look after their children may simply consider kindergarten as a disguised nursery, but the children are usually asked to learn arithmetic, spelling, etc. after they are 3 years old.

Zhou Libo, the founder of Shanghai-based Qingkou, he once mentioned the issues of children's education in "Mr. Zhou Live Show" hosted by him. He said that the children today have too much academic pressure and have lost the innocence that a child should have, every child looks "cool." He also cited an example: A little girl ordered a song called "Why do women trouble women" on the radio for her mother on Mother's Day. Why? It turned out that her mother discipline her very strictly, and she happened to be a very naughty child, as a result, being beaten becomes a widespread practice.

This story sounds funny, but somewhat sad. There are so many children that have been overwhelmed in childhood, they have lost the fun of childhood completely, can you say that they are happy? On June 11th, 2012, just after the end of the college entrance examination, in "Zhong Shan Talking" on the broadcast of Hunan Satellite TV, there were many videos regarding the efforts made by the parents in order to let their children pass the college entrance examination, the examples cited in the videos were also ridiculous: Frogs got poisoned due to children's college entrance examination; A wall of people got formed by the parents of examinees in order to block cars; Hiding the news of father's death for two months in order not to interrupt the efforts for the college entrance examination; A boy learned that his mother died in a car accident 12 days after the college entrance examination; A mother sent her daughter to the examination room in tears when she was in a car accident. A mother kneels because of her child not entering the examination room on time.

What we see with the naked eyes is not only a batch of students who have been "sacrificed" by innocent people, but also their parents, and even the "terminally ill" social system and the constant distortion of human nature.

Most of the students lost their creativity and vitality due to the unreasonable education. Students could only "read the books rigidly, "and leave the warning saying of "to believe everything in books is worse than to have no books at all" aside. The "champion" of various disciplines is therefore often laughed at as someone who "knows nothing but reading a book." An even more embarrassing thing is that many Chinese students with high scores were rejected by some foreign universities. The reason is that it does not reflect the sense of social responsibility, service awareness and commonweal that should be possessed by future social elites. Chinese students are widely recognized as the most diligent students in learning, but no Nobel laureate has been cultivated so far. On the contrary, let us look to the students in the United States, children are free and innocent, but a bunch of Nobel Prize winners have been trained (Yu,2011). Is it fair that the failure of Chinese education is to be paid by the innocent students eventually?

In China, the certificates act as a very important role. In all kinds of recruitment venues, people often see the job seekers holding a pile of documents, diplomas, certificates, etc. It looks like that one will have the ability to do his job well if he has the corresponding certificates, how ridiculous it is! This is due to the national standards of talents evaluation system. Employers often set the admission threshold based on certificates such as diplomas, as a result, the students, parents, schools are all regarding the diplomas, degrees and certificates as an important weapon. An even more unfortunate thing is that the students started to select their teachers after entering colleges and universities to get diplomas, certificates and a series of "qualifications" much easier. Students learn and imitate such unhealthy tendencies in society and send gifts to teachers to let their teachers to "take care of them" with regards to the diplomas and certificates. They often regard this as a "good" way to go along well with their teachers. One might ask: "who gave the teachers such a big right on earth? Why is the relevant department indifferent to this kind of social chaos? Even if one can get a worry-free work finally through the "network of relationships," are they useful to society? Can they contribute to society? China should think about it deeply.

After entering the society, most of the students will find: what they learned in the colleges are almost useless. What they learned at school is completely out of touch with social practice, the theories cannot be applied to realities, many books were read in vain. This type of education which is severely disconnected from the real productivity has poisoned a lot of young people who might have the ability to contribute to China's future construction. Some college students who have always been called "the God's favored ones" do not know what to do after their entering the society. Therefore, the diplomas, certificates and a series of "qualifications" are not so important because one should have the real ability to do his job well instead of owning a lot of certificates or diplomas.

The development of things is always interlocked, when the disadvantages of education appear, some of the consequences can be afforded, however, some of the consequences cannot be afforded by China. At present, some college students are overwhelmed, so they choose to commit suicide, they protest the injustice of this society via this special method, is the price they pay too high? Undoubtedly, it is stupid to choose to commit suicide. After all, wisdom is not equal to morality, intelligence is not equal to conscience. If there is a moral conscience, they should think about how painful their parents will be once they commit suicide. From another side, it shows that some children did not receive a good moral education in the growth process, what a pity! Children with self-awareness will gradually become aware of themselves as they grow up, and will gradually become developed in terms of conscience and morality. Children who lack self-awareness will be frustrated and will even go to extremes. Such kind of ludicrous events which happened in the colleges will make people unbelievable, however, this is not accidental. These are all caused by the unreasonable "Chinese-style education".

Education chaos: Rare fraud and rare shamelessness

With the continuous development of the Internet, a lot of internet buzzwords became popular and were applied to various fields. Education is no exception, for example, the word expert was replaced with "brick master," the word professor was replaced with "beast." This ironic and cynical is reflecting the education chaos to some extent. Experts and professors have begun to lose their popular feelings. This mess of education originated from some of the black sheep in education circles. As a result, some terrible rumors were spread out, with which the experts and scholars do not know how to deal.

Why are the scholars who were ever respected widely scolded by countless people? What needs to be emphasized here in particular is that some of the public servants in important positions get their degrees in the form of so-called "on-the-job" doctorates. The greater progress of administrative officials should be mainly relying on their diligent efforts and outstanding achievements. However, some people set aside their work and get a degree certificate easily without studying in school, this kind of action is extremely bad. Although the certificate is real, the holder's academic knowledge is fake. Look at the history of doctorate education and official history always and in all countries, it is not hard to find that the high-level administrative public servants obtained the doctorate degrees by using the public funds after their participating in work. This is due to the imperfect educational system in contemporary China, which is an ugly phenomenon of anti-social civilization. Furthermore, this is due to the official standard thought left over from Chinese feudal society. It is a blasphemy against science and academia.

This chaos of doctorate education is harmful. Those who obtained doctorates in a variety of irregular ways did not undergo a rigorous doctoral training. Without a rigorous doctoral training, how can they master the necessary scientific knowledge and scientific methods that a doctor should have? The doctorate is a recognition of the academic level as well as the academic process, not just the recognition of their work experience. Such practices will only let people get wrong academic titles for themselves and do not have the real scientific knowledge. This kind of negative impact on the academic field is huge and far-reaching in the long run and in the short term. If this kind of chaos of doctorate continues to spread, Chinese doctoral education will become a joke in the international higher education sector. China's doctorate will not be recognized by the international community, the integrity and international image of the people's Republic of China will be destroyed. In China, some civil servants got higher leadership positions by using these "Master" or "PhD" diplomas, thus they gained higher powers and more benefits, this phenomenon is even more detrimental to the glorious image of the China Communist Party (Tian and Dai,2012). How can the so-called "experts" and "professors" who arise under such circumstances be respected by Chinese people?

While the educational supervision is being strengthened, the phenomenon of rent-seeking and corruption in the education system are still emerging. This is a very weird social phenomenon. There always exist some nepotism networks in China. Once a chain is broken, it will lead to a terrible result like "dominoes." Therefore, these educators and politicians are willing to turn a blind eye to this to protect each other. At the same time, there are some problems which make the people indignant in the colleges and universities. For example, the education and scientific research funding were wasted seriously, because some professors and scholars fetch it via cheating, and these funds were used just for eating and drinking. They did some selfish things for themselves in the noble name of education, so do you think that they will be respected by the public people? Of course, not all professors and scholars are like those, there are still some good ones that contribute themselves to the education career. However, it will be even harder to win the popular feelings once this phenomenon exists in colleges and universities.

Let us look at the issue of academic counterfeiting, which is attracting more and more attention. People can see many fake academic qualifications and fake diplomas in society, which insulted this "holy land" of education. The famous fake fighter Fang Zhouzi disclosed a lot of scandal in academia, such as the Tang Jun "academic door" incident, He Haibo academic ongoing incident, Xiao Chuan Guo incident, Wang

Hui incident, Zhu Xueqin incident and so on. There are indeed many phenomena of academic fraud in the academic community in current China. So where is the problem? In fact, the peer evaluation and the error correction mechanism are either missing or non-existent. But can this be the reason for the socialization of academic issues? Can academic problems be diverted to other areas for "crackdown"? (Sun,2010) It seems that it is a very big task to fight against the academic fraud, according to the current situation of Fang Zhouzi, the fighting process in the future will be even more difficult!

Who is to answer for the unreasonable education system?

Some scholars think that the educational institutions are the carrier of education system and education norms are the core of education system. The school education system is the precondition for the existence of education system, and the educational management system is the guarantee for running the education system, education administrative system is a macro management system, school management system is a micro-management system within the school. Administrative and regulatory systems are the important parts of the education system and schools play a very important role in this regard. When facing the embarrassing situation of Chinese education, do the schools have the responsibility?

At present, most of the colleges and universities are practicing the academic year system, it will turn to credit system in future. Because the academic year system only requires a certain amount of years of study for the students, it is not comprehensive yet. The credit system requires the students to obtain the corresponding credit for each type of courses (such as social sciences courses, general courses, elective courses, etc.) The credit system reflects the individualized teaching to a certain extent, it brings some problems as well, for example, many students would choose some elective courses just to meet the requirements of the credit system, this is so called "gathering credits." Before and after obtaining the required credits, they have no interests in the courses they have chosen.

There exists a phenomenon of credits being obtained too many in the colleges and universities, thus many students think that it is a waste of time to choose these courses. Those who have already chosen these courses are likely to skip them eventually. This kind of "casting the net widely," only pay attention to the breadth of learning instead of the depth of learning, will result in the students' learning widely but not learning deeply. The older generation knows that a person must have a "skill" to gain a foothold in the community. Most of the university students who have just stepped out of school do not have any answers if they were asked what their professional skills or expertise are. As a result, there is no difference among various students. Is it a failure of the education system?

Chinese students were forced to learn a lot from an early age, and a large part of them did not know why. This is a blind learning, just to gain good scores and to get the praise from parents and teachers, as well as the envy of classmates. In this way, the students will have such a wrong sense of learning: to learn for the exam, to strive for vanity. In the end, this led directly to the decline of Chinese students' practical ability, the students will be unable to integrate into society and adapt to society. Whose fault is this? Parents? Teachers? Of course not! In fact, it is the product of Chinese traditional culture and the backward ideology from feudal society.

In fact, China's education has always been widely controversial. The United Nations investigator Katharina Tomasevski whose position is a special investigator in charge of education, has ever visited China for two weeks, after her seeing the weird phenomenon, she criticized that with regards to guaranteeing the rights to basic education, China is inferior to Uganda who is a poor country in Africa. "Education in China only accounts for 2% of GDP, which is much lower than the UN minimum requirement 6%." She said that "the government only provides 53% of the school's funds and the rest is borne by the parents of the students and the proportion of the government is lower than that in all other countries with compulsory education policies" (Wang and Liu,2004). Let us look at the United States, the efficiency of educational resources has been improved greatly because of the common cost sharing in the external system and the marketing management in the internal system, a situation of high tuition fees and high scholarships has been formed gradually (Wei and Wang, 2006).

Under the circumstance of insufficient education funding, the colleges and universities have thought of several ways to increase it. Therefore, this problem has been solved through enlarging enrollments. Most of the students who have been enrolled are children from the rich families, the colleges and some students have realized the goal of so-called "win-win" status. In this regard, the famous economics professor Lang Xianping has different opinion, he believes that although the goal of expanding enrollment of colleges and universities in China is to prevent the outflow of education funds, but China cannot save the wealth of the rich to sacrifice the interests of most poor students. Children from the rich families can find an excellent job easily after their graduating from universities, however, the poor children might not find a suitable job eventually. This sounds unfair! In the end, it will become the focus of public concern whether the education is fair or not.

In talking about this, the Chinese people want to say that one of the biggest drawbacks of China's education is that the country always wants to create a monopoly via administrative power instead of trying to maintain fair competition. It is very difficult to find a balance between marketization and state management. If it is overly market-oriented, the consequences of "industrialization of education" will emerge. If excessive administrative intervention is made, it will be easy to form a state monopoly and weaken competition.

Let us look at the original purpose of education. Einstein believed that the highest goal of education should be to train students who can serve the society and act independently and think independently. Einstein objected to compulsory education, advocated "free-for-all" and "self-responsibility" education and heuristic education that stimulated students' curiosity. There is a significant difference between Einstein's educational thought and the current education theory in China. Einstein's educational thought provided good enlightenment for the reform of

China's educational system (Wang, 2010). Has the goal of fostering successors been achieved? Have the talents been trained? In fact, the Chinese people have ever won the Nobel Prize. For example, Yang Zhenning and Li Zhengdao who ever won the Nobel Prize are the students from the Southwest Associated University, Ding Zhaozhong and Steven Chu are Chinese American. There are some Chinese who got the Fields Medal as well, such as Yau Cheng and Tao Zhexuan. However, the education they took has nothing to do with the China's primary schools, middle schools, and universities. Why China did not produce any Nobel Prize winner in the current primary schools, middle schools and universities? What is wrong with the China's education? It seems hard to make a complete answer.

Of course, there are many more things to do to save China's children and education. For example, China should expedite the reform of her education system to meet the requirements of social development. The family should strive to change the concept of narrow-mindedness and establish an equal human dignity and respect the value and significance of ordinary labor. The schools should eliminate unhealthy tendencies and create active learning atmosphere, and create opportunities and conditions for independent innovation. The teachers should really be good teachers and contribute to the teaching career to achieve a mutually beneficial progress in teaching. The Students should respect knowledge and respect themselves. The jobs that suit them are the best jobs, do not follow anyone blindly as their jobs may not suit you. Various kind of talents will be welcomed in this society but not just the uniform "standardized" people. Well, as you see above, a conclusion may be drawn that the responsibility of education is so great!

Education weakens China's opportunity to be the world leader

Higher education is an important part of national education. Its level of development is a crucial factor in measuring the overall strength of a country or region. Different from the credit system in the United States, colleges and universities in China have relaxed the guidance and management of students, lowered the demand for failing students in many courses, and implemented the so-called "cleaning test" to ensure that students will not repeat their grades, which is very different to the credit system in the United States. In the United States, the academic status of students will be evaluated through the credit system and performance points, the flexible management is carried out via performance points and credit system. This is one of the differences between China and the United States, which shows the enormous difference between exam-oriented education and quality education.

The Chinese students are taking exam-oriented education from primary school to high school. It adopts a top-down education mode in which teachers give lessons and students receive knowledge in class passively. This kind of education mode lacks interaction and exchange; thus, the learning enthusiasm has been reduced greatly. This is a binding education model with teachers' constraints in the schools and parents' constraints at home. The students lack self-discipline and over-depend on external power, which will result in the intolerance after their entering the society. Some students even do not know how to look for suitable jobs and let their parents arrange for them. In contrast, the students are independent under the American-style education, the parents in the United States are also more "ruthless" than the parents in China. By the age of 18, their children will be left for self-reliance. Not to mention the fact that even parents like China do their best to help their children find a job. This is extremely absurd and impossible for parents and students in the United States. If China wants to surpass the United States to become the world leader, at least there is still a long way to go in education.

In the current era of knowledge economy, the issue of education relates to the improvement of the quality of the entire nation as well as the development of the country and even its existence. To a certain extent, Darwin's law of "superiority and inferiority" still applies. However, the winners of the future world are no longer the slaughters of violent wars, but belong to the nation whose education is more popularized and whose culture is more developed. The world will be developed in the direction of "wisdom taking." After all, peaceful development is the theme of the world today. As announced by the Board of Education recently, "The only way to sustain and improve our competitive edge in the world is to devote all our efforts to reforming our education." The 21st century is an era of knowledge expansion the new society and the new era have given China a new historical responsibility. There are prophets who predict that future illiterates will no longer be illiterate people, but people who are incapable of action. Therefore, the Chinese people must develop their self-learning abilities in their studies. However, China's exam-oriented education ignores this point precisely.

Empowering the country by focusing on education is precedent in the world history. For example, Russia in the time of Peter I, Japan in the Meiji Restoration, Germany in early Bismarck, these achieved unprecedented growth because of their emphasis on education. A common characteristic is that they attach importance to challenging work, which unlike the China's current emphasis. Peter dressed personally, go to Western Europe to learn shipbuilding technologies, Japan sent many students, go to the West to learn advanced education, Germany is a learning-oriented country, never do things without outcomes. Unlike China, China overemphasizes the knowledge of the books, China has always had the reputation of "not hearing the word out of the window and reading the books of saints." But in the world today, China will not be able to become the world leader only by reading sages. To become the world leader, China must have an open-minded attitude, China must overcome the "shortcomings" in her development. As discussed before, China's education is weakening the opportunity to be the world leader for China, it is the time for China to consider what to do.

There is no doubt that education is relevant to every family, and even to the entire nation! Education is the foundation. The problem of education is more important than all other social issues. If the vicious circle of education continues, the ultimate victim will be everyone and the future of the entire nation! If the education system does not change, the victims will be succeeding generations of future generations. If the embarrassment of education continues, who are going to build China in the future? Mr. Yi Zhongtian, as a famous educator, he once said with emotion: "There is no hope for China's education, it is even worse than

Chinese football." This metaphor carries a bit of ridicule and sarcasm, but this is the cry of an educator. If so, what a sad it will be for China's education! After the founding of New China, the Chinese nation is no longer a "coward" to be on the verge of death. China has confidences to believe that the future of education in China will be getting better and better (Perry, 2014).

Chapter 9

The Two Sides of Economic Development

The national economy of any country is usually composed of many aspects, some various characteristics will be shown while developing the economy. In the face of the new trend of economic and technological development in the world today and the competition in overall national strength among countries, the high-tech competitions, cultural competitions and educational competition will dominate the development of the national economy. In these respects, there is still much room for economic development in China, so some people think that China will surpass the United States in 30 years or so and then become the world leader. However, some scholars also lamented that after China became the world's second largest economy, she is now in the most prosperous period. The China's economy has reached the bottleneck of her development. In recent years, the China's economy was in an era of unprecedented prosperity. After that, various social conflicts will occur gradually and these conflicts will be paid close attèntion to by all countries in the world. "Common fame is seldom to blame," China's economy will face more and more pressure and resistance. Can this be regarded as the two sides of China's economic development?

In fact, it should be regarded as the A / B aspect of China's economic development instead of being regarded as the two sides of China's economic development. Because there always exist achievements as well as problems, and there always exist the strengths and the weaknesses, at any stage of China's economic development. These relations cannot divide the "boundary of the Chu River" very clearly. The economic development refers to the process of economic development from achievement to crisis and then from crisis to achievement while developing both inside and outside the economy. At a certain stage, if the drawbacks of economic development become prominent, the corresponding crisis will become more obvious. If the economic development is not enough, there are still "hiding places," for the drawbacks and the crisis may not be so serious. Let us take the "opening to the outside world" as an example, this is a basic national policy started by China in 1978. Theoretically speaking, it would allow all kinds of commodities and factors of production in China to enter the stage of international competition to enable China's resources and the world's resources have shared each other and thus to improve the efficiency of resource use, reduce the cost of products, enhance the competitive advantage and promote the rapid increase of national competitiveness. However, after practicing for more than 30 years, it has not really achieved the original rational goal. On the contrary, during the process of opening to the outside world, some enterprises have developed a simple habit of learning and imitating, and this kind of habit even became a culture and a national habit, this can be regarded as the "path dependence." This kind of "path dependence" will be one of the greatest potential harm in the future economic development. Obviously, over-reliance on the external market has a negative impact on the internal market of China. Moreover, the resource and environmental problems that come with it have also jeopardized the further development of China's economy (Wang and Tian, 2012).

Maybe it is because the modern China was suffering from "closed doors policy" quite a lot, China paid special attention to her connection with the world after the reform and opening. In such a special country, it is quite easy to make mistakes from one extreme to another extreme. On the one hand China has made an important contribution to the world and benefited from the development of the world during the process of economy globalization. However, on the other hand, the external pressure China is facing is also getting bigger and bigger. Countries are beginning to make comparisons, compete, and they also have disputes over their interests. As far as economic development is concerned, China and the world have achieved a win-win situation to some extent. The world has provided strong technical support to China. China has provided the world with a big market and a cheap labor force. The so-called A-side and B-side of the economy are not only the good sides.

As far as the economy is concerned, the trade friction is a "stumbling block" to China's economic development.

Take the FDI as an example, on the one hand, the FDI brings advanced technologies and management experiences to China's economic development. On the other hand, maybe the rampant "pollution sanctuary" can explain some of the problems. Most of the scholars believe that the developed countries are all polluting the industrial enterprises heavily in the field of international direct investments in China. Due to the prohibitive cost of pollution control in their own countries and the stringent environmental regulation in their countries, China is relatively relaxed. Therefore, the developed countries will shift their heavily-polluting domestic enterprises to China and turn China into a "pollution paradise." Due to the different data selection, the results obtained will be different, so there exist the corresponding "pollution halo" hypothesis and "pollution neutrality" hypothesis. But what is certain is that this pollution problem exists in some areas.

Should China give up attracting foreign capital then? If this is the case, China is going to "give up eating for fear of choking," which will not be adopted by China undoubtedly. The Chinese people are not so short-sighted, the China's leaders will not be absurd. Will this issue affect the development of China's economy seriously? Does it play a key role in China's economic development? There are still many problems like these, and the environmental problems are only one aspect of China's economic development. In this sense, is China's economy on the verge of danger? If so, how to save the "cliffside" economy in China? Let us discuss these questions in detail.

Is China's economy at its most dangerous edge?

Lang Xianping, as an economist whose viewpoints and words were famous, he wrote a book titled "the China's economy has come to the most dangerous brink" in 2012. There are 5 chapters in this book, it described the current China's economic status, the gains and losses of China's economic reform and the "economic reform road map." Is

China's economy really on the verge of danger? A national discussion was triggered.

Some people said that Professor Lang Xianghui was alarmist and grandstanding, but Professor Lang responded that: "My prophecy has never been wrong, as early as the beginning of 2010, I have reminded everyone that the United States was going to wage a currency war, a cost war and a trade war against China. But there were so many people that thought my words were unfounded." (Lang, 2012) It was proved that many of Professor Lang's predictions were correct, for example, for the Financial crisis happened in 2008, the central government put forward "4 trillion rescue plan," in order to stimulate the domestic economy, Professor Lang supported this for sure, but also pointed out: "It is not reasonable to invest most of these 4 trillion to the infrastructure field, this is just like using tomorrow's overcapacity to solve today's overcapacity, which will result in more serious asset bubbles definitely." As time goes on, it seems that the inflation in the post-crisis era is confirming this prophecy. It is the ordinary people who pay for this, China should think about this phenomenon deeply.

It is not something as simple as shouting slogans whether China's economy has reached the most dangerous edge, it needs to be proved by facts. In 2011, the world economy was still in a recovery period of the post-crisis era. The China's economy was still being developed even under the pressure of low inflation. Let us look at some new data in 2012, the GDP was lower than 8%, which was the first time that it downgrades to less than 8 during the past three years. According to the data released by the National Bureau of Statistics on July 13, China's GDP growth rate was 7.6% in the second quarter. As you know, the rate of economic growth is like the water level line of driving a ship. If it is too low, the ship will inevitably run aground and the economy's intrinsic vitality will be inhibited(Wen,2012). The people's concerns about the future economic prospects was increased after seeing such kind of data. Therefore, it is the issue most concerned by all parties now that at what time the economic growth of China will bottom out.

On August 9, 2012, the National Bureau of Statistics of China released the economic data for July, the consumer price index (CPI) rose 1.8% from a year earlier, the CPI increase hit the lowest level in 30 months(Zhang,2012). The good news from the above two sets of data was that China's economy was in the process of gradual elimination of inflation. At the same time, the sad news was that the China's economy was in a gradual downward trend. Is this also suggesting China's economy has reached the most dangerous edge? On March 2, 2012, Michael Schuman, a veteran journalist of "Times," she published an essay on the future development of China's economy. In this article, she believed that if China does not change her economic development model, the economic crisis is going to emerge inevitably soon, China needs to solve the economic ills as soon as possible.

In addition, there is another phenomenon that often makes China feel terrible. At present, more than 80% of China's oil imports go through the Indian Ocean-Malacca Strait. The transportation route is the "lifeline" of China's economy. However, this "lifeline" has not only been plagued by the world's most rampant piracy activities in the northwest Indian Ocean, Southeast Asia, but also by countries such as India and the United States. In recent years, the substantial enhancement of China's dependence on foreign energy has highlighted the fragility of China's maritime strategy. From a strategic point of view, the stamina of China's economic development has been largely controlled by the comparatively weak control of the oceans, and China is not able to change this pattern easily in a brief period. So, China must have a new strategic thinking.

Let us be optimistic. In the short term, various potential factors that will drive China's economy to continue to grow should not be overlooked. Firstly, the self-regulation, self-repair function of the market. Such as the real estate, stock market and so on, they will stimulate the economic growth of other industries. Secondly, the policy of regulation and control, after all, the market is flawed, it cannot be regulated by the market itself completely, macro-control is also very necessary. In the long run, China needs to change the mode of economic development and adjust the structure of industrial development. If the economic development mode was changed successfully, it will be logical for China's economy to maintain a steady growth.

In this regard, it is quite difficult to answer, because different people will have different answers. Whether China's economy is already bottoming out or whether it can achieve a soft landing, what the Chinese people should understand is that there is no hope for a nation without a sense of crisis. The Chinese people cannot talk about the achievement only and ignore the existing issues. For those who only see the brilliant aspects of China's economic development and ignore the aspects of the China's shortcomings, it is strongly suggested that they should keep a clear brain during discussing the China's economy development.

Side A of economic development: achievements cover up the crisis

The development of human society is a process of recognizing the continuous development, that is, from practice to realization, and then from realization to practice, spiraling upward. It is the same for China's economic development where achievements cover up the crisis and crisis contains opportunities.

Since her opening to the outside world, the China's economy has maintained the sustained rapid growth for more than 30 years, which can be rarely seen in other countries. Many people think that China has formed a unique mode of economic development and they even regard China's rare economic growth as a "miracle." This miracle was determined by the superiority of China's economic decision-making system and her efficient economic policies(Zhang,2010). According to the common sense of economics, the "three wagons" that drive the economic growth of a country are consumption, investment, import and export. The production factors required for social productive activities are generally considered to include the four major categories of labor, land, capital and entrepreneurial talent. Based on the "three wagons" and the four major production factors, it is not hard to see the motive behind the "miracle" of China's economic growth.

First, let us talk about the first major element - the labor force. There is a view that the "demographic dividend" of the 1950s and 1970s was an important source of the miracle of China's economic growth in the past 30 years. According to estimates by the World Bank, the structural advantage of "demographic dividend" has contributed over 30% of China's economic growth. With the completion of the demographic transition, the "demographic bonus" which has supported China's economic growth for a long time began to decline. Firstly, the overall labor force is decreasing, according to the latest data, the proportion of China's working population began to decline. In 2011, the proportion of working-age population in China was 74.4%, a slight decrease of 0.10 percentage points from the previous year. The second phenomenon is the emergence of the "Lewis turning point." Thirdly, China's aging is going to deepen. The sixth census shows that China's ageing rate is 8.9%， it is estimated that the ageing rate will rise to 30% by 2050. The above three points will prompt a slowdown in China's urbanization process. It is estimated that the average annual urbanization rate will increase 0.8-1% or so in the future and it will be difficult to reproduce the "1.35 to 1.45 %" which happened during the Ninth Five-year Plan.

To a certain extent, the large amount of China's cheap labor is the major contributor to China's economic development, although such forces may become less. In addition, consumption power and land elements can be regarded as the resource endowments for China's economic growth, China has a large population, vast territory and abundant resources, this played a key role in the development of China's economy. Investments, imports and exports can be regarded as the economic benefits brought by China's participation in the globalization process, entrepreneurship can be regarded as a contribution to economic growth on the broader level of technological development, information progress and innovation ability improvement. Finally, in terms of factors, the superiority of socialism with Chinese characteristics can concentrate on key issues and play a key role in the overall development of China's economy. This is also a special advantage that the capitalist countries do not have.

To sum up, the five power sources or the five major advantages of "miracles" in China's economic growth are the labor force, resources, imports and exports, information technologies. Although it is a "magnificent" economic development situation, there are some potential crises. Let us discuss them one by one.

China has always been proud of her superiority of labor force, but it has been challenged again and again in recent years. Some analysts said that the rapid rise in labor costs in China has already threatened China's economic competitiveness. Therefore, it is pointed out that the labor costs will not be that low any more with the development of China's economy and the enhancement of overall competitiveness. Natixis Bank of France pointed out in its report in June 2012 that the labor costs in China will be equal to those in the United States within 4 years, will be equal to those in the EU within 5 years and will even be equal to those in Japan within 7 years, which will prompt many companies to shift their production centers to South Asia and Southeast Asia, because their labor costs will be much lower than China. The Boston Consulting Group reported that the costs of many American-made products will be equal to those of China. At present, many companies have already shifted their production centers, Germany Adidas company said that the wages of Chinese workers are not less than 258 euros, while Cambodia is 107 euros. If so, China's labor force will need to find innovative ways to seek more long-term development.

China has worries about the advantages of resources as well. Let us look at the economic growth of China for more than 30 years since her opening to the outside world, it is all at the expense of consuming a large amount of natural resources, the most serious of which is environmental resources. The extensive economic growth has led to excessive consumption of resources, over-exploitation, serious destruction of the ecological environment, deteriorating environment and imbalanced economic structure. This unreasonable growth at the expense of future generations is a kind of "suicide" economic growth. Take the real estate as an example, China's economic development is largely dependent on the wanton development of real estate, but the problem it brings is that a large amount of arable land has been encroached upon.

China has a large population, agriculture is the foundation of the nation and food security has become the most crucial factor in ensuring peace and security of the people. While the real estate's development brings economic prosperity, there are also a lot of idle real estates, the crisis of overproduction already comes. Some people may be puzzled, there are idle real estates, but why are the prices of real estate still so high? This is because real estate has a serious imbalance between supplies and demands. Usually people buy houses for their living, so most of the people who need real estate are working-class, while the real estate developers overbuilt elevated level houses to make more money, they ignored the development of residential housing. As a result, the land resources have been depleted, the environmental situation has deteriorated, and the economic growth is suspected of a bubble.

Let us look at the issues of China's imports and exports. There lurks some crisis in China's export-oriented growth not to mention the existence of trade disputes. In recent years, the "three wagons" of China's economic growth have been mainly driven by the imports and exports, which have led to over-reliance on the trade surplus and relatively insufficient domestic demand and investment. This is very dangerous. The so-called "pull one hair and the whole body is affected" can be fully verified in the subprime mortgage crisis in the United States. In addition, for the internationalization of the RMB, there are also similar security risks. The internationalization of RMB means that the circulation of currency will be more and more large, which will increase the difficulty of regulation and supervision and will naturally affect the stability of China's financial market.

As for the development of information technology, this is a good thing for the entire nation, but everything is not perfect. The informatization also brought some problems, for example, the "digital divide". That is, the different opportunities and positions in the information society of people with and without a computer, who have access to the internet and who do not have access to the internet, this will lead to huge economic differences and psychological grievances eventually (Chen,2000). This is a problem that exists in every country. As a result, there may be polarization and the economic conditions of those without knowledge will become more impoverished. The polarization between rich and poor has become another hurdle that hinders economic development.

There are some issues in China's political systems as well. While the wealth has risen sharply, the problems have also arisen. For example, excessive government power, abuse of public power and rampant corruption have led to the rapid growth of bureaucracy and the increasingly estranged relationship between cadres and the masses. Social class concepts have become prominent increasingly and social conflicts have become complicated increasingly. In the short term, the authoritative system can promote economic development, but in the long run, it looks like "quenching a thirst with poison." Unilateral economic reforms can no longer promote social progress. Without political reform, the fruits of economic reform will also die out. The achievements are gratifying, but the crises are still needed to be worried.

Side B of economic development: from crisis to achievements

From the side A of economic development, it is recognized that China's economy has been developed rapidly since the reform and opening. The country has become richer, the army has become stronger, the level of sciences and technologies has been improved, the people's life has become happier, and the market is more prosperous than before. However, the crisis behind the achievements cannot be ignored, such as high-intensity labor under high-pressure regimes and brutal exploitation, reckless destructive developments like environmental destruction and resource depletion, ignoring intellectual property rights like counterfeiting and piracy, etc. These crises will undermine China's international competitiveness seriously. The growth of the national wealth has failed to bring enough security to the Chinese people. Therefore, some people think that the "miracle" of China's economic growth is only a false prosperity, like the castle on the beach, vulnerable.

Perhaps this view is somewhat pessimistic. It is not a sad thing to realize that there is a turning point in the crisis. Well, then let us try to solve it, starting with the problems and crises of economic development and looking for opportunities for economic development. As a result, there will be another leap from crisis to accomplishment, as well as the re-sublimation of understanding and practice.

As you know, China is a manufacturing base, but the price advantage of China no longer exists. Many enterprises like the automobile manufacturers have shifted to Vietnam and Latin America as the labor costs there are much lower than that in China. In fact, this is both a challenge and an opportunity. China can take this opportunity to complete an industrial upgrade. The low labor costs is only the traditional advantage of China's economic growth. The modern economy requires China to have new advantages that can adapt to economic development. This is so called highly qualified labor forces. The replacement from the old labor forces to the new labor forces has explained the phenomenon of rising labor costs. Compared with the new labor forces, the old laborers have generally suffered from poor education and low basic knowledge, thus they can only have engaged in the most basic operations. In other words, they have no skills to do mental work, they can only do manual labor. This is also the labor base for China's initial primary export processing model. With the development of education, the educational background of workers is generally above high school, and a large part of them are trained in vocational and technical schools. In addition to the increase in labor and employment costs, it also forced the enterprises to improve the scientific and technological content, update equipment, and enhance the training of employees. To a certain extent, the "survival of the fittest" brought about by the competition increased labor productivity and created great benefits and have also boosted the quality of the labor forces. As a result, there is no advantage in the "quantity" of labor, but the advantage of "quality" has saved the losses in this respect.

In terms of resources and environment, there is an issue in China that economic construction and environmental protection are not racing together bridle to bridle they are not being developed at the same time. In some respects, there are many problems such as "to pollute it first and make the treatment later," "to develop it first and make effective use of it later." Fortunately, China have realized the seriousness of the problem. Therefore, China began to pay more and more attention to the harmonious development of human beings and nature, and proposed the strategic concept of "building a resource-saving and environment-friendly society." As a result, the sustainable development and scientific development are being attached more and more importance. If China work towards this goal, China's economy can be developed well for a long time.

In response to the problem of excessive dependence on foreign trade, China begins to focus on the development of domestic demand, stimulating domestic demand becomes another point of economic growth, which is safer and more controllable. Moreover, RMB internationalization can also be regarded as another big advantage. It has raised China's international status and gained universal recognition. At the same time, it is also a new measure for China's foreign trade to reduce the exchange rate risk arising from the fluctuation of the U.S. dollar. As a result, the dominance of the dollar will be weakened, because issuing the world currency is equivalent to collecting seigniorage from other countries.

The information technology itself represents the progress of the times, the emergence of the "digital divide" stems from the failure of proper allocation and correct using of this resource. For example, the country can take various measures such as social welfare, taxation and education popularization to narrow the "digital divide" between the rich and the poor to reflect the social fairness of a society. All the people including the rich and poor can enjoy the benefits brought by the advances in the information technology. When it comes to the issue of political system, the socialist politics with Chinese characteristics is also a great initiative. Practice has proved that this system is a remarkable success, but the emergence of some black sheep has reduced the government's credibility. Whether it is economic system reform or political system reform, it is a very big concept. However, it is generally agreed that the people who win the hearts and minds of the people will win the world, which is reflecting or explaining the so-called "water can carry boats and capsize." Therefore, increasing investments in grassroots democracy will be a major direction in the political structural reform.

In fact, the crisis be a turning point, the turning point can also become a crisis, it depends on how you deal with it.

The market economy is not able to save China

The theory of market economy was put forward by Adam Smith in England. Adam Smith's idea of market economy was first fully explained in his "Wealth of Nations" theory. It was for this reason that Adam Smith was known as the "father of economics" in the textbooks of western economics. Adam Smith believed that the national wealth came from the improvement of labor productivity, to improve the labor productivity, people should play the common utilitarian and rationalist nature, that is, everyone hopes to realize his purpose at the lowest price. People should build a unified market where all kinds of production factors and goods can be traded freely, at the same time, curb the state intervention so that the "invisible hand" can play an all-round role. Standardize the market to achieve the "natural order" via improving the corresponding laws.

The intrinsic mechanism of a pure market economy as a special system lies in the pursuit of the maximization of its own economic interests and the optimal allocation of resources under the guidance of market prices. However, the market price mechanism does not work in isolation. It needs some preconditions in the process of allocating the whole society resources. Firstly, everyone in the market economy should have economic freedom under the premise of not jeopardizing the interests of others, freedom of choice for individuals is based on the principle of voluntary exchange and voluntary cooperation under mutually beneficial conditions. Secondly, individual self-interest and mutual benefit between people can be unified.

In fact, people should understand that the market economy cannot operate spontaneously and orderly under the invisible hand. Because according to the theory of market economy, many conditions for operating the market economy are hypothetical. These assumptions sometimes do not exist, so it is unreliable. From the realistic point of view, the market mechanism has great limitations. It has political boundaries, distribution boundaries, social boundaries, ecological boundaries and ethical boundaries. For example, the market economy may not necessarily serve the interests of the nation when crossing borders, and the market economy cannot achieve fair distribution, the market economy cannot handle the social interests, the market economy cannot protect the environment and resources, and the market economy cannot raise the moral standards of the entire society. The problems caused by the advancing marching process of Marxism in China during these years have illustrated all these disadvantages of the market economy completely. As mentioned earlier, the education industrialization is a "bad result" brought by radical marketization.

Obviously, the market has its own limitations, the market is not omnipotent. The economic practices from various countries in the world tell us that the market economy will become the source of all evil and the resources will be destroyed if there is no national macro-management. Compared with the former Soviet Union, China adopted the policy of "both state and market" in the early and middle of the economic reform because China did not implement the theory of the market economy completely. While using the market mechanism, China also maintained her commitment to economic operation including the executive order, including regulation and management, which is why China has gained more successful economy so far. On the contrary, some socialist countries in Eastern Europe, such as the former Soviet Union, failed because of the so-called shock therapy that let the market economy control everything at the earliest possible time.

The success of China's policy and the unsuccessful reform of the former Soviet Union demonstrated that imposing marketization reform in the socialist countries will not work. This means that the market economy has a certain role, but not absolute, in the economic development of the socialist countries. It is also of significant importance that the government management and the coordinated development of other non-market economies are equally important. Market economy is not a panoply economic form, it has its own multi-functional defects. For example, the "survival of the fittest" in the market economy only favors the strong, which will exacerbate the polarization in the distribution of benefits and cause disparity between the rich and the poor. This is inconsistent with China's national tradition. The market mechanism may not be able to receive any result in the overall, long-term, non-profit social and economic activities and investment areas. Moreover, the impulse of the market micro pursuing the interest's maximization and the macro interests are contradictory. Pursuing the partial and short-term interests may undermine the interests of the overall interests and the long-term interests. Obviously, this runs counter to the thinking of the "Three Represents." In addition, the lagging of the market price signals can mislead the allocation of resources for some production projects. More importantly, if the market mechanism was introduced to the spiritual life, cultural life or political life, the market mechanism will be ineffective. They will go astray and fall into traps. For example, the current phenomenon of corruption that everyone hates should be said to be a by-product of the radical promotion of marketization in China.

Opposing to the fact that the market economy is the dominant body does not mean opposing the development of a market economy. According to China's national conditions, economic and social development should obey the idea of the market economy in the socialist society, that is, it should be compatible with the goal of promoting the balanced development of the society and economy comprehensively. One of the major gains made in the field of ideology during the 13th National Congress of the Communist Party of China is the formation of the socialism primary stage theory. In fact, according to the 13th National Congress of the CPC, the ideological line of socialism and development of the market economy, the Chinese people must adhere to the principle of "socialist public ownership" in economy and coexist in a variety of economic forms. This pattern is in line with China's national conditions and has the characteristics of reform and development. After that, it stressed too much on the role of the market in economic development and exaggerated the role of the market mechanism, it brought the state-owned enterprises that originally had the functions of production, management, social welfare, education, entertainment and entertainment into the front of the market. As a result, the state-owned enterprises failed to adapt themselves to the fierce pure market competition.

To put it simply, the current market-oriented situation in China is radical. For example, the auction of state-owned enterprises to private entrepreneurs, it needs to be known that the stock of state-owned assets is the wealth created by all citizens jointly, especially the peasants, who have made tremendous sacrifices for the industrialization of China. Will the state-owned assets be auctioned through the NPC for discussion? Obviously, the process of marketization which is different from that in Western countries is a natural process of progress, while the process of marketization in China is a policy driven by the government. In this process, many necessary elements for realizing a market economy are not available yet, which will result in a deformed bureaucratic market economy that does not coexist with the traditional social economy. Some industries or products that should not be marketed, such as education and health care, are marketed because of the government's need to establish a market system. As a result, not only the normal economic order in society is disrupted, but also the government and people are brought a certain degree of harm.

Obviously, the market economy cannot save China. However, it is undeniable that the market economy has a positive function. While paying attention to the development of the market economy, China should also pay attention to other non-market economies and continue to improve the functions of public investments. Undoubtedly, the market economy is a double-edged sword. It is necessary to give full play to the advantages of a market economy and to minimize its negative impact. The development of a market economy is not a matter of Chinese characteristics. A socialism with Chinese characteristics means that China should achieve a high degree of unity between the principle of socialism and the development of a market economy(Gu,2004). It is not only a great initiative but also a new topic to develop a market economy under the conditions of socialism.

The road to a strong country: strategic thinking on national management

Since the market economy cannot save China, then China will come up with a new strategic thinking that she will take the national management as a road to a strong country. To put it simply, the connotation of national management mainly refers to: the state acts as an operator directly or indirectly responsible for operating state-owned economy and its related business management activities. The ways and ranges of state operations will vary according to the nature of the country and their operating benefits. For example, the United States, the main industries in the United States are related to arms, aerospace, postal and other industries, her efficiency is very high. Of course, in some European countries, the industries they operate are also very good(Yu,1993). Some certain aspects of China's national operations have also created glory in history. Nowadays, radio and television, railway transportation and aerospace industries in China are basically operated by the state. Not hard to imagine, if these industries are not run by the state, "Shenzhou" series of spacecraft may be successfully launched in such a brief period? Can there be hundreds of millions of travelers riding the train back home safely with their loved ones during the peak of the Spring Festival every year? Undoubtedly, state management maximizes the interests of the people and the country.

In recent years, China's achievements have been well known to all people. As the economy continues to develop, the living standard of the people has risen dramatically. However, compared with the developed countries in the world, the economic gap remains significant. In a country with a large population and relative lack of resources, in the face of increasingly fierce international competition and the construction of a socialist economy, China must achieve the goal of producing high efficiency otherwise will fail to realize the goal of making the nation rich and powerful. Robin Bud and Michael Parkin, as the world's leading economists in Canada, they believe that economic efficiency can be achieved under two conditions: production efficiency and resource allocation efficiency. Facts have proved that China must take the market economy as a basis for adjustment and follow the law of value to achieve the two high efficiencies of production and resource allocation. At the same time, China must also use the macroeconomic regulation to standardize and protect the overall operation of the economy and to avoid any loss brought by the ups and downs (Bud and Parkin, 2004).

Products manufacturing and marketing are related to the people's actual life closely. The state is the representative of the people's will. The government's duty is to pay attention to the basic needs of the people, provide the public with necessary public goods, or create the conditions for convenience and paid public use of the semi-public goods. So that people can enjoy public education, social security, convenient transport facilities and public cultural and recreational facilities, and thus people can live in a clean and hygienic environment under the favorable market order and legal system, as well as capable of heating without any difficulties, gas, electricity, clean water, eating unpasteurized food, effective disease prevention services and much more (Chen,2007). These are all elements of public service that should be made available to every citizen. In view of the inflexibility of basic household items, we cannot make people consume less water or coal through price adjustment. If such basic rights are to be protected, obviously it cannot be handed over to the market for completion. This is the responsibility that the government must fulfill (Sha,2010). The government's economic work mainly consists of formulating policies, promulgating rules and directing production indirectly. To improve the service quality of administrative management means to formulate the correct policies and adopt suitable methods so that economic and social development will be coordinated.

The key to China's development lies in the strategy establishment for moderate development. While the market economy subject is pursuing the goal of "catching up and surpassing" to pursue the max profits, which takes the expense of the environment undoubtedly and runs counter to the goal of sustainable development. Look at the characteristics of China's economy since the reform and opening, China's GDP growth rate is falling compared with the past 30 years. On 2012, 2013 and 2014, the growth rate of China's GDP was 7.7%, 7.7% and 7.3% respectively. The development mode shifted from the rapid growth of scale to the intensive growth of quality and efficiency. The economic structure shifted from incremental growth to stock adjustment, China's economic development has entered a "new normal." Under the new normal, the most important feature of China's economy is its speed of "going down to the next level" and its effectiveness of "going up to the next level." It does not pursue rapid economic growth blindly, but resolve the problems left by blind pursuing high-speed development and innovate its development mode. China should start from the realities and take the path of development with Chinese characteristics. At the Fifth Plenary Session of the 18th CPC Central Committee held in 2015, Xi Jinping emphasized that China must establish firmly and implement effectively the principles of innovation, coordination, greenness, openness and sharing to achieve the development goals of the "Thirteenth Five-year Plan", solve the problems of development and lay a solid foundation for development. To implement the five development concepts is a profound change that affects the overall development of China. To act according to objective laws can make people succeed. In addition, the government's macro-control is very necessary.

To put it another way, people can think that the socialist countries have a relative advantage of administrative resources compared with the capitalist societies. The advantages of administrative resources are mainly reflected in the government's effective control of the economy and effective market intervention, specifically, the government can well formulate and implement the correct economic policies according to the actual needs, such as industrial policy, regional development policy, and industrial development policy. All these economic policies should be adjusted according to the needs, especially according to the economic laws.

The key to setting up a management mechanism for state operations in China lies in re-understanding the responsibilities of the central government and top leaders, it also lies in designing management standard and guiding management and behavior accordingly. China should gather the wisdom from all sectors of society and bring into harmony both the society and the people to give full play to the advantages of concentrating social forces on major affairs. To let the economic development be prosperous and orderly, the state management system must implement its activities. From the perspective of the world development, the developed western countries have been accelerating the growth of their state-owned economy in recent years, the industries and enterprises run by the state have emerged (Zong, 2003). Under the current circumstances, China should reiterate one of the principles in the state operation and the construction of the laws: To maintain the position of the large state-owned enterprises effectively in the leading market, China must not deflect or deviate from this general direction (Tian, Dai and Qi, 2012). In a nutshell, China's economic development still has a long way to go.

Chapter 10

Why did China Who Used to Be the Leader Fall Behind?

China should adopt a serious attitude toward her own history. Although there are a lot of glories of which she can be proud, she must not ignore or even negate the dark side of her own national history. China cannot say lightly like this: "Oh, we have to say goodbye to yesterday." How could China say goodbye to herself so easily? (Song, 1996) Because the history is an organic part of China nation and an important part of the entire Chinese people. So how can China forget her history so easily? On the contrary, China had better keep it in mind that she should remember the dark side in her history for further reference, which is so called "Experience should not be forgotten, as it may be a guide for the future."

If the ancient China used to be an eastern lion, the modern China can be regarded as a "tiger" that lags the western countries. As the old saying goes, "if the tiger went down to level land, he would be insulted by dogs." China might ask herself boldly and proudly: Was there any country that was stronger than China before the Opium War? No! But even if the strength of the ancient China was so powerful, it cannot last forever. As such, China must find out the reasons for the decline of China.

Some people once compared the history of China with that of the United States, the United States has a history of only 200 years, while China has a history of 5,000 years of civilization. After being compared, they concluded that the reason why the United States is more developed and advanced than China, is because the United States herself seize a variety of opportunities for development, but for China, it is because she has been stalled for a long time in the journey of modern development.

So why is there stagnation in the development of China? Or, what factors made China become backward in modern times? China, as a former world-class powerful empire, how could she lag so fast and so seriously? Even after so many Chinese people made such unremitting efforts, she still cannot get out of her predicament and get rid of her terrible destiny. Why?

As for these questions, different people have different opinions. Some people say that it is due to the China's political system, some say that it is because of the issue of China's economic system, what is more, some people even think that the reasons are relevant to China's historical destiny. Among them, the most talked about are the closed-door policies, backward technologies, backward ideas, and so on. Professor Wang Haiming from the Peking University pointed out that the root causes of China's backwardness cannot be blamed on history, politics, law or economy, but rather on the moral principles pursued by China. Coincidentally, there was another professor called Han Yuhai from Peking University, in her book named "Whose history is it in the past 1500 Years?" She listed a series of historical facts and denied the theory of closed-door policies, the theory of technological backwardness, the theory of ideological backwardness, etc. Then she discussed the reasons leading to the backwardness of modern China: grassroots unorganized; financial autonomy; national capacity continued to decline (Han, 2011). There seems to be a difference in opinion, but we shall know that the way of expression will vary even if for expressing the same opinion. We are just reminding the reader to think more about the essence of the problem when thinking about the question of modern China's history. So, what is the real nature of China's backwardness?

The famous Marxist basic theory tells us that the change and development of any thing is caused by the interaction of internal and external causes, the internal factor is the decisive factor, and the external factor works through internal factors. About the decline of modern China, we can also generalize the issue based on this view.

The arrogant "sauce tank culture"

Why did the United States develop faster than China? In fact, apart from other political, economic, military, scientific and technological reasons, the "short" history is also a crucial factor. The history of China is not only lengthy, but also has too many backward ideas. This is like we have two tanks, one is not filled with anything, the other one is precipitated a lot of "black sauce," if we want to put something new into the tank, we will not hesitate to put it into that tank which is empty. As for that "sauce tank," we might wonder: What would be the reaction after putting this new stuff in? Are they compatible? Or, we need to clean up these "black sauce?" Questions like these will come one by one, so no matter how hard we work, it will not be so efficient as the former.

Sometimes, it can bring uncontemplated results if looking at the problem from a different degree. For example, the education that the Chinese people accepted separates modern China's history from the world history. However, there are many relations between them. If comparing the modern China's history and the world history, there may be new discoveries. What is the world doing? What are China doing during the same time? To give a more interesting example, during the 14th-16th century European Renaissance, the art worlds such as Sanjeta-Finch, Michelangelo and Raphael turned out to be in contact with the four great Chinese genius, Tang Bohu, Zhu Yunming, Wen Zhengming and Xu Zhenqing, they were at the same period. In addition, in the 1740s, for both the Western countries and China, it was a very important era. The first bourgeois revolution broke out in Britain in 1640, which marked the beginning of Western society's entering the bourgeois revolution. The establishment of the Qing dynasty in 1644 marked the beginning of a new Chinese feudal dynasty. After looking at this period of history, people can find that at that time China was not far behind Britain economically, culturally, militarily and so on, at that time, the Britain just entered the stage of capitalist development. Despite the differences in social character between China and the West, there was almost no economic gaps (Wang, 1998). However, why did the nuances become more and more amplified later? Maybe it was due to the closed-doors policies!

When mentioning the "closed-doors policies," it is necessary to talk about China's "sauce tank culture." Mr. Bai Yang, the master of Chinese traditional culture and thought, he once wrote a very popular book: "The Ugly Chinese." After reading this book, the Chinese people were shocked, what is more, it reflected the "inferiority" of the Chinese people in this book, the backwardness of feudalism in China and the backward ideology, were derived from the traditional Chinese culture "sauce tank thought." Master Bai Yang pointed out that the Chinese people were deeply hurt by the nationality. Due to the "sauce" being too long in the sauce tank, the sauce was contaminated by the idea and judgment as well as the field of vision, and it is hard for the Chinese to jump out of the sauce tank. As the years went by, most of the Chinese people have lost the ability to tell the differences between right and wrong. All things depend on emotion and intuition without thinking deeply. All behavioral values were based on the moral and political standards in the sauce tank. Therefore, there was no mercy, no right or wrong for many people. In such an environment, people drew conclusions without sufficient understanding and analysis. In the long-term perfunctory, finally it turned out to be a serious retribution, that is, "the Opium War." It was also the Opium War that opened the long-term closed doors of China. Quite ironically, China's "outstanding" traditional culture which has always been greatly praised, was attacked so violently for the first time. However, it was delightful and a great honor for the Chinese nation because the popular discussion triggered by it has promoted another revolution in the civilization of the Chinese nation (Bai, 2008).

In fact, the culture was a very important factor for the decline of a country or a nation, although there were so many internal or external causes. It was an important reason whether the culture of the nation was powerful enough to withstand all kinds of intrusion. It was true that the history of China's culture was overwhelmed by that historical period. It was also exactly in such a reshuffle of world powers that China began to find the essence of her own culture and abandoned all kinds of Cultural dross, such as China's "sauce tank culture" in some areas. The wheel of history is always rolling forward, if there is life, there is struggle.

From natural disasters to man-made disasters: The impacts of civil strife

China has been an agricultural power since ancient times. This is an advantage, which proves that China has the natural and geographical advantages that other countries have never been able to own. But this is also a disadvantage at the same time. It is a mortal wound to rely on the traditional agricultural only. "Living by Heaven" means that if God wants to "give an opportunity," a good agricultural harvest will certainly come. However, if God "changes his face," in case of natural disasters, people will have to live a very poor living.

Natural disasters include floods, droughts, insect pests, which have been existed in China since ancient times. What is more, every natural disaster brought big harms to the Chinese people. Natural disasters occurred frequently and heavily, which was rare in the other countries at that time. People had no food and begged everywhere (Wen, 2004). As early as the Wei, Jin and Southern and Northern Dynasties, natural disasters caused by frequent weather disasters, harsh tyranny, and other man-made disasters caused great social unrest. These had a serious impact on the Central Plains where agriculture was very important to the ancient Chinese at that time: for example, crop failure, sharp reduction in agricultural population, shortage of farmland, ecological damage and so on(Xu, 2010).

In the Qing Dynasty, the types of natural disasters that occurred were even more diverse: droughts, floods, hails, frost disasters, snow frosts, earthquakes, landslides, black storms, locust disasters, epidemic disasters, etc. According to statistics, from the first 20 years of Daoguang to the thirteenth year of Tongzhi, natural disasters occurred in more than 10 areas throughout the country each year, while the four northern provinces were basically affected by the disaster every year (Li, 2008). It was reported that the Natural disasters continued and repeated throughout the entire Qing dynasty. In the case of droughts, its destructiveness is immeasurable because the technologies were not maturing enough at that time. The ancient people did not have the relevant technologies for artificial rainfalls, although it is now possible to temporarily relieve the natural "broiling" via the advanced technologies. At that time, they could only rely on the spiritual pillars of gods, so they had no way but to pray for rains, which was a true expression of reluctance to reality. Back to the subject, the largest and most devastating drought was the one in northern China during the Guangxu period in those frequent droughts happened in the Qing dynasty.

This drought happened in 1877 and 1878, mainly in Henan and Shanxi provinces, so it was known as "Jin Yu big drought."(Zhang, 2011) This drought lasted for a very long time and harmed a large area. According to the "ShangHai Daily" newspaper records, the flood victims in all cities of Shangdong province left their homes due to this drought. They prayed for rains, but it was helpless. According to statistics, from 1876 to 1879, the number of people affected by drought and famine in Shandong, Shanxi, Zhili and Henan provinces reached 200 million or so, which accounted for about 50% of the total population at that time. Approximately, there were around 13 million people that died of famine and plagues directly (People's Daily,2010). Such a serious disaster it was! It made all the Chinese people feel sad!

Natural disaster or man-made disaster? In fact, there were some relationships between these two. Natural disasters and man-made disasters have profound influence on social disorder, economic prosperity and ethnic distribution. There seemed to be a close causal relationship among natural disasters and man-made disasters, civil unrest and foreign troubles (Zhang, 2003). Taking the above-mentioned drought as an example, was it a natural disaster? Was it purely accidental? Of course not! The man-made causes of this "natural disaster" is as follows: Firstly, because the government increased the exploitation towards the people at the end of the Qing Dynasty, the peasants had no land to plant and could only cut down the forests and reclaim wasteland. As a result, the forest vegetation was destroyed, water and soil erosion became serious and the ecological environment deteriorated sharply. Secondly, as an agricultural country based on the natural economy, water conservancy projects were to be built to prevent drought and flood disasters and to ensure the yield. This was a key role that cannot be ignored. However, by the end of the Qing dynasty, water conservancy was deteriorating gradually, the project "twist pond ditches" was destroyed (Liu,2002). Of course, apart from the two listed reasons, there were some other human factors that destroyed the natural development. As such, once the natural disaster came, they had no way to resist at all. It was totally useless to just rely on a pious "heart" to pray for rains. It was a pity that the God had never been an easy "softhearted" demon. Once people break the natural laws, people would be punished finally. This is a natural law and a social law!

As the old saying goes, "troubles never come singly," in modern China, apart from all kinds of natural disasters, plagues, droughts and floods, there were all kinds of uprisings and man-made disasters. Let us take the peasant uprisings as an example, most of them ended in failure, and their negative impact on economy and culture should not be overlooked, although the Chinese textbooks only mentioned a little about this. Lots of peasant uprisings brought more wars to the ancient Chinese society. During the war, the rapid population decline and the shortage of cultivated land had hindered the social and economic development seriously. The peasant uprisings usually took place under the unbearable natural disasters and corrupt bureaucracies, where people can only survive in the cracks. From the first peasant uprising in Chinese history, that is, Chen Sheng and Wu Guang peasant uprising, to the Taiping Rebellion happened in the late Qing dynasty, all these were due to the natural disasters or corrupt bureaucracies. Coincidentally, the peasant uprisings in China often took place during the last years of the dynasty. This was because the peasants were unbearable and had to resist under the brutal exploitation from the ruling classes and bureaucratic landlords, then the economy and politics declined until the end of the regime.

History can be regarded as a mirror. The ruler must treat the ruled person kindly, otherwise he will perish. Due to the man-made disasters, it became even harder to resist the foreign invasions. "Flies do not bite the seamless eggs", it was a good opportunity for the Western countries, so it was inevitable that they would attack China then. The natural and man-made disasters in the history of China are sufficient proof of how difficult China was. Since ancient times, it has been difficult to maintain a prosperous regime.

Unexpected troubles: Disasters brought by foreign invasions

If it is said that modern China was at a disadvantage in international competition because of the military expansion from the West, the rising Russia and Japan became China's dangerous neighbors, which contracted Modern China's living space further. The complex geo-political characteristics of land and sea, the security environment around the periphery, and the Russia's pursuing her expansion policies, all these influenced and restricted the development direction of modern China, it was the geopolitical factor that led to Modern China's decline (Yin, 2006). As the other countries grew stronger, more resources were needed to support their longer-term developments. For modern China, who had the vast territory and the vast market, this was nothing more than a "fat meat" that the developed countries in the world coveted. Accordingly, almost each country wanted to bite this fat meat for a long time, if possible!

In modern China, the Sino-Japanese War was regarded as a watershed or a "turning point" in the history of China's developments. Before the Sino-Japanese War, China and Japan made simultaneous progress toward modernization. However, after the Sino-Japanese War, Japan took advantage of the blackmail extorted from China and developed her own commerce and basic education to squeeze into the ranks of developed capitalist countries rapidly. In addition to the casualties and property losses during the war, China also endured the most cruel and harsh unequal treaties and carried overloaded foreign and domestic post-war debts (Jin, 2000). Of course, this was only one aspect. The humiliating history in modern China was not made by one or two countries, it was formed by all the western powers. Apart from Japan and Russia these two neighboring countries that had the geographical advantages, there were some other countries such as the United states and some European countries, they also wanted to "rob the owner while his house is on fire". The most typical example was that the "Eight-Power Allied Forces" invaded China jointly. If there was only a single country was to invade China, China had sufficient confidence to resist. However, under the suppression from all powers, China would be unable to fight against them easily.

Taking the example of Japan's full-scale invasion against China in the 1930s, the war interrupted the original modernization process in China completely. Due to Japan's occupying, China lost one-third of her forests, iron mines and coal mines; 4/10 railways; 7/10 soybean production; 2/5 export trade;93% oil and 55 % gold. According to statistics, by the end of 1932, the Chinese government lost 17.8 billion yuan in the northeast China. During the eight years invasion, Japan occupied over 47% of the total Chinese cities, including more than 80% of the big cities. Almost all of China's modern industries were in these cities. According to figures released by the Chinese government in 1995, China's direct property loss during the Anti-Japanese War was 100 billion U.S. dollars and its indirect loss was 500 billion U.S. dollars (Ka, 2008).

In addition to the economic losses, there were also the lives of the 300,000-defenseless people who were shocked by the Nanjing massacre, which were unbearable pains for the entire China. Apart from the war, Japan also infiltrated and corrupted China continuously through cultural and political factors. The Chinese people should keep in mind the lesson of history. Even under a peaceful environment, the Chinese people should be on guard against Japan absolutely. The event of Diaoyu Islands was just showing that Japan would not compromise easily and she would continue to occupy China's territory. This incident was still ongoing and escalating. On August 15, 2012, Japan detained Chinese people protecting Diaoyu Islands, which infuriated and harmed the entire Chinese People seriously. China will never compromise in any attempt to carve up China's territory!

Russia was also an aggressive country. As early as the Qing dynasty, the Russian invaders began to take the opportunity to intrude into the northeast of China, occupied the Heilongjiang River Valley and some other places. Wherever the invaders went, there must be a lot of people that were murdered or raped. After 1840, when western powers invaded China, Russia also invaded and occupied as many as 1.5 million square kilometers of China's territory through a series of unequal treaties. On the one hand, it reduced the space of Chinese people's survival and development. On the other hand, the natural resources in the territory have been plundered, which affected China's future development seriously. Although the relations between China and the Soviet Union were relatively friendly during Stalin's time, after Khrushchev came into power, the rupture of the Sino-Soviet relations proved once again: there only exist permanent interests and no permanent friends. This seems still true today.

On June 25, 1950, the Korean War broke out. To protect her position and interests in Asia, the United States sent troops to intervene immediately. The United Nations Army headed by the United States even attacked the border between China and North Korea. What should China do? Since ancient times, China knew the truth that "if the lips are gone, the teeth will be cold," Accordingly, China must protect her own interests and thus sent troops to fight against the United Sates. This was so called the "War to Resist US Aggression and Aid Korea".

Due to the War to Resist U.S. and Aid Korea, China's economy was dragged down for several years. Hundreds of thousands of people had been killed in foreign lands. These were the serious injuries caused by the war. China shall draw lessons from the history. The United States has not given up any kind of pressure on China from the ancient times to the present. For example, she forced the appreciation of the Renminbi, this was a premeditated interference on China's economic. As anyone knows, the exchange rate issue is one of China's internal economic system issue and should be solved by China herself, this has nothing to do with the United States.

China used to be the world leader, but in her history, there were lots of internal worries and external afflictions, which made her difficult for economic development. At the same time, the economic and political malpractices began to emerge gradually.

The declining economy

When the economy reached the most prosperity period, it is also the beginning time of the decline. The small-scale peasant economy in China could be regarded as a probable reason that lead to the decline of the world leader at that time. Because the feudal system was no longer able to adapt to the trend of the times under the prevailing world conditions. The economy based on the production of self-sufficient handicrafts lagged the western world.

China lost the world leader position, what were the reasons? In addition to the political and military reasons, the declining economy was a very important aspect. During the Qing Dynasty, there was a pure agricultural economy in China. China did not know the industrial and economic structure in Europe and the United States. Under the precondition of a decline in the natural economy, those rulers in China "closed their doors" and adhere to their own backward thinking which was not correct at all to some extent. At that time, the Qing dynasty's "closed doors" policy was widely adapted, the Qing dynasty wanted to contain the forces of Western colonialism outside of the south gate of China and at the same time limit the frequent commercial activities of foreign businessmen in China(Wang,1998). This was done to protect the natural economy from the impact of the capitalist commodity economy, because there were no other effective ways except this. As a result, they took such a negative attitude of "closing the doors". But then again, the long-term closed-door policy had also led to people's loss of international markets and unfamiliarity with modern technologies and ideas in the world. And this may also be an essential factor behind the backwardness of China in modern times (Wu, 2011). While foreign capitalism developed rapidly, China's natural economy lagged far behind the western world.

There were some differences between the natural economy and the commodity economy. The natural economy was a form of production that met the needs of the producer or economic unit itself, that is, a self-sufficient economy in the popular sense. It was a product of the low-level social productive forces and the underdevelopment of social division. It has the characteristics of small-scale production and backward production technology. Take the commodity economy as an example, the modern Chinese commodity production technology has been stuck based on manual production, compared with the western mechanism industrial products, there was an obvious disadvantage. In China, the development of commodity economy reached a new peak during the Tang, Song and Yuan dynasties, stagnating or even shrinking in the middle of the Ming Dynasty, and finally failed to break through the fence of natural economy (Zhao, 2003). China's natural economy also opposed the foreign capitalist commodity aggression stubbornly before and after the Opium War. However, after all, China's cotton textile industry could not compete with the large-scale production of foreign machinery. As such, the natural economy could not resist the capitalist economy. Since the 1960s, with the continuous expansion of the treaty ports and the increase of the output of foreign capitalist goods, China's natural economy, which lasted thousands of years, had finally begun its initial disintegration. The disintegration of China's natural economy also marked the gradual collapse of the economic base that once prided itself as the world leader. Therefore, China lost the position of world leader.

In fact, China's economy had fought against the western economy a little bit, at the end of the Qing Dynasty, the industrial development was carried out as well, however it was too late. In the final analysis, human factors may not be as important as people think. Under such a historical background, no matter how wise those leaders in authority were, it was hard to escape the fate of economic decline. At most, this is one aspect of the incident. Those leaders were not completely blameless. In the latter part of this article, the political factors will be also mentioned, which accelerated the decline of China's world leader position.

The conservative politics

Since ancient times, many people think that the Qing government's closed-door policy is the reason for the decline of China. However, apart from this reason, there are some other reasons listed above, such as internal and external problems and economic self-decay, which also played a key role. Only when all the factors are combined that the event will develop that way, this is determined by the principle of universal connection of all things in the world. It is a result of various synergies, this is what we call "history".

Although the political factor is not the only or the ultimate reason that lead to the loss of China's world leader position. It is always helpful to repeat the various influences brought by China's conservative politics. In the 1980s, Chinese political academics defined the concept of "politics." That is, "Politics is an activity that is mainly implemented by the government and involves various social fields and occupies a major position in various social activities." Conservative politics, it means preferring to maintain the status, maintaining the current interests and fearing to break the existing order. The "closed-door state" in modern China is just an example of conservative politics. On the contrary, there is another politics called liberal politics, it means maintaining an inclusive mentality, learning and working hard to catch up with the trend of social development.

The inclusiveness of the United States is enough to "taste" the "sweetness" brought by the enlightened politics. For the decline of modern China, the academics generally agreed that the backwardness of China in the late Qing Dynasty originated from China's stubborn and backward system of monarchy which lasted for thousands of years, and the closed-door Chinese society was not opened until China was attacked by western powers. Then China started to integrate into the world economic market (Huang, 2009). This "arrogant" policy contributed to the arrogant mentality of the ruling class. On the one hand, the closed-door policy made it hard for the advanced system to enter and thus the differences between the small-peasant economy and the western industrial technology were getting bigger and bigger. On the other hand, the ruling class did not know the power of gunboats and the accuracy of rival's location. Taking the Opium War as an example, the emperor and ministers did not know where the United Kingdom was located.

The "anecdotes" about the Qing emperor were much more than the above one. There was a very interesting and controversial anecdote, that is, half a century before the Opium War, the British government let the Magarni Mission come to China to give his birthday to Emperor Qianlong. According to the China's courtesies at that time, ministers need to kneel with their knees, the upper part of the body bent over the ground, touch their foreheads three times, and then stand up so that they can kneel for a second time. On the contrary, in the United Kingdom, ministers only need to kneel on one knee, which had discrepancies with Chinese manners. As for what ceremony the Magarni Mission did in the face of Emperor Qianlong, both China and the United Kingdom remained silent and unable to verify. However, what is certain is that this meeting failed and eventually broke up. The Magarni Mission returned to their own country under the urging of the Qing government. We might say that the Magarni Mission was originally "coming with evil intent," because the colonial expansion in Europe made the United Kingdom want to bite the "fat meat"- China. However, it was undoubted that Emperor Qianlong's "stubbornness" accelerated the British invasion towards China and provided a reasonable reason for the colonial expansion.

It is recognized that the "closed-door" policy reflected the arrogance of feudal rulers essentially. Due to this kind of arrogance, the Qing dynasty was under a closed development pattern for an extended period. Both the government and the public ignored the rapid changes in the world. The feudal ruling class's ignorance of the outside world and political corruption accelerated the decline of the Qing dynasty undoubtedly(Wang,1998). "The sea is full of diversity, with great contents." China has taken a profound lesson from history in this respect. Therefore, China is now holding the attitude of modesty and inclusiveness to the trend of the world, therefore China became the second largest economy.

How difficult it is to rejuvenate the nation!

Although China has surpassed Japan and became the world second-largest economy, she still has not finished the important mission of rejuvenating the nation. It is a goal of the entire Chinese people to realize the great rejuvenation of the Chinese nation. However, what is the "national rejuvenation?" This is not defined by the government officially. Some scholars have summarized its historical connotation in such four sentences: the historical vision and cultural feelings of the past and the future; the overall concept and value aspiration of unity and reunification; the tenacious will and grand ambition; the national confidence and world feelings (Zhang, 2011). Therefore, the national rejuvenation is a very broad concept, there is no way to explain it in detail but can only be understood as a relative concept. Whatever the definition is, the national rejuvenation that the Chinese people want to realize will certainly continue to move forward based on regaining the past glory. The wheels of history will be rolling forward without any retrogression. Therefore, if China do not want to be eliminated, she should focus on economic and political construction to realize the "national rejuvenation."

When mentioning the national rejuvenation, the Chinese nation used to be very prosperous and powerful in her history. At the same time, the history of the Chinese nation is also a history written by those people that survived numerous suffering. "National Rejuvenation," according to the literal understanding, it means returning to the former prosperous state of China. The earliest people that mentioned it was Mr. Sun Yat-sen, who emphasized the ideas of Three Principles of the People. "Three Principles of the People" is an idea that explores the road to rejuvenation of the Chinese nation (Liu, 2012).

Now, as a national dream, how long will it take to realize the Chinese nation rejuvenation? On August 3, 2012, Yang Yiyong, the director of the Institute of Social Development, he said that the Chinese nation rejuvenation index was 0.6274 in 2010, 62% of the revival tasks was done. No matter whether this indicator is correct or not, it is strange to quantify the national rejuvenation. As you can imagine, the discussion on national rejuvenation will continue gradually and profoundly.

The development of China's economy should be attributed to "one correct road and one correct flag." In fact, this road is the "road to socialism with Chinese characteristics." Professor Zhang Ke Rong, who studies the history of modern China, he believes that the contemporary significance of the national rejuvenation has focused on the "path choice" issue, that is, how to achieve the goal of national rejuvenation. Apart from the fundamental road to democratic revival (the road of socialism with Chinese characteristics), the fundamental leadership of the national rejuvenation (the Chinese Communist Party), the fundamental method of national rejuvenation (the path of peaceful development), and the powerful impetus (reform and opening) of the national rejuvenation are also included (Zhang, 2011).

The road to national rejuvenation will never be accomplished overnight, lots of difficulties will be encountered in the future. Although the above-mentioned natural disasters, plagues and foreign troubles have become history, no one can predict whether there will be new internal and external disturbances in the future, which will hinder the progress of national rejuvenation. The economy and politics have always been the protagonists in history. The quality of development will affect the national rejuvenation process directly. Most important of all, the "sauce tank culture" in China is still in the corner of society. The negative impact of this respect should be alert constantly and China should pay more attention to it. All in all, the national rejuvenation will be just around the corner, if China makes her heroic effort to develop the economy, politics, culture and society these four aspects.

Part III: What could be If Not to be No. 1

Chapter 11

Who is the Current World Leader?

As it has been stressed in recent years, the world is a whole mutually related one and like a global village. There are no so-called first and secondary. However, there are still various kinds of rankings made by the public. Facing such a problem, each country has the right to speak and the answers given can be totally different. Therefore, people may ask: Who is the world leader in the world today?

The Americans will be proud to say that the United Sates is the current world leader. The United States is not only the world's largest economy, but also the world's largest military power. In this regard, the British people may not be very glad and they will proudly recall their British Empire of the 19th century, because the United States picked up a big bargain after the World War with regards to the hegemony of the world. The Japanese may not be convinced. They may say that as early as 1988, Japan had the global economic power, although this throne was gotten by the United States. Well, then the Chinese must have something to say, if people want to mention who is the No.1, China should be the first one, just take a look at the prosperity of Tang Dynasty you will know the reason. Besides, there were four inventions in China, which brought significant effect for the entire world after these four inventions were introduced to the European countries and America. Similarly, the Russians may be flushed and the Germans may be angry ... a controversy is doomed to occur with no results. It is understandable that the British Empire was very powerful in her history, but she was still declining as time went on. So, did the Japan. China used to be brilliant in her history but she still cannot escape the terrible fate ... All these have proved such a rule: there is no permanent No.1 in the world, everything is changing from time to time.

Facts speak louder than words. No matter how unwilling to admit or reluctant to give in, the United States is the indisputable leader in the world today. Let us discuss it in detail below:

The world leader was generated from the wars

Almost everyone says they are strong, because anyone likes to boast about themselves. In such an impetuous society, there are only a few people or country that have a clear self-awareness. However, the Chinese people must admit that the strength of the United States is indeed strong. Of course, the Chinese people are not the so-called pro-Americanists, nor are they dissatisfied with their own country. On the contrary, it is precisely because they are full of enthusiasm for the motherland that they do not want their countrymen to lose morale in the gentle countryside that they themselves imagine. As the old saying goes, born into misery and died in peace, both China and the United States know this truth clearly.

When people enter the "United States of America" in Baidu Encyclopedia, it will then show the encyclopedic card about "the United States." What is different from many other countries is that the detailed introduction about the "wars that the United States has participated in" is amazing. As everyone knows, the United States is a young country with a history of only 200 years. However, the history of the United States is more like a history of wars.

When mentioning the establishment of the United States, it is quite necessary to talk about the American War of Independence, which is also the largest anti-colonial war in world history. It is because North Americans were unwilling to continue being oppressed by the exploitation from the British colonies (Zhang, 2017). Finally, the victory of the American War of Independence made the United States get rid of British colonial rule and achieved national independence.

The American War of Independence was not the end of the United States war. On the contrary, it just opened the long scroll of the United

States war. In the following, there were lots of wars, such as the westward movement in the 19th century, the two world wars in the 20th century, the Afghanistan war and the Iraq war in the 21st century, etc. There is no way to list all the wars. Some wars were just and some wars were unjust, just look at all these wars that the United States has participated in, people may draw such a conclusion: her world leader position was generated from wars.

Some people say that most of the wars launched by the United States were aimed at fighting over natural resources. Some say that most of the wars launched by the United States were aimed at diverting domestic crises. While the others say that the United States will not stop the wars if the United States dollars is still the dominating currency in the world. There is no uniform answer to this question. Naturally, different conclusions could be drawn according to the different perspectives of the problems. There is a significant difference between the motive of the war launched by the United States and the self-proclamation by the U.S. government. People often hear from the U.S. government that the United States wants to save those people who are currently in poor, it sounds like the people in other countries are extremely hard to save without the United States. As a result, the United States has always regarded herself as an international policeman and has put on a layer of justice for the wars she has launched or participated in. When necessary, the United States will not justify any country before waging wars against the destination country.

Of course, most of the people are peace-loving. Especially for the Chinese people, the meaning of peace is well-known to all. Logically speaking, this Nobel Peace Prize should have been rewarded to the Chinese leaders, but not. The 2009 Nobel Peace Prize was issued to the United States president, that is Obama. In the first year that Obama took office, neither the peace process in the Middle East nor the reduction of offensive nuclear weapons have achieved any positive results. Instead, the troop surge in Afghanistan has increased the extreme instability in the region. In this context, the Nobel Peace Prize was awarded to Obama, so most of the people really did not know the thoughts of the Awards

Committee. Perhaps it was telling us: Even if there are so many wars occurred recently, we cannot forget the most important thing, that is the peace! Peace and development are still the main topics!

The development will not last too long if there is no sufficient economic and political power. The United States is not so short-sighted, nor so stupid. The wars can be used to attack the destination country, but it requires more "civilian officials" to defend the country. The "general of wars" is used for the military strength of national defense. Therefore, if one wants to say that the United States is the leader of the world today, he needs to look at her economic foundation first. Because the economic foundation determines the superstructure, this is the vivid fact that the Marxist theory tells us.

The economic strength of the United States

After the United States experienced the Great Depression brought by the global financial crisis, some people may want to ask: Is the U.S. economy declining gradually? The U.S. economy has ruled the world for such a long time, is it over now? As everyone knows, the economic foundation determines the superstructure, it will need lots of facts to conclude whether the economic foundation is powerful or not. Most of the people think that the United States is still a supporter for economic hegemony and can cite a great variety of reasons to deny the saying of the "U.S. economic decline": as the world's largest economy, the U.S. gross domestic product still accounts for about one fifth in the world; the living standard in the United States remains one of the highest in the world; the population of the United States is growing; the United States is the issuer of the world's leading reserve currency; the United States has the world's largest and well-developed higher education system which attracts the world's most outstanding talents; the United States will reborn in the economic crisis that happened every 10 years...there are lots of reasons like this. Some people say that the competition is now only in the first half, the United States will completely rebound in the second half. President Obama has encouraged the people in his State in January

2012: "Those who tell you that the United States is declining are undoubtedly lying." (Wu,2012)

It is undeniable that the United States has never recovered from the financial crisis. Although the leaders of the United States are now applauding the situation, however most of these activities should be attributed to the general election that is being held in full swing. Of course, the negative news about the U.S. economy is far from being taken by voters in their massive canvassing speech. The public opinion on the U.S. economic situation is more of a foggy sight. Finally, these veils have become clearer and clearer after the election. For the inspirational words of Obama, people must admit: The United States leader Obama is so powerful! It is not the case, when this kind of inspirational words were spread out widely and frequently, then things will become true. The truth will become fake, and the fake can be disguised as truth. True or fake, the "public" is always ignorant onlookers.

It would be totally wrong if people draw the conclusion according to this one-sided fact, although there are so many disappointments, the top executives in the United States are concealing it carefully and avoiding mentioning. It seems that the economic glories have become history? Of course not! A country that can experience so much wind and rain and still stands tall, it must have its own advantage naturally. The data from the Federal Bureau of Economic Analysis show that the national income growth rate for the fourth quarter of 2012 will reach 4.4%. The output of manufacturing industries will increase significantly, which will also increase people's confidence in turning employment abroad into manufacturing from abroad. The United States is adjusting her industrial structure and promote productivity growth via this economic crisis. These manufacturing enterprises were on the brink of bankruptcy three years ago and are now in short supply.

According to the rankings of world competitiveness issued by the International School of Management Development (IMD) on May 31, 2012, Hong Kong, China, the United States and Switzerland are the most competitive countries in the world (The Xinhua News Agency, 2012) As the world's largest economy, the United States ranked second in 2012. However, she is still the center of world competitiveness due to her unique economic ability and vitality.

The scientific and technological strength of the United States

The level of science and technology in the United States is unparalleled by any other country, not to mention the three scientific and technological revolutions in history. For example, the Apple Corporation in the United States. When walking in the street, you will see that almost everyone has got an Iphone whether he is old or young, boy or girl, rich or poor. The enthusiasm for Apple products is already beyond the imagination of the world people. Nowadays there are lots of Iphone Fans in the world. It is undeniable that the Iphone is really the best mobile phone in the world, which have changed our lives completely! Indeed, the world changes rapidly because of technology.

As a Chinese, it is really a pity that the Chinese people could only copy the appearance from Iphone but no ability to copy the core technologies that Iphone owns, this is so called "cottage products," which is cheap and affordable but fake. In China, the "cottage" culture can be regarded as the sadness of China. What is even more puzzling being that those who own the "cottage" products even feel proud of them, they do not feel shamed at all. In the buses, subways, shopping malls, almost everywhere, the "cottage" products can be seen.

Speaking of science and technology, we must say something about the intellectual property protection. Why can people in the United States take the lead in science and technology and achieve the strongest? That is because people's IPR is well protected! Perhaps it is unfair to answer this question, after all, paying attention to education and personnel is also an important internal cause for the development of science and technology. However, it is undeniable that intellectual property protection plays an irreplaceable role in scientific and technological innovation. Let us take the Rolex replicas as an example, if in China, you can easily buy a Rolex replica without any problems. However, in the United States, selling replicas is extremely forbidden and will be fined heavily when being found by the relevant departments. As you see, the United States pays more attention to the intellectual property protection than China. In this respect, we should give a thumbs-up to the United States!

The government should be the main promoter of science and technology innovation. For any country, if she wants to have a technological innovation environment, she will inevitably need the state support. The government plays a key role. The U.S. government attaches significant importance to the construction and promotion of the "innovation culture," and regards the investors and scientists who promote scientific and technological innovation as the heroes of the country (Huang, 2017). On January 25, 2011, President Barack Obama said in a speech to Congress: We are a country that has created a car and realized a computer for each desk, a country that owns Edison, Wright Brotherhood, a country with Google and Facebook. We are now living in such a country where innovation has not only changed our lives, but what is more, it is the way we make a living (Zhan and Wang, 2012). With the government support, science and technology talent support and other factors, so the United States can maintain her position as the world's number 1 scientific and technological power for a long time and can become the target for other countries in the world to follow.

The solid military strength

When it comes to the U.S. military, her solid military strength may let people feel creepy. Looking at the history of the U.S. foreign wars, which one is not massive and consumes a large amount of manpower, material resources and financial resources? The inherent expansionism in American culture must be traced back in her history. When the United States rose, the United States did not step into imperialism, the Americans have never denied their foreign expansion behavior. The strong military strength of the United States comes from her strong political and economic strength. There is no other country in the world that can mobilize the global resources for its own use as free as the United States, no matter how powerful its economy is.

According to the economic knowledge, it seems that most of the time, when the United States is engaged in military expansion abroad, there is a major crisis in its own country. This is not by accident, nor is it speculation. Because, as we all know, when a country's economy is sluggish, on the one hand the war can partially divert the crisis, on the other hand it can stimulate domestic demand. If there is a war, the consumption will be unavoidable, thus the domestic demand could be stimulated naturally. This logic may sound ridiculous and may even make people think weird. How could a country save its economic crisis at such a cost? However, the facts are incontrovertible. What the leaders think cannot be imagined by ordinary people like you and me?

The form of wars also changes from time to time, and the dominance of the U.S. dollar is a solid foundation for the expansion of the wars in the United States (Ma, 2017). Starting from the "Star Wars" in the Reagan era, the U.S. wars are no longer based on the balance of interests dominated by the "consumption of power and benefits in kind", but are translated into the calculation of interests led by "monetary debt and its exchange rate relief." No matter how profound and massive the difficulties are, if the United States controls the "dollar debt hegemony," the United States is the only country that has the least fear of war. Because every war will bring a "war bonus," and the other side of the war must end up at the expense of consuming state power and national wealth. Because of this, when the U.S. subprime mortgage crisis broke out, it is said that Rand's policy proposal for the U.S. government is: Why spend 700 billion U.S. dollars to rescue Wall Street? The effect of starting a war would be even more immediate(Ma,2010). Undoubtedly, can we find a better way except the war? The war is still the best choice for the national interests of the United States today.

Backwardness is to be beaten, this is an everlasting truth. China has practiced this iron rule well, it is also a history of humiliation. Therefore, in order not to be trampled under the horseshoes of others, China must manage her own national defense and build up her own military forces.

The education system

One of the biggest differences between the U.S. education system and the education system in the other countries is that education in the United States is done for every American. However, in China, "quality education, but not exam-oriented education," this is only a slogan, there is no real activities. What is the real quality education? Let us look at the students in the United States, the education in the United States does not require that every child should be trained as a scientist. The main purpose of education is to tap the talents of every child and to be truly interest-oriented.

The United States is one of the most developed countries in the world in education. One of the characteristics of the U.S. education system is its strong educational scale, another characteristic is the local education authorities' emphasis on educating students' analytical ability and original ability. In addition, there are two distinct characteristics of American higher education (Hou, 2018). One is the decentralization of rights. The other is the credits recognition among different universities. A student can successively accumulate and calculate credits at several universities, the education system in the United States is a concentrated expression of Western educational thought. Western education believes that all theoretical knowledge is ultimately attributed to the application, so American education is more focused on developing students' abilities. The theories are only used as a supplementary tool to guide students. Therefore, American schools have very rich classroom activities and extracurricular activities. This is undoubtedly a great advantage that should be supplemented by Chinese students who have acquired a great deal of theoretical knowledge.

The talents have something to do with the education all the time, they are just like the twins. When it comes to the education, it is necessary to talk about the talents as well. If education is fundamental, talent is the key. To enhance the development of science and technology and increase the national productivity in China, it is necessary to attract talents. Attracting talents means not only retaining their own talents, but also attracting foreign talents. Only in this way can they be inclusive and harmonious.

Let us talk about the methods for introducing foreign talents in the United States, there are four aspects: Firstly, the immigration law will be revised constantly in order to attract outstanding scientific and technological talents from all countries in the world so that there is a real capacity to keep useful personnel in the United States. The second method is to retain students as talent reserve force. Here mainly refers to the use of various grants, scholarships, concessional loans and other generous conditions to attract foreign students to the United States. Thirdly, the "green card" policy provides convenience for foreigners. An important U.S. policy to attract talented people is to grant non-U.S. Professional workers permanent residency rights in the United States, commonly known as "green cards." The fourth method is to create a superior social environment to retain talents, to build the good material conditions for the subsequent development of students and create a superior environment for survival and development via issuing high salaries, research funding, rewards, etc. (Global finance and economics, 2008). As for attracting the foreign talents, China should pay close attention to her own talents.

In contrast, although China attach importance to talents as well, it is just a slogan. China has a policy for issuing Green Cards as well, however after more than a decade of implementation, only thousands of people have obtained green cards from China. Many outstanding talents who originally belonged to China have become a member of another nationality simply because of studying abroad for convenience of life. All other nationalities are regarded as "foreigners" and cannot legally stay in the homeland permanently where they are born. Compared with the extraordinary talent strategy of the United States, is the Chinese government too stingy?

There are still many more macroscopic problems except the above mentioned. As the Chinese old saying goes," capture the king before the thief," therefore, the most important aspects have been showed to the readers. After all, we came to know and understand the world, but not to explain the world.

The overbearing international strategies

The global strategies of the United States have evolved from its inception to its formal formation and has undergone a development from fragmentation to systematic integrity and from military strategies to global strategies. In general, the U.S. international strategies are such a gradual and progressive historical process that it expands from its homeland to overseas and then expands from overseas to global. Of course, the United States' global strategies is not static. It is constantly adjusted with the strength of international development.

With regards to the international strategies, different leaders have different opinions. During the Bush administration, the new strategic goal of the United States was to establish a "new empire." Moreover, Clinton's remarks showed such an essence: Does the United States want to "lead" or "rule" the world? The new Conservatives represented by Bush were pursuing the goal of "ruling the world." This is also the most expanded global strategy in the history of the United States (Jiang,2005). Bush issued many amazing remarks during his tenure. What he wanted to convey was nothing more than that: the market economy and the bourgeois democracy in the United States were the most superior economic and political systems in the world. The United States should enhance her own military economy constantly. At the same time, people from all over the world should also be encouraged to get rid of other social systems, especially the socialist system. They should learn and practice the market economy and bourgeois democracy in the United States. If they were in favor of this global strategy of the United States, the United States should assume her obligations (Liu,1993). These can explain the "new world order" advocated by the Bush administration. The "new order" advocated by him was essentially "the U.S. order".

The Obama's global strategy can be roughly summarized as the following: To shift its strategy to Asia Pacific without giving up Europe. On January 5, 2012, the U.S. President Barack Obama spoke at the

Pentagon in Washington about the military strategy for the next 10 years. According to Obama's speech, the United States must turn her attention to the war in Iraq and Afghanistan and put an end to the policy of adapting military force to participate in long-term nation-building to be able to protect U.S. security with a smaller conventional ground force. Undoubtedly, China will become her number one formidable opponent in the United States' Asia-Pacific strategy. The United States was feeling that the Chinese military had become a major force. But the only way the United States can encourage the like-minded people to check and balance China jointly was that the United States should control her own behavior. As these countries will make China their own major trading partner, they cannot take risks (Chen and Ren, 2015).

The alliance among the English-speaking countries, the Pacific navy and the Pacific allies will bring a good security environment to the United States. To maintain such an environment means that the United States cannot act recklessly and cannot feel uncomfortable with her allies. Some scholars have mentioned that the U.S. international strategy can be summed up in one sentence: threaten the big powers with soft weaknesses and seduce the small ones with interests. Presumably this statement will be well reflected during the Obama administration.

Since the Trump came into power, frequent activities have provoked great attention from all the parties involved. At the beginning of his taking office, he withdrew from the active promotion of the TPP when Obama was in place and UNESCO, the Paris climate agreement and other global or regional agreements, ostensibly to engage in trade protectionism and the implementation of globalization strategy, but in fact he was implying the strategy of " destroying first and then establish it" to promote the United States to re-establish a new system around the world and help the United States to dominate the global economic governance system better in the near future. Obama's "Asia-Pacific rebalancing" strategy will also be changed at the hands of Trump. The original "three legs" called economy, military and politics, have been half destroyed so far. Economically, withdraw from the TPP. Politically, the political shift in Philippines has caused the United States to lose her priority in Southeast Asia. As a result, Obama's Asia-Pacific rebalancing strategy has come to an end completely. However, this does not mean that the United States will give up her efforts in the Asia-Pacific region, the Trump's Asia-Pacific policy will be revealed in a new way gradually (Zhang, 2017).

It was extremely difficult for the United States to become the world leader. Now although many scholars think that the status of the United States will fall soon, it is still too early to think that the United States is going downhill. Whether it is European countries, Japan or China, who wants to surpass the United States, it will still be very difficult. As the saying goes: Only when you can bear loneliness can you keep it forever! Therefore, when fighting each other, China must also make a detailed strategy. The best way to do this is to take the economic construction seriously and prove the country's prosperity with facts.

Chapter 12

The Embarrassment of Being No. 2

February 14, 2011 is a traditional western holiday, namely, the Valentine's Day. However, Japan released her economic data was not "sweet" at all on that day. According to the economic data, the gross domestic product was 5.4742 trillion U.S. dollars, which was lower than China's data announced in January 2011, that is, 5878.6 billion U.S. dollars. As a result, it was obviously that China had surpassed Japan and became the second largest economy in the world, while the Japanese economy was No.3 in the world. Of course, the United States is still the No.1 in the world.

Why was this result not "sweet" for the United States? Because there were some subtle international relations and it had something to do with China. If the No.2 is very obedient, the No.1 (United States) should be very glad. Japan was the former No.2 of the world economy, she was of course quite obedient to the United States, but for China, the situation will not be the same, China will not be so obedient as Japan. Therefore, the United States was so anxious after China became the No.2 in the world. Otherwise, how come there are so many "China threat" theory and "China hegemony" theory?

It is necessary for China to think about herself as she is now the second largest economy in the world. After all, what the public need is a real benefit, a change life that can be seen and touched. Although the total economic output is already in the second place. The living standard of the Chinese people has not changed very much. Nowadays, lots of countries recognize China's development, but China cannot get dizzy with success. For China, she needs to be praised, but at the same time, the criticism is also needed. As the old saying goes, the real warrior dares to face the sad life. Accordingly, let us look at the embarrassment of being the world's second-largest economy.

The "poorest" No. 2 in the world

According to the data of GDP per capita published by the World Bank, the average GDP of the United States was $55,904 in 2015 and was $57,467 in 2016. However, for China, it is really an embarrassment, the average GDP of China was as low as 8280 US dollars in 2015 and was 8123 US dollars in 2016. As you see, there is such a significant difference between the United States and China. According to the total economic output, although China ranks second, it is even more embarrassing for China to measure the gap in per capita GDP. The gap in people's real life is even more immediate. Taking a step back, even if Japan ranks third in the world, her GDP will still be ten times higher than China's. Nowadays there are still 150 million poor people in China (Zhu and Liu, 2011). China has become the second largest economy in the world but it does not mean that China has achieved the common prosperity! China still has a long way to go.

Now, some people may say that the United States and Japan have their own advantages. However, China does not have such kind of advantages, what is more, China has a population of 1.3 billion. Although China's economic aggregate is very large, it is still very poor in view of the large population.

The real power of a country should not only focus on "big", it is also necessary to emphasize "strong." China is now the world second-largest economy, this only focuses on "big," it does not mention the "strong" at all. However, there are some people who love to take this for granted. They think that the second-largest economy represents China's strength. "Big" and "strong," they do not have the same meanings. The difference between them is quite large.

Given the current dilemma, China should admit that she is not strong enough, although "strong" is one of her goals all the time.

The collective development of hundreds of millions of Chinese compatriots is the goal China pursue. As Mr. Deng Xiaoping said, the common prosperity is the ultimate goal of the entire Chinese people. Professor Ito Takashi, a professor of economics at the University of Tokyo, he once said: "It is meaningless to say that China's per capita

GDP is low, and the per capita income of China's coastal areas is almost equal to that of Japan.

However, as a Chinese, this argument cannot be viewed from the standpoint of Japan. Because the Chinese nation is a whole entity, the prosperity of a single area does not mean the prosperity of the entire China. The gap between the rich and the poor in China is so great that the inland area and the coastal area are far away from each other. As a result, the per capita GDP of China is not so high.

Development at the expense of resources

What is the support behind China's economic aggregate? Is it sustainable? For the moment, China's overall GDP has been bought at the expense of very large ecological resources. At present, the proportion of the first and second industries in China's industrial structure is quite high, the proportion of the tertiary industry is obviously low, the internal structure is irrational and the efficiency is quite low. The rapid development of China's energy requirements has continued to increase, although the energy demand structure is being adjusted, but the current energy conditions determine China's higher energy consumption model, at the same time, China's energy efficiency is far lower than the world's average due to the limited level of science and technology (Sun, 2011).

For example, to produce one ton of crude steel, China needs 1.5 tons of coal, the United States needs 1 ton, and Japan only needs 0.6 ton. The low efficiency of energy use in China has become a fundamental problem. The resulting environmental pollution is a serious threat to people's health (Zhu, 2012). During these years of economic development, China has taken an extensive economic development path with high energy consumption. For example, the annual consumption of crude oil, raw coal, iron ore, steel, alumina and cement in China occupies 7.4%, 31%, 30%, 27%, 25%, and 40% of the total consumption in the world, but the GDP created is only equivalent to 4.3% of the world's total annual GDP. Obviously, China's annual gross domestic product created is not proportional to the amount of resources consumed, resulting in huge waste of resources.

The purpose of economic development is to meet people's material and cultural needs, but unrestrained and development and waste of resources will push China into an impasse in a brief time! Under the prohibition of the state, some local governments still pursue their own interests to increase the GDP and do not hesitate to pollute the environment. This is a very complicated issue, but if you look at this issue from a business standpoint, the problem will become very simple. Chinese businessmen will think that the environment is belong to everyone, but the efficiency is belonging to their own. To achieve the so-called benefit targets, the environmental resources are wasted very much.

Some people who work in the banks know that the banks have indicators and tasks that emphasize performance. If the task has not been completed, it means that the year-end prize will be empty. Therefore, the bank clerks encourage people to open accounts at the bank, whether you have money or not, this kind of bank accounts are usually useless.

The Chinese people are not living in the era of planned economy anymore, so it is not necessary at all to make such kind of indicators. Why do the companies and individuals still emphasize the number that has been exaggerated for no reason? Just think about it, it is at the cost of resources.

China cannot consume too much resources any longer, because she should think about her next generation. So, what China needs is the sustainable scientific development.

What is China's economic responsibility?

It is always right to look at things from both sides. Just like the ranking of the world economy. China has become the second largest economy in the world. On the one hand, it can contribute to China's rising position in the international community. On the other hand, the countries in the world are also eagerly to ask China to make more contributions in the world economy, politics and some other aspects, assume more political obligations and international responsibilities, and require China to make more concessions in many areas such as trade and investment, climate change, and energy development, which is squeezing the development space of China's economy.

The "Wall Street Journal" reported that the developed countries want to urge China to take greater responsibility in some areas, such as reducing carbon emissions and reforming foreign exchange policies. Ma Jiantang, the head of the National Bureau of Statistics of China, he said that the China's GDP surpassing Japan is "the result of the Chinese people's hard struggle and continuous progress under the leadership of the Communist Party of China, but on a per capita basis, China is still a poor country in the world." Some countries in the West have frequently attacked China with various economic responsibilities such as the creditor's responsibility, the responsibility of the energy consuming country, the responsibility of the carbon-consuming countries, and the responsibility of the saving country, to allow China to assume more international responsibilities. "Singapore United Morning Post" once reported in 2010 that the current order is in a state of chaos because the global economy has lost its balance. To restore this order, every country has responsibility. There are many countries including developed and developing countries, that have asked China to assume more international responsibilities.

Sun Lijian, a professor from the Fudan University, he said in an interview with the Xinhua News Agency reported that the above requirements show the consistent attitude of foreign institutions: They ignored the reality, their intentions are very clear. They are going to pull China into the ranks of major powers and let China to assume more responsibility in the development of the world economy regardless of China's actual national conditions. They put China's total energy consumption at the top of the list, but the fact is that China's total energy consumption has not surpassed that of the United States. It is obviously that they just want to ask China to take more responsibility, which is not what China should bear. China cannot afford it now! There are also many problems in China that need more energy to solve, such as the gap between the rich and the poor, the employment and the education, etc. All these require China to spend a lot of manpower, material, and financial resources to solve it. Therefore, China must tell the international community that China is still a developing country. China is willing to assume more international responsibilities and become a responsible enormous power. However, China needs a path of free development, as a developing country, China cannot take all the responsibilities from the various powers. China really cannot afford it!

The curses of being No. 2

In the various stages of history, there were several countries that have acted as the No.2, these countries have ever been beaten by the world leader. Such as the former Soviet Union and the Japan, it seemed that there was a curse near them (Lin and Ying, 2010). China is now the second largest economy in the world. Will there be such kind of curse as well?

From World War II until 1981, the former Soviet Union economy was second in the world at that time. According to statistics, the gross national product of the Soviet Union was equivalent to only 37% of the United States in 1950, it was 65% in 1970, and exceeded 70% by the end of the 1970s. However, in the 70s and 80s, it was the time when the curse really came. The irrational issues of the Soviet Union's industrial institutions became apparent gradually. In addition to hardware, the Soviet software facilities did not keep up with the needs of the people. Due to the industrial malformation, the people were often unable to buy things. For example, food and light industrial products can only be supplied by tickets. People often line up for the purchase of necessities. By the end of the 1980s, the socio-economic situation of the Soviet Union had become even worse. According to reports, the daily necessities of daily life in the Soviet Union were very scarce and the housing was very tense. If they would not have to line up in the future, they will certainly feel lonely. After the end of World War II, the Soviet Union became No.2 in the world within half a century, she was then the only country in the world that could compete with the United States. But then the Soviet Union failed to surpass the United States, she failed to be the world No.1, and lately Japan surpassed the Soviet Union quickly.

With regards to Japan, she surpassed China via the Sino-Japanese War. In the later period the Japan's economy was quite terrible due to the failure of the Second World War. Then the United States started to help Japan, so Japan changed from a defeated country to one of the United States allies, Japan received substantial assistance from the United States, and made rapid progress in technology. With the gradual rise of the economy, she surpassed the former Soviet Union in the 1980s and became the world's second largest economy. Despite this, Japan's throne was not stable. Because she relied on the United States too much, she will be very terrible once the United States stopped helping her.

So, how can China break this kind of "curse?" Can China learn some lessons from history? First, China has the similar issues like the former Soviet Union, that is the structural contradictions problems. To adjust the industrial structure and the economic structure is also the slogans of China. It is undeniable that the development of the service industry still lags, and this is an important industry that can absorb a lot of labor. This will solve the employment problem in China. All the problems in China are interlocking. Just like the domino, the most important thing is to find an entry point.

Not only the structural contradictions in China are prominent, but also the structural contradictions in the entire world are prominent. In the entire world economy, China is undoubtedly a "big manufacturing country," and the United States is a "consumer power." On the one hand, China produced too much, on the other hand, the economic bubble in the United States is too serious, therefore there was a global financial crisis in 2008. Secondly, the Chinese nation is an industrious nation. China emphasizes "do it yourself, get plenty of food and clothing." Therefore, the loss of self-development characteristics should certainly not happen in China. However, the slogan does not rely on shouting. What China must do is to accelerate the pace of independent innovation and to be a truly innovative country. Only by this can China break the "curse" of the world No. 2.

The troubles of being No. 2

Originally, as a developing country, China should enjoy various kinds of preferential treatment. However, in the eyes of other countries, China has become the second largest in the world, and thus China should not enjoy so many benefits any more. Some western political forces have tried to disassociate China from the camps of developing countries by speculating "second largest economy in the world." They are compressing China's rights as a developing country while at the same time divorcing the relations between other developing countries and China (Chen, 2010). It is obvious that the developed countries want China to make more efforts and get less benefits. They can also make things difficult for China by this way. It is not hard to imagine that there will be more and more international disputes and frictions in the future. From the above examples, it is very clear that they want to fabricate "China's economic responsibility theory".

China's foreign policy has been to keep a low profile for a long time. In the United Nations General Assembly, China has ever been a permanent member who abstained from voting. But unexpectedly, in the eyes of other countries, China is now the world largest exporter and the second largest economy. Some people explained that these milestones mean that there are fewer and fewer places where China can hide. Not to mention that China has become the target of public criticism, but the pressure and frictions she faces have really increased. The pressure from the United States, the unwillingness from Japan, and the vigilance from some other neighboring countries, all these are showing that China is going to face more and more pressures and frictions.

"The Times of India" interpreted China as the "second in the world" from a political perspective and called on India to prepare for the response. China has become the second largest economy in the world, the Indians are certainly not the only people scratching their heads and keeping an eye on what will happen next. The most unrecognizable aspect of this matter is how it will affect China's strategic decision. The current signal shows that China is not only on the world stage, but also her surrounding neighbors are becoming more and more hardened, she is not only asserting sovereignty in the South China Sea, but also the Sino-Indian boundary issue will become increasingly intransigent and will undermine the Indian-Palestinian reconciliation process. To cope with the challenges of the "central state," India must first increase its own economic data. In 1990, India's total economy was 80% of China's, but now it only accounts for 1/4 of China's. In addition, India will also abandon the Cold War strategy, strengthen its full cooperation with the West, and deepen its cooperation with Japan and Southeast Asian countries.

These figures on the total amount of the economy and the resulting title of "the world's second largest economy" have led to such a strong confrontation and reaction. Many countries have rapidly increased their vigilance, the entire city is on alert. Is it true that the gap between China and the United States is so big on the day before and after the release of this series of figures? These countries may be overestimating China, or they are deliberately hyping it.

Be careful about the ulterior praise

The great man of the Chinese nation, Chairman Mao Zedong once said that when the Chinese Communist Party is about to become the ruling party, China must always be vigilant to resist the attack of sugarcoated shells. When the outside world becomes tempting, China should maintain self-awareness. This was the case in the early years after the founding of the People's Republic of China, and it was also the case during the modernization period. Self-inflation was unnecessary. It is a long-term plan for the rejuvenation of the Chinese nation to recognize the problems and make a clear progress.

China has been highly developed for more than 30 years. China was a poor country that needs international assistance, however, China has now become the world second largest economy. On July 30, 2010, Yi Gang, the deputy governor of the People's Bank of China, he stated in an interview with the media that China has become the second largest economy in the world. One stone provokes a thousand layers of waves, the foreign media will use this as an opportunity to hype the second largest economy in the world vigorously. Although the GDP of the United States in 2010 exceeded 14 trillion yuan, which is more than the sum of China and Japan, but according to the financial institutions such as the World Bank and Goldman Sachs, China may surpass the United States and become the world largest economy by 2025. Any Chinese who are still awake should ask themselves: Is that really the case? China is not a country that is childish and ignorant. The Chinese nation is a historical country that has experienced many vicissitudes. China will not repeat the mistakes she made in the past. Is the price paid by the Chinese people less? Is the development of the economy "quick and good" or the development of the economy "good and fast?" Now that China has a more accurate position, China must focus on "good" first. Although it is only a matter of ranking, it is enough to highlight China's speed and pay more attention to the valuable spirit of quality.

There are some elements about "fast" that have been internalized into every corner of life and even the mind intentionally or unintentionally. China often lament that the rhythm of life is too fast to keep up with the pace of the times. In all aspects of life, the elements of "fast" can be seen. For example, the "fast food" for dinner and the "flash marriage" in China. When they lose their abilities to control themselves during the high-speed rotation, it is the time for them to pay for "fast". The "prosperity" in the early years when China was just established has already given the Chinese people a profound lesson.

All in all, the above points are said to be the embarrassment of the world No.2, but in the final analysis it is the challenge that China will face after becoming the second largest economy in the world. This is also a critical issue that needs to be addressed in China's "12th Five-Year Plan." China is now at the cost of resources, what is urgently needed is to realize the "low-carbon economy". This is also the inevitable path for China's economic transformation. China must strive to develop and grow her economic peacefully.

China is a country with a population of nearly 1.4 billion. No matter how small the issue is, if being multiplied by 1.4 billion, it will become a big problem. Similarly, no matter how large China's economic aggregate is, if it is divided by 1.4 billion, it will become a very low per capita level. Regarding the title of "the world's second largest economy", China should maintain a high degree of sobriety, but not be fooled by the western media, China should also see many challenges in China's economic development. China should develop herself in accordance with her own steps, speed up the transformation of economic development methods, improve the quality of economic development, promote the improvement of the people's living standards and quality, and increase their economic strength comprehensively so that China can become the second largest in the world (Chen, 2010). As a Chinese people, he should not allow himself to stand in an embarrassing position forever and bear various untrue titles. Everything will come to fruition one day; the entire world will cheer for China on that day!

Chapter 13

Challenges from Japan

Nowadays the total amount of China's GDP has exceeded that of Japan and China is now the second largest economy in the world. This change has caused an uproar in Japan, which has brought new variables to China-Japan relations. The relations between China and Japan is very complicated, because all kinds of phenomena and contradictions are intertwined. Some people may want to ask: Will Japan be willing to lag China economically? Of course not! Therefore, China will face more fierce chases and challenges from Japan definitely!

Of course, not all the Japanese are against it in the face of the rise of China's economic. There are some observers who believe that the changes in the ranking of the world economy only show the pure symbolic meaning and cannot change the essence. In addition, the economist Takkashi Shiono from Credit Suisse Japan Branch said: "China's economic growth has a very positive meaning for the Japan's economy. Although some Japanese people may be a bit embarrassed, however this is a huge opportunity for the Japanese companies" (Blair,2010). At the same time, this conclusion was also recognized by Dr. Martin Schulz, a senior economist at the Fujitsu Economic Research Center in Tokyo, Japan, who believes that the faster the Chinese economy grows, the better the Japanese economy will be. Popularly, China and Japan are "brought out of their mother's womb" because their innate geographical position determines the relationship between them. Japan can gain huge benefits from it with the development of China's economy.

If all the people are looking at the fact that China is the world's second-largest economy from a positive perspective, China will not be as timid as this. In fact, most of the foreign media view this normal economic phenomenon in a form of hostility or vigilance. They think China is now declaring world hegemony to the world, they may have forgotten China's diplomatic determination. China does not like hegemonism and will never seek hegemony. As a Chinese people, it is necessary for him to know that there are some countries will put pressure on China, especially Japan, which lag China temporarily. Chairman Mao Zedong said: "if people do not offend me, I will never offend him." The China's act of upholding world peace is the best proof.

With regards to Japan, the third largest economy in the world today, there is so much to say. However, in view of the limited time, and considering the excessive sensitivity of some issues, let us just focus on the economic historical sources of China and Japan and some series of chain reactions because of China's rise, and some strategic adjustments of the Japan's economy.

The economic miracle of Japan in her history

The real glory of the Japanese economy was after the Second World War. Some people may find it strange that Japan was obviously a defeated country in the second world war, how come there was such a glory with regards to the economy? This is because the United States helped her a lot after the Second World War. Accordingly, Japan turned from the role of a defeated nation to the role of an "American allies" quickly.

The post-war Japan's economy can be divided into three periods. The first one is the post-war revival period from 1945 to 1955, then the period of rapid development from 1955 to 1968, and finally, the stable period after being the second largest economy in the world. Lately, it was replaced by China in 2011 and fell to the third in the world, which ranked behind the United States and China.

During the post-war revival period, Japan's economy not only achieved economic democratization through the "disintegration of the fiscal gates" and "labor reform", but also laid a solid mass foundation for her economic growth. Japan's economy also adopted material resources, financial resources, and human resources since 1947. The "inclined mode of production" that had been put into the production of coal and steel accelerated the speed of economic recovery. Japan's economy suffered from inflation in 1948, a lot of people were forced to save their money into the banks, lots of capital flowed into large enterprises, which created a "period of panic in stabilization." At that time, Japan made a fortune suddenly because of the Korean War in 1950, which also eased domestic economic problems. The consumption of war has stimulated the growth of demand, accelerated Japan's economic production activities, and restored Japan's gross national product to pre-war levels.

During the period of rapid development after 1955, Japan's actual average growth rate was 8%, in the following 25 years, Japan's economy continued to develop and then reached the highest rate in the world. In 1955, Japan's gross national product ranked seventh in the capitalist countries, 13 years later, it took the second place formally and became the second largest economy. In the past, Japan was one of the "moderately developed countries," however, she has now become a world-wide "economic power" after experiencing historical economic development miracles.

Of course, flies do not bite seamless eggs. If there were no problems for Japan's economy, it will be impossible for China to surpass her. When Japan's economic bubble burst, Japan's economy will then begin to decline. Now, Japan's economy seems to stand at a crossroads: is it continuing to decline, or is it moving steadily?

Japan's advantages: Innate advantages and acquired advantages

Regarding the big issue of population, Japan is undoubtedly innately superior. The fact that China's population is more than ten times the population of Japan shows these two points: Firstly, Japan's per capita GDP has an absolute advantage. Even if China's total economic output is larger, it will be minimal if divided by 1.4 billion. Compared with Japan, it is much less. Secondly, Japan's economy has the advantage of "a small boat and a good boat." For example, in the market economy, the efficiency is very important, because Japan's economic volume is small, so she can improve efficiency through all kinds of methods. But for

China, it is different, because China has a population of 1.3 billion and the total economic volume is very large.

Since the Meiji Restoration, Japan has formed Yamato ethnic culture, the core of this national culture is "collectivism." This had a profound influence on the development of Japan's economy and society, and has thus become the acquired advantage of the Japan's economy. The Meiji Restoration was in the latter half of the 19th century. Because of the catalytic role of Western capitalist external pressure, there occurred a self-sustaining crisis in Japan in order to overcome the crisis of becoming a colony. Under the dual nature of the national revolution and the democratic revolution, the reform movement was then becoming westernized and the modernized. In the process of the long development, the Yamato people created a unique Japanese civilization by drawing on foreign civilizations and integrating them well with themselves. At the same time, it also reflects the spiritual outlook and psychological quality of the nation.

The most important thing for a nation to be different from the other nations is its unique psychological quality. The spiritual qualities of the Yamato people have given the world a way of thinking. Some people say that they are productive but they are not good at thinking, they are respecting groups and ignoring individuals, emphasizing commonalities and discrediting individuality. Indeed, the Japanese people have a powerful sense of collectivism. They believe that solidarity can achieve success. They also value the concept of harmonious coordination and thus produce strong national cohesion. This point can be seen from the rise of Japan and her outward expansion and post-war rebirth. Regardless of the impact of her influence, cohesion should be worthy of recognition for a nation. The resulting Japanese nationals are highly obedient and have strong discipline and overall mobilization. The Yamato nation has strong centripetal force and a keen sense of national identity. All these are the acquired advantages of Japanese Yamato ethnic culture. After the war, Japan also made efforts to introduce advanced science and technology and management strategies from the western countries, it was integrated with traditional cultures to become a new kind of Japanese-style civilization with oriental characteristics.

Obviously, the joint effects of inherent and acquired advantages can promote the development of the country's economy better. Otherwise, it is impossible to complete all the historical missions after considering the congenital deficiency or acquired disability. In short, Japan's ability to embark on a successful modernization path is precisely because of the inherent advantages of Japan's small countries and their unique cultural characteristics.

The strategic adjustment of Japan's economy

After the burst of Japan's economic bubble in the 1990s, Japan's economy was in a stage of "downturn." Gradually, after entering the 21st century, it is not easy for the Japanese economy to have high-speed development after World War II. At present, whether the Japanese economy can continue to recover or not has become the focus of the public attention. Faced with this, some media reported that Japan's economic recovery needs at least three conditions: Firstly, the export environment; Secondly, the rapid growth of production; Thirdly, the effect of stimulating the economy fully (Martin, 2010).

From the perspective of export environment, Japan's dependence on external markets is more serious, and whether the economy can improve mainly depends on the international market. If the U.S. economy does not recover, Japan's exports will be difficult to expand and it will be difficult to stimulate domestic economic growth. The unemployment rate will remain high. This will inevitably lead to a decline in the average employment income of the entire society, a decrease in purchasing power, and a difficult reversal of deflation. Japan's lack of social spending may create a liquidity trap. Therefore, it is difficult to predict whether Japan's exports will continue to increase in the future. Bank of Japan Governor Shirakawa said that the underlying reason for Japan's current deflation is definitely because of the weak demands. In the context of deflation and the appreciation of the Yen, Japan's economic outlook has become even more uncertain. In response, Shirakawa emphasized that on the one hand

Japan should adhere to a loose monetary policy, on the other hand, Japan should do her utmost to overcome deflation.

From the point of view of production and inventory adjustments, the Yen has continued to appreciate recently, which is extremely detrimental to exporters. Deterioration of corporate performance will inevitably affect many aspects of employment, wages, and equipment investment, thus affecting national consumption, and finally dragging the economic recovery. At the same time, Japan's economy is really on the track of self-discipline recovery and needs a new round of domestic inventory adjustments. The time for inventory adjustment is beyond the expected long-term, this will also become one of the risk factors for Japan's economy to resume growth.

Judging from the effect of economic measures, in the context of the high unemployment rate and the severe national income situation, if the Japanese government fails to introduce further targeted policies and measures, the domestic economy will no longer be effective in pulling domestic economy. Therefore, stimulating domestic demands will be one of the main directions for Japan's economic development in the future, and her complementary policies will surely go hand in hand.

The adjustment of Japan's economic strategy and the adjustment of her political policies also need to complement each other. What policies will the Japanese government introduce to guide market expectations and stabilize market confidence? For now, there is no positive answer.

The ambition of Japan

Although Japan has a small territory, her ambition is not small at all, she has great ambitions. In fact, as an island nation, Japan has a wealth of tidal and wind power resources, and solar energy is also very advanced, but Japan will never be satisfied with her projectile land. She also hopes to obtain more natural resources from the outside world. After all, due to the limitation of land area, her resources are relatively poor compared to other countries, and the natural disasters in this island country are frequent. This makes the Japanese nationality contain a keen sense of crisis. Once this awareness expands, it becomes an uncontrollable big ambition.

When mentioning the wars between Japan and China, there are two representative wars that must be mentioned. One was Sino-Japanese War, which ended with China's failure. The other was the Anti-Japanese War, which ended with Japanese surrender. The Sino-Japanese War, which broke out in 1894, was an unjust war of aggression. After the victory of the Sino-Japanese War, Japan became a powerful Asian country, thus freeing herself from the semi-colonial situation completely. Japan made a fortune in this war and it was the first time that it had tasted the sweetness of aggression. This has also stimulated Japan's desire greatly to expand her aggression.

China's War of Resistance Against Japanese Aggression was described by Japan as the Sino-Japanese War and was also the "second Sino-Japanese war" by most western countries. Regardless of its name, the nature of the war cannot be changed. The War of Resistance Against Japanese Aggression began in 1937 with the "Lugou Bridge Incident" and was triggered by the Japanese Empire's invasion of China. It took eight years and ended on September 2, 1945 with Japan's surrender. Although there are only two relatively large "Sino-Japanese wars" are summarized here, the small wars they contain are numerous.

China has suffered from Japan's repeated aggression in modern times. In Japan's mainland policy, the demise of China is her established national policy. The most important reason is because of China's backwardness. Although Japan is a small country, her economic strength and her weapons and equipment are much more advanced than China. Although China is a big country, the number of troops is far better than that of Japan, but economic strength and the military's weapons and equipment lag far behind Japan (Zhong, 2010).

Under the cover of the Japanese government, many Japanese people believe that they were not wrong when they launched the war. They may continue to do so. This is their nature that cannot be changed. China needs to sweep away the negative, impetuous, ambiguous sentiments that pervade China's society. If China really has the determination to get rid of unhealthy habits from top to bottom, China will be able to regain her glory. In addition to China's own efforts, the Chinese people may still have a huge doubt: Nowadays Japan refuses to admit her aggressive activities, what is the reason? Why is Japan so rampant? In fact, it is not difficult to find out if you think about it carefully. In addition to being blessed by the United States, it is also one of the reasons that the aggressor countries have not committed any substantive punishment for the crime of Japan's war.

After the Second World War, Japan was growing up under the protection of the United States, so Japan's ambition would naturally swell gradually. In recent years, under the provocation of the Japanese right-wing forces, regarding the Diaoyu Islands issue, there were lots of conflicts with the Chinese government. Moreover, as for Sino-Japanese relations, the United States should be ashamed because she could benefit from it. The stalemate among China, the United States and Japan, these three countries will remain for some time. Especially after the United States has shifted her global strategic objectives to the East Asia region, the United States needs Japan and China to contain each other's strengths.

In fact, the expansionist attitude of Japan can be easily imagined. The ambitions of Japan will gradually show in future international exchanges. The fundamental reason is the sense of misery of Japan. Once this sense of urgency is amplified, it will bring more and more wars to the world. The Japanese diligence can also prove this very well. They always rely on diligence and historical opportunities to reform and innovate technologies constantly.

Disputes on the Diaoyu Islands

When mentioning the Sino-Japanese relations, we must mention the long-standing dispute over the Diaoyu Islands. The Diaoyu Island and its affiliated islands are located at about 92 nautical miles northeast of Keelung City, Taiwan Province, and about 73 nautical miles from Japan's Ryukyu Islands, but separated by a deep-sea trough. The Diaoyu Islands consist of Diaoyu, Huangwei, Chiwei, Nanxiao, Beixiao, and three small island reefs, with a total area of approximately 6.3 square kilometers. Among them, Diaoyu Island is the largest, with an area of 4.3 square kilometers (Zhong, 2012). The Diaoyu Islands have been China's territory since ancient times. Like Taiwan, it is an inseparable part of the Chinese territory. China has indisputable sovereignty over the Diaoyu Islands and its adjacent waters (Zhong, 2010). During the last century, Japanese officials used the following three principles to negotiate with China on the sovereignty of the Diaoyu Islands: Firstly, the so-called sovereignty over the Diaoyu Islands originated from the "principle of privatization" in international law; Secondly, Japan regained the sovereignty of the Diaoyu Islands according to the "San Francisco Contract" and the "Okinawa Return Agreement." The third is the so-called time efficiency.

In fact, the above three points are not enough to judge the facts(Wang,2012). Despite this, Japan's occupation of the Diaoyu Islands will probably not be easily eased. The escalation of disputes between China and Japan over the Diaoyu Islands issue is a concentrated expression of the Japanese people's extreme concerns about China. In contrast, China does not pay much attention to this dispute. Only officials emphasized that "Chinese sacred territory will never allow anyone to buy or sell." However, it is very difficult for China today to form a national gathering power. Therefore, among the Chinese who protected the Diaoyu Islands, the Taiwanese was the majority.

The national consciousness of the Japanese society is too strong. China's victory in the War of Resistance was finally achieved with the support of the United States, the Soviet Union, and other countries, Japan is still interested in China. Regarding the Diaoyu Islands issue, the Japanese people even thought that it was an opportunity to fight against China. There may be occur another war between China and Japan, because both the Japanese government and the people are willing to fight China. The Japanese government's hard-line attitude toward the Diaoyu Islands issue is the response of the Japanese public. Why does the Japanese public have such a mentality?

As we can see from the report of Japan's NHK TV station, the Japanese government's attitude towards the Diaoyu Islands disputes has become increasingly tough. Japanese Prime Minister Noda Yoshihiko stated publicly in the House of Representatives' plenary session that if there is a difference between "Japanese territory and territorial waters" including the Diaoyu Islands, when necessary, Japan will consider dispatching the Self-Defense Forces. Although Noda Yoshihiko emphasized that "usual crisis management and preventive diplomacy efforts are also important", "the government must respond with a firm attitude". This is the first time that the Japanese government has indicated that it will dispatch troops to resolve the Diaoyu Islands dispute. On the "Diaoyu Island Incident" in 2012, we saw the ulterior motives of Japanese Prime Minister Yoshihiko Noda. The various acts of the Japanese government and people are also continuously irritating the Chinese people and the government: Japan's right-wingers went to the Diaoyu Islands to perform "sweethearted" activities; The Japanese government detained the Hong Kong "Diaoyu Islands Protecting" person for no reason; Governor Shintaro Ishihara of Japan proposed to "purchase" the Diaoyu Islands, and on September 3, 2012, the Japanese government used the so-called "land owner" for about 2.05 billion Yen (about 166 million China Yuan) and reached an "agreement" on "acquisition of the island." No doubt, the "Island purchase" farce played by the Tokyo Metropolitan Government and the Japanese Central Government was approved by the Japanese Prime Minister Noda Yoshihiko. Another Japanese NHK TV station reported on September 20 that Japanese Prime Minister Noda Yoshihiko also announced on the evening of the 19th when he participated in Asahi TV program that the Diaoyu Islands "had no sovereignty problem".

It seems to be the Japanese government's toughness toward China. However, it satisfies the Japanese people's strong dissatisfaction with China. With this kind of boost, there will probably be another war between China and Japan. The Japanese people are unbelievable. They do not hate the Americans who beat them. This is also the case in business, they are afraid that the Chinese will earn the Japanese money.

Now, Japan is certainly not satisfied with her status as No3 in the world, and may also want to regain her status as No2. Japan is a true tiger in Asia. In Asia, only Japan can compete with China.

But the Chinese do not have the same attitude towards Japanese people, this is a fact. Just like the modern history between China and Japan, the Japanese always harass China. Moreover, due to historical reasons, the result of the friction between China and Japan is always terrible, the victory of the Chinese Anti-Japanese War as mentioned above is not a true victory for the Chinese people, so the Japanese are still unconvinced with China. There are a lot of people who want to stir up the Sino-Japanese war. This is the reason why the possibility of another war between China and Japan has always existed, if there is a fire line that can break out. The battle between China and Japan in the future will surely be like the modern history. It cannot be China's declaration of war against Japan. It is precisely that Japan may declare war on China. This is the grim reality facing China and Japan today.

Can the Sino-Japanese War be avoided?

Economic and political issues have never been able to be seen in isolation. Apart from the economic relations between China and Japan, there is also a complex political factor. This will also have a profound impact on the future economic cooperation and development of China and Japan. To be more extreme, if there is a war, what the economy will be? Take the Sino-Japanese War as an example, China's history textbooks describe in detail the background, passage, and influence of the outbreak of war. What about Japan? After the introduction of the war, several questions were utterly listed: (1) Do you think that Japan and China will not break out of the war in the last two decades? If there is a war, where do you think China will attack Japan? (2) What kind of measures do you think should be taken...(Zhong, 2010). Well, as you see, the Japanese government do not treat the facts seriously. They seem kidding.

All along, the good-hearted Chinese people are always good at thinking about issues from the best aspects of their affairs. For example, whether China and Japan will have a war in recent years, China's answer will always be: No! Because peace and development are the theme of the development of the times today! However, the Chinese people may want to ask: If the war is going to happen, is it still necessary to repeat the historical tragedy? China should be more concerned about the more serious international security issues.

Let us return to reality, China and Japan are still in the traditional security dilemma of East Asia. Historical issues and Taiwan issues may cause new conflicts at any time. Disputes surrounding the ownership of the Diaoyu Islands, the development of the East China Sea oil and gas fields, and the division of the outer continental shelf are now visible (Wang, 2011). Well, since the facts are like this, let us come together to supplement this important lesson for the people! If the Sino-Japanese War is to happen, what should China do before that?

If China do not want to fight, what should China do to avoid this war? As we all know, weak countries have no diplomacy, and China's history has verified this long ago. What about the actual strength between China and Japan? Or, who will benefit more? In fact, as far as the war break out, for the time being, regardless of the issue of winning or losing, it is not an easy task for any country. It will also be a protracted war, and it is very likely that both sides will lose. So, what should China do in the face of this kind of war?

As the saying goes, "capture the ringleader first to capture all his followers." Beyond China-Japan relations, we must first resolve the issue of excessive American intervention. Fortunately, the world is a big family, China can fully mobilize the strength of other countries, such as South Korea, to exert pressure on the United Nations (in fact, pressure on the United States) to maintain peace in Asia and even peace in the world. The excessive expansion of Japanese military forces is prohibited.

In addition to starting with external factors and seeking international assistance, the most important thing is to start with domestic development. Marxist theory tells us that internal factors are determinants of all things. External factors can only play a role of delay or acceleration. "If you do not fall, no one can knock you down!" China must use her major energy and strength to make her own country powerful (Cai, 2008).

China must give Japan such a gesture: China is not so easy to bully! The Chinese people should unite with strong national cohesion against the samurai spirit of Japan's Yamato ethnic group. China will not lose to Japan. In addition to be a giant in language, China must also be giants in action! If China is as powerful as the United States, how will Japan react? But at least it is certain that Japan will not take the initiative to provoke a new war between China and Japanby then. Therefore, whether the Sino-Japanese war can be avoided or not, the answer depends on the world and the China herself!

Who else would Japan challenge?

In addition to China, who else would Japan challenge? We all know that since the Second World War, Japan and the United States are allies. So, will this relationship change substantially? Will Japan challenge the United States? Of course, if Japan were to take the initiative to provoke the United States, it seemed a bit overwhelming. But if the United States stops her aid to Japan, will Japan be forced to rise? In fact, the relationship among any country is based on interests. If the interests are in conflict or disagreement, it is only between the enemy and the friends. As the saying goes, there are no permanent friends, no permanent enemies, only eternal interests. The Japan-US relations are certainly no exception.

Many facts have proven that the Japanese Democratic Party had criticized the Liberal Democratic Party for its approach to the United States before it seized power. When the Democratic Party took power, Yukio Hatoyama put forward the idea of "East Asian Community" in a high-profile manner. He wanted to "move from the United States into Asia," and his diplomatic gesture turned gorgeously to Asia(Da,2011). It has been vividly described the relationship between Japan and the United States as a "noisy husband and wife." If we use the relationship between husband and wife to describe the relationship between Japan and the United States when the Democratic Party came to power, we can generally draw a story about one party fighting for greater freedom and arguing with the other side. Now, it happens to conflict with another family member, and it also increases the willingness to return to the other half of the family. The other half is to consolidate the couple's feelings and accept it. However, the original contradictions have not disappeared and may erupt in the future. Moreover, as one side's power is decreasing, more and more people cannot take care of the other side. The other side must always consider what to do in the future (Sun, 2010). Therefore, the Japan-US relations is still weak. We can only wait and see how it changes in the future.

In addition to the United States, we also must talk about the relationship between Japan and Russia. Due to the proximity of geographical location, the relations among China, Japan and Russia are also very delicate. The contradiction between Japan and Russia originated from China. The two Japanese-Russian wars in history have occurred in the northeastern region of China. At the time, they were also a "dog bite" war. Japan, which has a small land and is poorly resourced, is always sensitive to disputes over islands and sea power. However, she faced the most complex island and maritime disputes. She has serious island and maritime disputes with her three neighboring countries - China, South Korea and Russia. Among them, what Japan values most is the four northern islands. For a long time, Japan has made significant efforts to recover the four islands from Russia, and she once gained the support and sympathy from many countries in Asia(Wang,2008). Now, on the surface, Japan and Russia are not offensive to each other, in fact, in the dispute between the four islands of the North, the relations between Japan and Russia is very delicate, and this kind of relations will continue to exist.

After looking at the relationship between Japan and neighboring countries, it does not seem peaceful. Japan not only has conflicts with China and Russia, but also has subtle political conflicts with South Korea, North Korea and other Asian countries. In response to the North Korean nuclear issue, Japan has made public opinion constantly about rearming itself. In 2003, the Japanese Defense Agency announced that once it becomes aware that North Korea may launch a missile attack on Japan, Japan may implement a "preemptive" military strike against North Korea. Specifically, if North Korea begins its military preparations for Japan, the Japanese military will mobilize the military to conduct "a purely self-defense counterattack." Once North Korea begins to add fuel to a missile aimed at Japan, it will be considered by Tokyo as "the signal of the outbreak," the Japanese army will take the necessary measures against Pyongyang. After North Korea conducted an underground nuclear test in October 2006, Japan announced that it had taken six months of economic sanctions against the Democratic People's Republic of Korea. Sanctions include: North Korean ships are prohibited from entering Hong Kong; North Korean imports are completely banned; 24 luxury goods are prohibited from being exported to North Korea; North Korean citizens are prohibited from entering Japan. On April 11, 2008, the Japanese government extended the deadline for sanctions against the DPRK for another half year by the same reason (Feng, 2008).

Although the Japanese government partially lifted (note: not completely lifted) the economic sanctions against North Korea, it still cannot change the relationship between Japan and North Korea. On December 2, 2016, the Japanese government formally decided that she should strengthen Japan's separate sanctions. The Japanese government's separate sanctions include: (1) expanding targets for re-entry of visiting North Korea's General Association of North Koreans (North Korea General Association) cadres, foreigners' nuclear and missile technicians in Japan; (2) North Korea ships are prohibited from entering Hong Kong; (3) Expansion of assets frozen by groups and individuals involved in nuclear and missile development. On July 28, 2017, Japanese Foreign Minister Kiichi Keikyu stated that Japan will impose new sanctions on North Korea. The relationship between Japan and South Korea has been deteriorating. Japan has also tried every means to target North Korea through various means.

Here we briefly elaborated the grudge between some major countries and Japan, and we do not need to exhaust all the relations. Because the above relationships have been enough to show the great ambition of Japan. Japan is an extremely crisis-conscious country. Of course, this is inseparable from the mentality of the small country. Moreover, people in Japan not only have a keen sense of crisis, but also have an extraordinary level of diligence. Of course, these two are also related to each other. Nowadays Japan is being protected by the United States. But who can guarantee that Japan will not be strong enough to shock the United States? At that time, it is worried that the world will face a chance to reshuffle again. Japan's growth is not only a challenge to China, but also a challenge to the world! In short, one sentence: Japan does want to dominate the world.

Chapter 14

Would the United States Want China to be No.1?

It is an indisputable fact that China has become the second largest economy in the world. The United States, as the world largest economy, she is certainly worried about this fact. So, does this indicate that the United States is worried about her world leader position? Even if China will continue to be strong, will the United States promise to give up her world leader position? In the United States general election that ended in 2016, various candidates including Donald Trump and Hillary Clinton were playing the games to refuse China to be too strong. Is this telling the world that whether the Democratic Party or the Republican Party is in power, the United States is bound to contain China?

For China, what is urgently needed to be resolved is how to keep the relationship between the United States and China. If it is not handled properly, China will be very difficult to be the world No.2. Whether her attitude is moderate or tough depends on China's economic development. Optimists in the western countries believe that the rapid development of China is an "opportunity" for the United States because China's accelerated development can provide the United States with a huge commodity market and a steady stream of capital; While some pessimists compared the rise of China to the rise of Germany at the end of the 19th century and compared the current Sino-US relations with the English-German relations at the end of the 19th century(Lin,2008). Judging from the current situation in international relations, the U.S. authorities and most of the people hold the latter attitude, that is, pessimistic attitude.

On August 18, 2010, AFP (Agency France-Presse) reported that China replaced Japan and became the world second largest economy. This news shocked the United States and thus she began to worry about her status as a world economic champion (Chang, 2017). After learning about the news, Krugman, the Nobel Prize winner in economics in the United States, he wrote on his blog: What China is doing is equivalent to a kind of predatory business policy. He made an appeal and hoped that President Barack Obama will take a harder stance against China on the issue of the RMB exchange rate. China's becoming the second largest economy in the world seems to make the United States "unhappy." With regards to the RMB exchange rate, this should only belong to China's internal economic policies, it has nothing to do with the United States at all.

In fact, the United States will not give up her world leader position easily. Then, from what aspects will the United States hinder China's development? As the old saying goes, "he who has a mind to beat his dog will easily find his stick." The history of the modern world shows that once the United States want to block a country's economic and social development, she will never lack the reasons! Let us discuss it in detail.

Instinct to maintain the position of the world leader

People have human instincts. Animals have animal instincts. As countries, they are a collection of people with instinctive reactions. The relationship between the United States and China is becoming worse after China became the second largest world economy, because the United States knows that China will replace her world leader position one day. From the history, the United States has been blocking the other countries all the time, as she do not want any country to replace her position. This can be regarded as the instinct of the United States.

The United States surpassed Britain in 1872 and became the world largest economic power. As a result, the United Kingdom became the "target" of the United States. This can be regarded as a "retaliate" or a "winning pursuit." So, the American hegemony is based on the historical heritage of the British Empire. The so-called freedom, democracy, culture, and law in the United States are basically copies of the British Empire model (Zhang, 2001).

After the second World War, the economy of the United Kingdom was very bad. The Bretton Woods Conference in 1944 announced the end of the sterling hegemony. Afterwards, the United States exported the dollar and replaced the pound gradually through the "Marshall Plan." After the "Third Point Plan" launched, the British forces were gradually driven out of the Middle East. In 1956, Britain joined forces with Egypt and attempted to recapture the Suez Canal. This was the last effort of the British government to maintain the empire's glory and highlight the remnants of the Empire. However, the United States did not hesitate to attack, to obtain creditors and cut off the supplies of funds and even threatened to sell the British pound, and forced Britain to withdraw its troops. Therefore, it can be seen from the above that the United States wanted to keep her world leader position all the time.

Since the Soviet Union was established, the socialist system has greatly liberated and developed the productive forces of the Soviet Union. The economic strength of Soviet Union was No.2 in the world by 1938. The United States was No.1 at that time. As a result, the instinct to maintain the world leader position began to work again! Economically, the strategic goods were refused to be delivered to the Soviet Union since 1948. What is more, the arms races and national conflicts were also the tactics that the United States adapted. At that time, President Reagan's economic adviser said: "We should keep armaments at a prominent level so that Moscow will not be able to catch up with us. At the same time, we will stop supplying what they need to survive. The "Star Wars" plan proposed by the United States dragged down the Soviet Union eventually. After the Soviet Union disintegrated, the Cold War between the United States and the Soviet Union was then over.

For Japan, the former world second largest economy, the United States loves and hates her. "Love" is referring to that the United States wants to use Japan as a "pawn" in her Asian policy. "Hate" is referring to the fear that Japan's wings will be hard on that day and thus Japan will not listen to the U.S. any more, and when the time comes, the United States will end up badly. In the late 1960s, Japan became the world's second-largest economic power. From the 1970s to the 1980s, the economic competition between the United States and Japan was extremely fierce. The famous "Plaza Accord" was an iron-clad fact (Li and Cui, 2016). In September 1985, the United States invited the finance ministers of Japan, the Federal Republic of Germany, Britain, and the Central Bank of France to hold a meeting at the Plaza Hotel in New York.

Based on an overestimation of Japan's economic strength and the special relationship between the Japan-US military alliance, Japan agreed intervene in the foreign exchange market and make the Yen appreciate substantially. Undoubtedly, the United States used this fact to cope with Japan's trade deficit. The depreciation of the US dollar against the Japanese Yen solved the problem of the US's huge trade deficit effectively. Moreover, who would dare to say that there was no relationship between Japan's late bubble economy and the Plaza Accord? The Japanese economy has fallen into a recession, and the United States' attitude toward Japan has only eased a little. It seemed relieved. Let us look at the current Sino-U.S. economic relations, it is such a coincidence that the U.S. has begun to want the RMB to appreciate and join the other countries in putting pressure on the Chinese government.

The high-sounding "democratic" banner

In recent years, the United States has frequently used so-called "democracy" and "human rights" to extract economic and political interests constantly from China and other Asian and African countries. The strategy of "promoting democracy" has become an important part of the global strategy of the United States after the Cold War. Regarding the high-sounding "democracy" flag promulgated by the United States, other countries have no choice but to fight back. Now, the United States is going to contain and postpone China through the so-called "democracy" and "human rights" once again.

The strategy of "promoting democracy" is an important part of the United States' global strategy after the Cold War. The Bush administration regarded "promoting democracy" as an important way to realize the new international order under US leadership; the Clinton administration regarded "promoting democracy" as one of the three pillars of the U.S. global strategies, along with maintaining security and expanding economic growth (Liu, 2009). Even if the current Obama administration downplays the strategy of "promoting democracy," ostensibly, it is only a plan to slow down and is not the ultimate strategic choice.

Basically, every president will have a massive foreign war during his reign. Let us look at the so-called "human rights defense" bloody war launched by the United States under the high-sounding "democracy" banner. Let us look at the Gulf War. During the period from August 2, 1990 to February 28, 1991, there was a time between the multinational forces composed of 34 countries headed by the United States and Iraq during the period when President Bush served as President of the United States (1989-1993). This is the so-called Gulf War. The fuse was that the Iraqi troops invaded Kuwait on August 2, 1990, overthrew the Kuwaiti government, and announced the annexation of Kuwait. Of course, it was undeniable that Iraq's invasion was in violation of international norms and was inhumane, and it was bound to be widely condemned by the international community. However, the U.S. sanctions imposed on Iraq for more than a decade to control Iraq's oil exports. What the United States wanted is the rich oil resources in the Middle East. Once the Iraqi army expanded, it will undoubtedly challenge the global strategy of the United States. The United States then used the banner of "democracy" and "humanity," but it was doing non-democratic and inhuman activities. This made it unreasonable for the Iraqi people, who were implicated in no way!

Let us look at the NATO air strike against Yugoslavia. From March 24 to June 10 of the year 1999, when Clinton served as president of the United States (1993-2001), NATO forces headed by the US armed forces intervened in the Kosovo issue and imposed a large-scale air force joint air strike against Yugoslavia. This was a typical local war under the condition of informatization, and it was also the first time in history that an air strike has been used to achieve the purpose of war (Hua, 2010). The excuse for war was an ethnic conflict within the Federal Republic of Yugoslavia. The United States launched such an air strike with the name of "democracy." The scene of the war seen by the People's Daily reporter was even more bloody and tragic. On the tractor that was struck, the driver was burned into coke, and the deceased's stump arm was hung in the carriage and was recognizable from several vehicles. The bodies of the dead can be seen to be mostly women, children and the elderly. On highways and fields, there are blown-up daily necessities, bedding, books, and photographs. Looking ahead, we can see that the site of the explosion is an undeveloped area with no buildings around it. NATO is obviously aiming at massacring civilians. The so-called "accidentally injure" is totally untenable (Lv, 1999). Now you see, where is the "democracy" and the "human rights"?

Let us analyze the war on the invasion of Afghanistan. On October 7, 2001, that is, after the September 11th incident. At the time when George W. Bush served as President of the United States (2001-2009), the United States used forces to implement her Asia-Pacific strategy under the pretext of fighting terrorism. There was an exaggerated name for this war: "persistent freedom." With the evolution of the war, there were more and more analysts who awaken from the dream. They thought that Afghanistan was evidence of "from the failure to the fear" and this war was launched by the United States. It was difficult to disapprove of this evidence because there was no way to protect President Bush and his speech. Bush had said that "war has opened the way for Afghanistan to peace and democracy." (Gala, 2006) It was also "peace" and "democracy!" But now, look at the status in Afghanistan. Are people rich? Is it democracy?

Let us analyze the U.S. war on Iraq. From March 20, 2003 to August 2010, there were two presidents during this period. This can also be the "chicken ribs" that President Bush "left" to the President Obama. Some people say that the Iraq war was the "second Gulf war", but Iraq was a war that should not have happened. The main reason for this war in Iraq launched by the United States, Britain, and other countries was that it accused Iraq of concealing weapons of mass destruction and secretly supporting terrorism. However, this accusation has not been accepted by the international community. What is ridiculous is that the United States did not find the legendary "weapons of mass destruction" in Iraq. It just entered Baghdad under the banner of "human rights" and "democracy," and did not bring the Iraqi people with them.

The newly appointed Trump administration promulgated the "Muslim ban" at the beginning of his administration. There are seven countries that affected by the ban – Iran, Sudan, Syria, Libya, Somalia, Yemen and Iraq (Qing, 2017). On the same day, German Chancellor Angela Merkel expressed his worries and doubts about the "Muslim ban" in the United States, arguing that this approach is not conducive to global counter-terrorism. Merkel said: "We must fight against terrorism resolutely. But that does not mean that we can doubt the entire community that has a certain belief. The United States is currently skeptical about Muslim groups, or citizens from specific countries. The first decision violated the principles of the international community in aiding refugees and violated the principle of international cooperation. The US's "democracy" and "human rights" are based on the "Urban supremacy," and it is customary to "democratic" slogan, pursuing the maximization of self-interest. From Trump's words and deeds, he can realize his strong attitude towards North Korea. The North's military sanctions may have been secretly prepared by the United States. In recent years, the two US strategic bombers' actions against North Korea may be the most straightforward proof that the United States has been waiting for the best time to send troops to North Korea to complete her battle under the name of "defend democracy".

If we really want to sort out the "different minds" of the United States, there will be lots of books we can write. It is rather dramatic that the United States has always claimed to be the country that understands democracy most and understands human rights most. However, it even happened to have an unexpected Occupy Wall Street movement. The American people could not tolerate the huge social contrast and they all went take a statement on the street and ask the U.S. government to give them a justice! The system that Americans once took pride in fooled them. The democracy that the United States claims has failed at its own door. Democracy has become the democracy of the rich, and the ordinary people have become victims of this kind of democratic system (Zhou,

2012). Their own systems are full of loopholes, and they are trying to impose this system on other countries! As China, which is now regarded as a "thorn in the eye" by the United States, the Chinese people must be highly vigilant against the true interests of "pseudo-democracy".

The harmfulness of Foreign Media

Of course, we are not opposed to foreign media reporting truthfully on China's negative news. If it is real and reliable, we should be pleased to accept it and strive to improve it. With the expansion of the media, the power of the media has also become more and more powerful. However, if this powerful and credible platform is turned into a battlefield for crowds and fights, it should not be. Sometimes the media will unreasonably exaggerate many facts to attract the public's attention. If there are many hypotheses, it will be accepted by the public.

The concept of "demonizing China" was first proposed in the book "Behind Demonizing China" co-authored by Xinhua News Agency reporter Li Xiguang and others in 1996. At that time, it was an anti-China wave set against the United States, while some Americans media took the opportunity to make a big fuss and broadcast many negative reports that were detrimental to China's national image (Guo, 2012). "Demonization" does not mean "negative" but it means "defamation." From this, we can know the intention of "demonization".

Western media added emotion habitually to the negative reports of China, either by far-fetched explanations or deliberately distort the facts and commit evil intentions. From August to September 2007, the world's largest toy manufacturer, Mattel Inc. announced three recalls of toys made in China because the lead in the paints of toys exceeded the standard. The incident was immediately rendered by foreign media and public opinion and directed at Chinese toy manufacturers. It is clear to those who understand the inside story, on August 27th, the director of the General Administration of Quality Supervision, Inspection and Quarantine of China told the world that 85% of the 20 million Chinese toys recalled by Mattel were produced according to the requirements of the United States. The problem lies in the design. Non-manufacturing.

The close negative reports from the US media have already passed a message to consumers: There is a problem with the quality of Chinese toys(Wang,2007). On September 21 of the same year, the fact that Mattel Corp apologized to China on this incident demonstrated the malicious rendering of the Western media on this incident.

In fact, the apologies should not only have made by the United States and Thailand companies, it should also be made by the United States media! After the "March 14th" incident happened in Lhasa in China that caused serious riots, the Western mainstream media such as CNN and BBC adopted "military repression" or "armed control" vocabulary reported immediately. To cooperate with the report, they also selected some photos for publication carefully (Wang, 2007). These false reports have aroused strong indignation from the Chinese people. The scrapped pictures were ignored by news facts and hurt the feelings of the Chinese people. Their intentions are sinister and well known. In addition, Western media have frequently flooded China with food safety issues, environmental pollution, and human rights issues. These acts of foreign media are a true portrayal of foreign anti-China forces. They do not want China to be strong enough to threaten its rule, especially threatening them to continue to advocate and believe in the capitalist system. To put it plainly, the media is also serving the political system.

China threat theory?

If the responsibility of misrepresentation in foreign media is to be pursued, the American media should be blamed certainly. Why does the United States hate China so much? Need to rely on the power of the media extensively to exert unwarranted pressure on China? In fact, from the point of view of the "China threat theory" that the United States has always advocated, these problems will become very clear.

The "China threat theory" can be known from Wikipedia. "It is a recourse to containment of China in international relations. China's economic rise after reform and opening has become an influential power in the international community. The expansion of armaments, especially the joint maritime defense capability of the Hainan Air Force in the East

China Sea and the South China Sea, has caused worries and doubts in relevant countries." Visibly, it is a public opinion weapon and psychological tactics fabricated by Western countries to contain China's development and has strong negative influences.

In fact, the "China threat theory" has a long history. It can be traced back to the middle of the 19th century. This period can also be considered as the first stage of the development of the "China threat theory." During this period, based on the needs of colonialism and imperialism, Western powers began to colonize overseas frantically under the drive of capitalism, and at the same time they began the earliest advocacy of the "China threat theory." To the second stage, from the middle of the 20th century to the 1990s. At this stage, the Chinese nation has struggled for a hundred years. Under the leadership of the Communist Party of China, it overthrew the external oppression of colonialism and imperialism eventually, won national liberation and independence, and established a socialist system. The Western world is based on ideological considerations. They promote the "China threat theory" greatly. At that time, the Western camp led by the United States hatred the Red regime. So, it blocked the new regime completely (China Youth Daily, 2012).

The third stage was happened after the Cold War. The "China threat theory" proclaimed by the United States has occurred from time to time, and there were many names. There were "ideological threat theory," "civilization threat theory," "military threat theory," and "economic threat theory. "And" ecological threat theory "and so on. Among them, "economic threat theory" is the main argument (Li, 2008). At first glance, the first phase seems to involve economic "threat" and the second phase is more of a political "threat". At this stage, it seems that it has returned to the economic "threat". In fact, the economics and politics have no clear boundaries. Especially for complex international relations, every economic nerve touches the sensitive nerves of politics. At the same time, every political change has profoundly affected the rapid development of the economy.

In the face of the tumultuous "China threat theory," one might ask: why is the "China threat theory" so deeply rooted in the American concept. Why does the United States turn a blind eye to China's unremitting efforts to integrate into the international community over the years? What is the true intention of the "China threat theory" that the United States has repeatedly advocated? (Zhang,2011) You can think of the answers to these questions as "institutional" differences or "ideological" differences, but all problems boil down to one point: the difference in interest! This is the so-called "no eternal friends, no eternal enemies, only eternal interests!" Of course, the Sino-US relations cannot be exempt. From this perspective, the "China threat theory" is essentially the "results of the concrete interest estimation and appeal" of the United States. It is "a US policy approach" and is a tool for the United States to safeguard its political, economic, and security interests (Zhu, 2005).

It can be seen from the above that if there is a dispute between the United States and China, then the United States will not stop her advocacy of the "China threat theory". To this end, China must face it calmly. The reason why the above-mentioned situations occur is mainly due to the strong reluctance to see the weak grow stronger gradually, and vested interests do not want to see the relative decline in the long-term political, economic, and technological advantages, so they complain and dissatisfaction, even "demonizing" China, just for their own interests (You, 2011). In the face of interests, there is no absolute right or wrong. Therefore, China has nothing wrong with this behavior of the United States.

As a matter of fact, the United States has made a big mistake in defending her position as the world leader. She always points the finger of the problem to other countries without thinking of herself! As everyone knows, the two major powers of China and the United States can only strengthen cooperation and common development in the competition. Any attempt to suppress China from the outside will not succeed. The biggest threat and challenge to the United States are not from China or other external powers, but from the political, economic, and social issues that are plagued by domestic conflicts (including ridiculously high fiscal deficits and debts, unending bipartisan disputes, and extremely severe poverty. Rich polarization and excessive overseas expansion, etc.) The United States can only avoid decline if she solves her problems one by one (Jiang, 2012).

The United States continues to grow

The United States is a belligerent nation, so it is aware of the truth that "backwards must be beaten." In terms of economy, in addition to using the power of the United Nations, the United States is relying more on the shock of her own power to gain world discourse. In front of the fact that China's economy is getting stronger, how can the United States be willing to see her world leader position fall from her hands? Therefore, in addition to relying on external forces to suppress potential adversaries, the United States is also secretly trying to seek self-development and expansion in the struggle!

Although the U.S. economy was hit hard during the global financial crisis, many evidences have shown that the U.S. economy is gradually recovering. In January 2012, the latest data released by the US Bureau of Economic Analysis (BEA) showed that in the fourth quarter of 2011, the US economy achieved a growth rate of 2.8% (annualized rate), which was the largest increase since the last year and a half (Shu, 2012). The recovery of the U.S. economy has a few major motives. (1) Consumption keeps growing. The three major carriages of economy: consumption, investment, and export. Among them, consumption is the most important part of stimulating domestic demand. Therefore, if the U.S. economy wants to recover, it must start with consumption. (2) Production keeps expanding. Naturally there is a need to have supply relative to it. Otherwise, the so-called demand is only a "potential" demand, and it cannot produce any substantial economic effect. According to a report from the American Institute for Supply Management (ISM), in January 2012, the U.S. manufacturing industry experienced the fastest growth rate in seven months; the non-manufacturing activity index also climbed from 53 to 56.8. (3) The employment market has stabilized. Due to the impact of the financial crisis, the United States' unemployed army has become a major headache for the government. Only when the people have jobs can we guarantee social stability (Ma, 2018).

Therefore, the necessary policies for stimulating employment can provide immediate relief. The economic chain is like one link, employment, demand, supply, etc., are all on the same chain, and the joint action of all factors can bring about the continued prosperity of the United States economy. Perhaps the above-mentioned three points cannot fully play their role in the United States after the financial crisis. They may even encounter difficulties. However, the United States is still the world most powerful economy. This is unmatched by any other country. The three major advantages are: Firstly, the foundation is good and the family is strong. From 1890, the total economic output of the United States surpassed that of Germany and ranked first in the world. It has now been 122 years. Secondly, there are many R&D investments, strong innovation capabilities, and high labor productivity. Thirdly, the use of the U.S. dollar as an international currency has helped the United States to pass on the economic crisis and the debt crisis effectively.

Judging from the historical financial crisis and macro-policy response, the developed countries, especially the United States, as the major reserve currency issuing country, she has not only the possibility and motivation to defuse the crisis through inflation, but also has successful historical experience (Wang and Zhou, 2012). In summary, under the premise of making effective use of the three major advantages of the U.S. economy, the three major forces of U.S. economic development will work smoothly. Therefore, the U.S. economy's improvement is only a matter of time. Do not underestimate the status of the United States, at least for now, she will not fall!

Overall, although the momentum of China's economic development is strong, the US will not let China become the No.1. However, the United States may not be so hostile to China. At least, from the perspective of the "China threat theory" to the "China responsibility theory," this has fully demonstrated the willingness and attitude of the United States to try to cooperate (Zhang, 2012). Although the "China Responsibility Theory" is also a "heavy burden" imposed on China by ulterior motives, the essence of the United States' "China Responsibility Theory" is to use the American model to shape China and demand that China cooperate with the United States. To safeguard the international system led by the United States jointly.

Chapter 15

So What if not Acting as the World Leader?

The pain of being the world leader, the tiredness of being the world leader, these are always widely known. However, while the world leader is infinitely scenic, there are also "second philosophies", that is, not being the first, not being the third, but being the second. In political history, this coincides with Deng Xiaoping's policy of "hiding your position and keeping yourself up and making a difference." This is a manifestation of China's foreign policy of not seeking hegemony and urging you to stay ahead (Tang, 2017). It must be admitted that to be the No.2 is inevitably embarrassed, there will be many benefits, but at the same time there will also be many conflicts. As far as China's current state of development is concerned, to be the world leader is still not qualified. So, what will happen to China in the coming period, even if she does not want to become the world leader?

From the long history of China, her policies are not to be promoted to be the world leader. China was forced to fight. However, the Chinese nation can still resist all foreign aggressors with strong national cohesion. So, China will be the victorious finally. China is moving forward steadily! When China defeated the aggressors again and again and cleared the internal troubles, China discovered her own flaws and China knew that it was a difficult and prolonged process to move forward with the world. Looking at today, when China achieved a little achievement, China was just arrogant and she could not be overwhelmed.

The U.S. history during the past few years has clearly demonstrated to us that it is not easy for acting as the world leader. Before the Second World War, the United States pursued "isolationism," meaning that she did not participate in world affairs, and she was only at ease with her own national strength. After the end of World War II, the U.S. economy and military were all in the world's leading position. At the same time, because of the Bretton Woods monetary system, the US dollar and gold-based financial exchange standard system was established and established firmly (Qiu and Zhao, 2017). For a long time, this monopoly of the U.S. dollar has "reasonably" provided the U.S. with a steady stream of financial support, making it very easy for the U.S. to obtain huge economic benefits. However, behind this huge economic interest, the United States must invest huge other forces to maintain her position as a world leader. The famous "Triffin dilemma" may illustrate such issues well.

In 1960, Professor John Terry from the Yale University in the United States pointed out that the Bretton Woods system is based on a country's currency as the main international reserve currency. In the case of stagnant gold production, the supply of international reserves depends on the balance of payments in the United States entirely: If the balance of payments in the United States remains positive, the international reserve assets will not meet the needs of international trade development; if the balance of payments in the United States remains in deficit, there will be an excess of international reserve assets. The crisis threatens the international monetary system. The dilemma lays the foundation for the collapse of the Bretton Woods system. In order to maintain her position as a world leader, the subprime mortgage crisis in the United States seems to be confirming that the world leader is overburdened (Triffin, 1997)!

China cannot be the world leader

When the countries all over the world are clamoring that China will soon become the world leader soon, apart from some people who have already been "victorious" and have taken it for granted that the world belongs to China's nationals, the other is totally different from this. The voice also appeared at the same time. The Chinese people began to think, and very calmly or even firmly believe that: China cannot be the world leader! Then, what are the fatal problems in China that will make China be difficult to become the world leader?

In fact, in the face of various praises from the other countries and the media, it is not surprising that the Chinese are starting to get turbulent.

In China, most of the Chinese people see a prosperous scene of prosperity. No matter what the occasion, people talk about achievements first and talk about problems later. The achievements are described very widely and heavily, while the problems are always understated, sometimes even people feel a bit of cliché. In China, there is really no such thing as a so-called positive assessment. What is missing is self-criticism. When talking about this, the Chinese people must remember why Premier Zhou Enlai was so respected by the people. Premier Zhou's personal charisma must be a great cause. Among them, Premier Zhou always takes the lead in putting forward his own questions, criticizing and self-criticizing when he starts making statements at every meeting. In this regard, everyone need to act as the "Premier Zhou," especially those officials who need to make decisions for the people. If this can be done, it will be obvious that those ugly incidents of embezzlement and bribery will vanish naturally.

Moreover, the power of the ordinary Chinese people's speech is always "being blocked." This involves the institutional problems. China's democratic centralism was originally a very good one. However, in the implementation process, it looks different. In terms of votes, the voters who had the rights to vote could use the ballots in their hands to reflect the will of the nation, but there are some "black-box operations." For example, if the name of a candidate is announced to the public in advance, others will avoid talking and only let the people fill in the name of the person. This kind of thing is common in China. Therefore, netizens began to show their own "alternative votes" and stated that they were "represented" to use the right to vote jokingly. If such problems cannot be properly resolved, even if China will realize the direct elections for the entire people one day, it is still not a real election.

In addition, even if China has surpassed Japan and become the world's second-largest economy, China's economic development remains problematic. In a public opinion survey, for the question of who is the world's number one economic power, only 43% of the Americans thought that it is China, those who hold opposing views occupies 38%. Only the Chinese themselves are particularly "quiet": In the survey, only

6% of Chinese respondents believe that China has replaced the U.S. position, which is the lowest among all the countries visited (Huang, 2012). Because the Chinese economy cannot grow indefinitely at an annual rate of 8% to 10%, and not to mention the true level represented by this figure, China also faces a dreadful population with environmental issues. In terms of energy consumption, China's dependence on energy consumption is still dominated by coal resources, while clean stone, natural gas, etc., have not been popularized due to excessive cost. In addition, the large population base of China provides the living needs of 130 to 400 million people. The amount of consumption involved is also huge. This demographic advantage may bring about positive effects such as economic growth and the expansion of domestic demand, but it is not hard to imagine the negative effects that come with it. How to deal with domestic garbage and industrial waste? Where does the resource come from? How can we insist on not harming the sustainable development of future generations? How to solve the clothing, food, housing, transportation and employment problems of so many people? In addition to developing new energy sources, using innovative technologies, and reforming the new system, China has no choice.

In addition to the various questions about China's internal environment, China's external environment is also very complicated. There are different degrees of territorial disputes between China and too many countries. China's territorial disputes with countries such as Russia, Japan, Vietnam, the Philippines, Brunei, and India have come to an end (Gong, 2012). To keep quiet, most of the time China is compromising, so China has "shelving controversy and common development". Is not that how you break your teeth? The Chinese people know that "shelving the disputes" does not mean that the disputes have been resolved. Sooner or later, these disputes will "jump out" themselves, but the timing of "jumping out" will vary according to different "people".

Gross economic growth is not everything

What China has always emphasized is that China has surpassed Japan and become the second largest economy in the world in terms of total economic output. Please note that it is the total economic output! One of these words cannot be ignored. The first is the economy, which means that in science, technology, military, education, and other fields, the distance between China and the world current leader is far more than a "separation". The second is the total amount, which means that in such a populous country as China, there will be no more gross increase, and once it is apportioned, it will become "not enough for outsiders".

Let us first talk about economic issues. More and more public opinions, including textbooks, have emphasized that the world situation of the single-level hegemonic countries in the United States has changed or will eventually change. In contrast, the forces of the third world countries, such as China, are gradually increasing. The BRIC countries, etc., are even the "BRIC Four Countries" (now known collectively as the "BRIC countries") that have been extended through South Africa. The world is moving toward multipolarity, although this process may be very long. In the growing process of the Third World, China will inevitably become a topical country. As mentioned earlier, more and more remarks have been made that China will surpass the United States as another world power that can compete with the United States. However, facts have proven that although China is now a big country and is the second largest economy in the world, her political status in the world has also improved, but China is still far worse than the United States.

Because China is only an economic country, it is not an economic power. Moreover, China's political and military strength is still far from the United States. In addition, even in the economic aspect that China herself is proud of, there are potential hazards of losing economic advantages. Therefore, although China's current economic development momentum is good, it is mostly the result of cheap labor. Several years later, because of China's family planning and rising labor costs in China, the number of young laborers that will follow it will become smaller and the aging will become more and more serious. This will inevitably increase the pressure of rising labor costs. By that time, the most favorable conditions for China's rapid economic development have disappeared. What else do we have to support the development of the entire national economy? What is it like to compete with the United States? What is more important is the need for political and military strength to provide strong protection. Only by doing so can China have the hope to become the world leader (Zhang, Chang and Xu, 2016).

Let us talk about the issue about the total amount of economy. This issue may have been involved, but even so, there is still a need to revisit the issue of total volume. Perhaps in the less populous world, where the largest economic aggregate is, it also represents the nation's wealthiest people, but in a populous country such as China and India, this is far from the case. The total amount of money can represent many apart from the most obvious national income, which means that per capita income may not be appreciable, the total product represents a possible lack of supply; the total employment represents a large gap in the job ... and the most important potential meaning represented by the economic aggregate. The gap between the rich and the poor in China is getting bigger and bigger. The poor are too poor and the rich are too rich. The middle class with the most purchasing power is not yet formed. This is a very embarrassing situation. Obviously, if you only feel complacent about the increase in the total economic output, you must be too silly.

The Chinese people have the final say

"The duck knows first when the river becomes warm in spring." Whether a country is strong enough to take on the responsibility of being the world leader. The people in this country are the ones who have the rights to speak.

There is a widespread belief that it is not China that has survived the financial crisis but that China has helped the Americans survive the financial crisis! In other words, from this perspective, China is qualified to become the world leader. At least when the United States encounter crises, only China can aid. However, China is not really making progress, but also depends on the lives of most ordinary people. This is the vision that a true world power should have. It is also what China has been pursuing and working hard for.

It is true that China's economic aggregate can now be said to be very large, but it only represents "fast" growth, it does not mean that people's lives are prosperous. For the common people, the true sense of well-being comes from real personal experience, such as per capita income, per capita purchasing power, social equity and social harmony. The increase in total economic output may be due to input and output in infrastructure with a relatively large share. For example, electricity, water power, and street lighting public utilities mainly focus on GDP, which affects the actual purchasing power of the common people. For the happiness of the common people, these are all "returns without success".

When talking about happiness, one should think of the CCTV happiness survey that has received so much attention recently. The specific situation is that in the 2012 Mid-Autumn National Day holiday, in order to welcome the convocation of the 18th National Congress, CCTV has not been idle, and the "happiness survey" is in full swing. In this major grassroots survey, CCTV reporters targeted ordinary people and asked questions about "are you happy?". To everyone's surprise, everyone began to talk about the "weird replies" to ordinary people. For example, when a working man faced this problem, he replied, "I am happy and not happy." Another helpless worker said, "This is too complicated." It is ridiculous that an 18-year-old university student queuing up to buy a train ticket complained in an interview that "please line up in order." For such "weird replies", how will the national leaders feel?

For us, these answers are undoubtedly the expression of true feelings. They are real people's livelihoods, but they may not have reached the intentions of those who planned the investigation. Happiness is not as abstract as what people think. It is subjective. It should be real and determined by objective living conditions. In terms of actual purchasing power, the size of the total economy does not mean that people have very strong purchasing power. The common concern of ordinary people is whether the demand for basic consumer goods can be met. These consumer goods will play a key role in the future market demand and the stability of future economic development. Of course, this is a problem that must be paid attention to in stimulating domestic demand (Bai, 2015).

Imagine that if China's GDP only grows at a rate of 8% or 9%, then the Chinese people will feel that the benefits of growth will be very small. A very important economic reason is the structure of wealth in the private sector. We all know that for any family, the income that can be spent each year should include two parts: the first part is the labor income and wage income; the second part is the income of asset wealth appreciation. In the United States, the rate of general asset growth is rising at about twice the rate of GDP. However, only ordinary people enjoy the income from labor, and the channel for asset income is basically blocked. The long-term downturn of the stock market is a very serious problem of poor investment channels. Therefore, for individuals and families, the rise in wages is the main channel for sharing economic growth. However, what the people think is often not what officials think. The rising wages cannot catch up with the price increase.

Why so? This is because as officials themselves, they will generally spend the wealth represented by these economic aggregates on projects that they can see and feel, and these are often characteristics of infrastructure and large industrial facilities. In contrast, if officials spend money on invisible, intangible education and medical care, the people can feel it, but others cannot see it, and the leaders at the next level cannot see it. Obviously, officials will think for themselves. If this is not good for their next promotion, they will certainly not do so. When a foreigner comes to visit, he will not say that "the changes you bring during the mayor's business are really big." So, everyone's goal is to see the "image project."

However, a society's growth always depends on continuous investment and reinvestment, and consumption cannot keep up. It may be a few years, but it will continue to rely on this model for a long time. Under the current state-owned arrangement, under the taxation power and structure, China's GDP has grown at a rapid rate, but the ordinary people do not feel the benefits corresponding to the rate of GDP growth (Chen, 2008). Therefore, many things should find reasons from the root, such as why domestic demand is insufficient? Why do people feel that they are happy in the eyes of their hearts, but instead they have various questions and answers?

The pace of advance cannot stop

If China does not want to be the world leader, what will happen to the world? What will happen to China? In fact, the answer is: The world is still the world, and China cannot be China any more. Because, if China is not going to be the world leader, it is not so important to most people. What is important is that when the wrong leader is coming, the pace of progress of the country cannot be stopped, nor can one of the problems that need to be resolved be ignored. In this way, the position of the world leader will be a matter of course, rather than "an uncrowned king", which will be criticized by the world.

In the process of rapid economic development in China, the problems exposed are increasingly prominent, such as environmental issues that China often refers to. Despite the environmental problems, high pollution is not unfamiliar to everyone. However, what are the hazards caused by pollution? How serious is it? It is often easily overlooked by the Chinese people. On June 12, 2008, the Pearl River Delta Air Pollution Prevention Summit Forum was held in Guangzhou. Zhong Nanshan, academician of the Chinese Academy of Engineering, pointed out at the forum: " The lungs of those Guangzhou people over the age of 50 are all black!" According to statistics from clinical and surgical methods, he found that the lungs of Guangzhou residents had been lost due to the inhalation of enormous amounts of pollutants into the lungs. The self-purification ability was threatened. "Whether sick or ill, Guangzhou people over 50 years of age are black." (Shi, 2009) It can be seen how great the environmental damage is to people's health! The environmental issues are urgent, it is everyone's responsibility to protect the environment. There are many things that the Chinese people need to do to address environmental issues and achieve sustainable development. These are not the only things that can be resolved naturally after China becomes the world leader.

In addition, China's "gap" problem is also widespread. The gap between urban and rural areas, the gap between the rich and the poor, and regional disparities have made the Chinese people realize how important fairness issues are in China (Song, 2014). In the early years after the founding of the People's Republic of China, in the face of the devastated land in China, they have repeatedly stressed the issue of efficiency and emphasized that some people should be rich first. Today, the situation changes, people do allow some people and some regions to get rich first, but the first rich to bring about riches does not seem to be as smooth as expected. Even more so in the economy, some coastal developed cities have taken the lead in enjoying the diverse benefits of China's external development (Fu, 2010). If we simply compare China's developed regions such as Shanghai, Beijing, Hong Kong, and Macau with the developed countries, the economic disparity will obviously not be too great. If we want to discuss the level of culture and civilization, Hong Kong and Macao regions will have a special cultural and political background. It is also different from the Mainland, and these economic centers and political centers in the Mainland are only part of the vast land of China. None of them can fully represent China. In this regard, education and culture are particularly important. Spiritual food and material food are equally important to the people. In the next 100 years or even longer, China should focus on continuously investing heavily in strengthening education and cultural development. This is a top priority and concerns the grand cause of national rejuvenation.

Politically, China has her own advantages. China is a socialist country. China can concentrate her efforts on key issues. Similarly, in terms of culture, China has her own inherent advantages, but the advantages are not obvious at present and have not been transformed into other advantages, which has led to the overall development of the overall economy and society. In the military and economically, in other aspects of the national economy and the people's livelihood, it is obvious that China is at a disadvantage. The gap between China and the world is realistic, regardless of whether you are the wrong leader.

Defeat the rivals without comb is the best strategy

There is a saying in The Art of War by Sunzi: it is not the best soldier but the best soldier, if a soldier does not fight. In fact, the so-called "no war" is only a strategic choice, and China has never been a belligerent nation. The United States is not very happy to play the role of a world police officer. Of course, China would give both hands in favor (Wu, 2012).

China has not echoed the issue of the "two-nation group" that the United States once proposed, and it has not been very clear that this is a huge conspiracy. The so-called "two-nation group" (G2) refers to the cooperation between China and the United States and leads the world affairs jointly (Wang, 2008). The earliest proposed concept of the "G2" between China and the United States was Fred Bergsten, the director of the Peterson Institute for International Economics in the United States. Subsequently, the American economic historian Neil Ferguson also proposed a "new concept," namely, "Chimerica." Ferguson believes that China and the United States have now entered the "communism era": The United States is the world's largest consumer country, and China is the world's largest savings nation. The two sides are cooperative in the way that the United States is responsible for consumption and China is responsible for production. Whatever the "two-nation group" or the "central China," it means the same thing. However, in a developing country like China that insists on not forming an alliance with any country or group of countries and pursues an independent foreign policy of peace, the mainstream ideological community naturally disagrees with this claim. However, there are also some supporters who believe that the two countries' groups are a clever idea. It does not mean that China has been constrained.

From a broader international perspective, some experts and scholars believe that no country can use force to invade China, but China needs to go to the world to protect widely distributed national security and interests. This expansion is not aggression and does not infringe on the interests of other countries. It also protects world peace and stability. One example is China's escort fleet in the Red Sea. They are not a threat or even a threat to pirates unless they attack (Ding, 2010). While seeking to rise peacefully in China, the United States is not stupid, because once the "two-nation group" is formed, the United States can use its efforts to fight hard, and it is difficult to guarantee that China will not become an "executioner" of the United States. In addition to the need to strengthen vigilance against the "two-nation group" of China and the United States, China must guard against those who urge the United States and her allies to confront China and urge China to take on enormous international responsibilities. In short, in the face of world ranking competition, China can show weakness and are willing to show weakness. The world current leader is the United States. We are still far behind.

Although the general economic slowdown in the United States and other advanced economies does not mean that the U.S. as the world's number one power and her leading role in the current international economic and political order has undergone a disruptive change. Now, China should still demonstrate the fine traditional virtues of the Chinese nation, and it must not be insulted or threatened. Moreover, the developed countries led by the United States are still the dominant force in the world economy. They have advanced technology, abundant financial resources, and high-quality labor resources, and they have strong self-repair and adjustment capabilities. China wants to replace the United States, or want to Combat with the United States to co-manage the world order, this fundamental change in the world economic landscape will probably be a long-term and complicated process.

Let us look at the strategic transformation of the United States. President Obama rectified Bush's unilateralism policy in a very timely manner and made the United States achieve new results in consolidating the strategic relationship between traditional allies and expanding new allies. The U.S.-France-Germany-Japan strategic friendly relationship with the United States as the axis has been upgraded. The United States' diplomatic strategy of strength and China's non-alignment policy have caused China and Russia to lack sufficient strategic allies to change the unipolar political strategy dominated by the United States(Yan,2011).

Therefore, from the current situation, China's unilateral power cannot change anything. China can only do her own duty first.

China is a developing country. Apart from their hard-hitting strength in the economic, military, and political fields, the most important thing is to focus on the development of soft power. With regards to the development of ethnic culture, this kind of development strategy makes effective use of the development routines that allow others to avoid shortcomings. Therefore, China believe that for a developing country, the key to a strong country lies in a firm national spirit and a national culture that leads the world. The history of the United States is short but the United States advocates grasping the future. The American Hollywood movie culture is just the proof! The German spirit of Germany made its two defeats rise magically. Russia is a nation that rejects the golden mean of independence and self-reliance on the dream of an empire, but it is a pity that the population and geographical limits have constrained the realization of the ambitions of the great powers of Russia! Japan relies on the solidarity spirit of the Yamato nation. However, the culture of the glory of the Japanese nation is a double-edged sword that brings both a rapid prosperity and a catastrophic disaster to Japan. The history of Chinese culture is profound and it is completely capable of conquering the world. During the Tang Dynasty, the envoys of various countries came to Changan to worship. This is due to the value and charm of the Great China culture. Of course, this also requires strong military support.

The soldiers who did not fight for war and the "Second class philosophy" had equivalent results. As the saying goes, "without a step, without a thousand miles." The "Second class philosophy" is a realistic choice. The need for survival is also a wise move. When faced with an extremely unstable external environment, China needs the United States especially, that is, the world current leader. We all know that the United States has always been happy. To achieve the rise of the Chinese nation and realize the Chinese dream, China should secure the throne of the world leader at an early date. What China need is the power to defend her own authority in the future. Therefore, national defense construction is of utmost importance. At the close of the Nineteenth National Congress, Xi

Jinping proposed to adhere to the road of strengthening the Chinese army with characteristics, promote the modernization of national defense and the army comprehensively, adapt to the development trend of the new military revolution in the world and the needs of national security, improve the quality and efficiency of construction, and realize the Chinese dream (Yu, 2018).

Under the new situation, China can only adhere to the diplomatic line and principles and China must oppose hegemonism and power politics. International relations are also closely related to the strategies and tactics of various countries (Li, 2017). China must be good at keeping her talents under control, and make a difference under constant controversies. China must strive to grasp numerous opportunities for development, and at the same time. International strategy and foreign policy are not moved by outside rumors, try to make China invincible. Learning to be a No.2 is a business strategy. China should learn the valuable experience from the current world leader.

In short, development is an absolute truth! In the current China, the rich people are still only the in the initial stage. The Chinese people must be intelligent and honorable. They should treat people respectfully. With the growth of China's economy, culture, and military and other comprehensive national strength, international hostile forces will inevitably seek to disrupt international economic hegemonists. The existing international peace environment also has some factors that can be reversed. Therefore, the crisis of the international environment facing China is absolute and long-term. The vigilance in peacetime must not be relaxed. However, no matter how the hostile forces block it, China must continue to take the road of reform and peaceful development. All the Chinese people should be convinced that a peaceful and prosperous China will surely rise and will certainly make an important contribution to the global prosperity.

Bibliography

Bade, Robin, and Parkinne, Michael (2004). Principles of Microeconomics (2nd Edition). Beijing, PRC: Renmin University Press.

Bai, Baoli (2015). Our country has the guaranteed system of crossing the "middle income trap". People's Daily, October 14, 2015.

Balifskaya, Na, Ye (2006). Institutional Theory of Educational Reform: China's experience and Enlightenment: reading the Theory of Chinese Educational system. Educational Research, 2006(4): 94-95.

Bao, Erwen, Jiang Yaping (2003). From the Gulf War to the War of Iraq War, J. J. Ring, July 2003.

Blair, Kevin, (2010), Gavin Blairn on China's economy ranks second in the world: How does Japan view it? American Christian Science Monitor, August 17, 2010.

Bo, Yang (2008). Ugly Chinese. Beijing, PRC: People's Literature Press.

Brantly, Womack (2007). United States and China' s Rise: Parity and the Mohe of Civilizations. Foreign Affairs Review, 2007(6):16-25.

Cai, Fang (2016). How does China give impetus to global economic growth? The People's Congress of China, 2016(21):13-13.

Cai, Jiangnan (2008). Strengthen ourselves, no one can knock us down. Jiefang Daily, April 22, 2008.

Cao, Zheng (2016). Misunderstanding of Democracy: Comments by Foreign Scholars on China's Authoritarianism. Reform & Openning. 453(24):39-42.

Center for Defense Policy Research, Academy of military Sciences (2012). Take it easy to deal with the "China threat." China Youth Daily, April 06, 2012.

Cha, Zheng (2015). Study on the sustainable development of China's economy under the new normal state. Economic & Trade Practice. 2015(15):6-7.

Chang, Zheng (2017). The rise of China is different from the United States and Japan. Leadership Science, 2017(29):61-64.

Chen, Baosen (2000). The two-sided international trade of the "new economy" in the United States. International Trade, 2000(7): 32-35.

Chen, Changsheng (2007). The Chinese government's public service: Institutional change and regional comprehensive assessment. Beijing, PRC: China Social Sciences Press.

Chen, Jian (2012). Diplomacy: make the world harmonious. Beijing, PRC: Renmin University of China Press.

Chen, Jiangsheng (2014). Chinese strategic issues should be studied after becoming the second largest economic entity in the world. Studies on Mao Zedong and Deng Xiaoping Theories, 2014(10):45-46.

Chen, Jun (2010). An analysis of the advantages and disadvantages of economic globalization. Journal of International Trade. 2010(8):70-73.

Chen, Shiyang (2010). Who are making it hot topic on Chinese economies as the second. Beijing Physical Education University Newspaper. December 30, 2010.

Chen, Weiying (2012). Double reverse or devastated global PV market, experts suggest making the worst plans. China Enterprise News. 2012-08-30.

Chen, Wenling, Ren, Haiping (2015). The adjustment and influence of the global strategy in the United States. Globalization, 2015(2):78-92.

Chen, Xiangyang (2004). The national traditional strategic and cultural resources of China's peaceful rise in the 21st Century. Journal of Jiangnan Institute of Social Sciences, 2004 (4).

Cheng, Shi (2005). "pendulum" trade policy under American economic hegemonism. China Business Newspaper, August 7, 2005.

Cheng, Weili (2017). Cooperation is still the main theme of economic relations between China and the United States. Outlook Weekly. 2017(15):29-29.

Chu, Xiaohui (2018). Trade frictions between China and the United States are escalating! Why did China choose to fight back in the middle of the night in April 1st? Sina News, April 2, 2018.

Cover Article (2008). American national talent strategy. Global Finance, Aug. 29, 2008.

Dai, Xu (2009). C Shaped Enclosure: China Breakthrough under Internal and External Troubles. Shanghai, PRC: Wen Hui Publishing House.

Deng, Bangfeng (2013). Analysis of the Reason and Result of the Policy of " closed door state " in Qing Dynasty of China. Technology Management. 2013(14):68-69.

Deng, Xiaoping (1993). Address to the third plenary meeting of the Central Advisory Board. Selected Works of Deng Xiaoping, Vol. 3:87, Beijing, PRC: People's Publishing House.

Deng, Yunte (1937). The History of Disaster Relief in China, Shanghai, China: The Commercial Press.

Ding, Li (2010). Is China being surrounded? Economic Observer, September 21, 2010.

Ding, Li (2010). Is China besieged? Economic Observer Newspaper, September 18, 2010.

Du, Zhigang (2011). Is Japanese-US relations really rocking solid? The Northeast Forum, 2011(12): 012.

Fan, Hao (2018). Cultural consciousness and confidence of modern Chinese ethics and morality. Journal of Southeast University (Philosophy and Social Science), 2018(01):5-14+146.

Fan, Hengshan (2017). The important characteristics of the relationship between China and the world in the new era. Leadership Science, 2017(24):21-21.

Fang, Tie (2000). The Reasons for the Song Court to Take the Dali Kingdom as its Vassal State and its Policy of Control Through Conciliation. Journal of the Central University for Nationalities. (06):47-51.

Feng, Wuyong (2008). North Korea and Japan's relations have turned around. Beijing Youth Daily, June 15, 2008.

Freud. Translated by Lin, Chen, Zhang, Huanmin, Chen Weiqi (2011). The Ego and the ID, Shanghai, China: Shanghai Transition Publishing House.

Fu, Xuan (2016). The study of revenue and corvee in Shanbei during the Ming dynasty. China, Yan'an: Yan'an University, 2016,27-33.

Fu, Yong (2010). Why didn't the rich former leads latter. West China Development, 2010(8):94-94.

Fukui Fumimasa (2010). The Thought and Religion of the Cultural Circle of Chinese Characters, Wuhan, China: Wuhan University Press.

Gallas, William (2006). The American invasion of Afghanistan caused a "long tragedy." Global Vision, October 8, 2006.

Gilpin, Robert (2007). War and Change in World Politics. Shanghai, PRC: Shanghai People's Publishing House.

Gong, Jianhua (2012). A study of the marine political strategy in the South China Sea --- China's action of South China Sea Dispute. Pacific Journal, 2012(3):75-87.

Gu, Lei (2012). On the peaceful rise of China. The rule of law and society, 2012(01):146-147.

Gu, Yumin (2004). Market economy is a double-edged sword. Liberation Daily, 11 December 2004.

Guang, Wen (2008). The World Bank Forecasts that the Size of China's Economy Exceeds the US in 2030. International Project Contracting & Labor Service. (4): 58-58.

Guo, Junwei (2012). How to treat western media as "demonizing" China. Young journalist, 2012 (3): 29-30.

Guo, Lijun (2011). Win-win situation between China and the world—Commentary on the 10th Anniversary of China 's Entry into the WTO. Guang Ming Daily. 2011-12-11.

Han, Yuhai (2011). Who wrote the history of 500 years: China and the World since 1500 (3rd Edition). Beijing, PRC: Jiuzhou Press, November 2011.

He, Lan (2005). China's Foreign Relations after the Cold War. Beijing, PRC: China Communication University Press.

He, Ru (2014). Study on cultural exchange between China and foreign countries in the Silk Road of the Tang Dynasty. Northwest Agriculture and Forestry University. 2014.

Heng, Zhanwei (2017). The study of national cultural genes should attach to the core concept. Journal of Historical Science, 2017(11):12-16.

Hou, Jie (2018). American higher education certification system and the enlightenment. Contemporary Education Science, 2018(01):90-94.

Hu, Jintao (2007). Upholding the Breat Banner of Socialism with Chinese Characteristics and Strive for a New Victory in Building a well-off Society in an all-round Way. Beijing, PRC: People's Publishing House.

Hu, Shi (1999). Ancient Chinese Philosophy. Hefei, PRC: Anhui Education Press.

Hua, Ji (2010). NATO airstrikes on Yugoslavia. PLA Daily, October 21, 2010.

Huang, Fangni (2012). Who imagines China as the world leader. Fragrant grass: Classic Reading, 2012 (04):42-43.

Huang, Junying (2017). The research and reference of American innovation and entrepreneurship policy. Science & Technology and Economy, 2017(1):31-35.

Huang, Tiannan (2009). Later Qing Dynasty decline from economic perspective. Market Forum, 2009(04): 9-10.

Ji, Baocheng (2006). The industrialization of education should be over. Southern Weekend. March 23, 2006

Ji, JinSan (2011). A study on the present situation and strategic countermeasures of regional economic development in Western China. World of Economics, 2011 (4).

Jiang, Lingfei (2005). American Global Strategy. Asian Tribune, Aug. 29, 2005.

Jiang, Xia. Containment of China is an impossible Mission: On Milles' theory of offensive realism and the theory of China threat. Journal of Hubei Institute of Administration, (2012)3: 38-4343.

Jiang, Yue (2015). Bronze Age: A book tells the civilization of three era. China, Beijing: Qunyan Press, 2015.

Jin, Puseng (2000). Sino-Japanese war of 1895 and China's foreign debt. South East Academic, 2000(1): 107-111.

Jin, Weixing (2006). The Versailles-Washington System and the Change of Chinese Diplomatic Policy. Journal of Soochow University (Philosophy and Social ScienceSocial Science Edition). (3):121-129.

John, Hobson (2010). The Miracle of Chinese History. Studies of Chinese ancient civilization. 2010(11):28-29.

Ka, Xiuyue (2008). The influence of Japanese War of aggression against China on China's modernization. Newspaper of the Chinese Academy of Social Sciences, September 17, 2008.

Lachman, Gideon. Translated by He, Li (2011). When China Becomes Number One. Financial Times. 2011.6.9.

Lang, Xianping (2012). China's economy has reached its most dangerous edge. Web Guide, May 10, 2012.

Li, Gang (2015). China: An Active Advocate of Global Economic Governance Reform. Social Outlook. (07):33-35.

Li, Hua (2008). Natural and man-made disasters and abnormal life of the elderly in North China. Lanzhou Journal, 2008(9):136-138.

Li, Jin (2016). Study on the relationship between the market economy and the nation state under the economic globalization. Modern Economic Information. 2016(6):17-17.

Li, Jin (2008). Comment on American Theory of China Economic threat. Master's degree thesis of Class 2005, Diplomatic University, May 2008.

Li, Liping (2005). A brief discussion on China's economic development strategy under economic globalization. Utilities Accounting. 2005(04):14-16.

Li, Suqin (2009). Financial hegemony, economic virtualization and the occurrence and adjustment of economic imbalance between China and the United States. International Economic and Trade Exploration, 2009(9): 63-68.

Li, Xiaoxiao (2011). Five5 Years Later, China's Economy Ranks First in the World. Is the Prediction of IMF Reliable? China Economic Weekly. 597(18):46-47.

Li, Ying, Cui, Lin (2016). The enlightenment of Japan's long economic downturn to China's economic development. Practice in Foreign Economic Relations and Trade, 2016(2):93-96.

Li, You (2017). Research on the position of national image in contemporary China. China, Jinan: Shandong University, 2017.41-43.

Lian, Dong (2000). The necessity of opening to the outside world from the history of the closed door in our country. Journal of Chifeng University. 2000(6):16-17.

Lin, Chenyin and Yin, Xiaolin (2010). The second mantra: When China becomes the second largest economy. Rule of Law Evening News, August 30, 2010.

Lin, Hua (2007). Revitalize the Time-Honored Brands and Develop National Brand of China, Beijing, China: China Food.

Lin, Limin and Chang, Shanshan (2008). International Strategic thinking on China's growth into the second largest economy in the World. Modern International Relations, 2008 (10): 32-40.

Lin, Yueqin and Zhou, Wen (2011). BRICS Economic and Social Development Report 2011. Beijing, PRC: Social Sciences Literature Press.

Lin, Yueqin, Zhou, Wen (2012). Blue Book of Emerging Economies----Report on Brics Economic and Social Development. Beijing, China: Social Sciences Academic Press.

Liu, Jian (2009). An Analysis of the trend of the Strategic Conception of American Democratic Union. Modern International Relations, 2009 (11): 45-49.

Liu, Jianfei (2009). The world pattern in the context of the global financial crisis. Contemporary World, 2009 (8):4-8.

Liu, Ruoyu (2012). China and the World: Finding the Way in the Transformation——A Sidelight on the 2012 Annual Conference of the International Finance Forum. China Financials. 115(11):82-84.

Liu, Shihui(2002). The importance of environmental protection in the light of the hazards of natural disasters in the late Qing Dynasty. Chengdu Normal University Journal, Vol.21(3):36-9.

Liu, Xuyi (1993). The Bush Administration's global strategy. American Study, 1993 (01).

Liu, Yuanjun (2012). Sun Wen's thought and the road of Chinese revival. Journal of China Political Science and Law University, 2012(1):125-129.

Lou, Xiangpeng (2009). New Thinking to Make the Company Bigger and Stronger. Oriental Enterprise Culture. 62(11):44-46.

Lu, Dadao (2016). The global concept and global strategy of contemporary China. Scientia Geographica Sinica. 2016(4):483-490.

Lu, Jin (2015). Discussion on the Development of Political Multi Polarization in the Contemporary World -- Global Civilization Conflict and the Establishment of a New World Order. Modern Economic Information. (15):436-436.

Lv, Yansong (1999). Step into the Kosovo War: at least 150000 people in Kosovo have taken up arms and are ready to fight NATO. Global Times, April 23, 1999.

Ma, Guoshu (2010). Why is America at war all the time? Global Times, August 7, 2010.

Ma, Jun (2017). The number of China's trade remedy cases reached a historic high in 2016. China Tendering. 2017(3):12-12.

Ma, Weicong (2017). The new hegemonism of the United States after the Cold War. Win the Future, 2017(13) :0174-0174.

Marx (2002). Critique of Political Economy, Karl, Mars and Frederick, Engels, 03, Beijing, China: People’s Publishing House.

Mei, Xinyu (2011). Ten years of China's WTO entry: Winning import and export and boosting the global economy. China Comment. 2011-09-01.

Meng, Qinglong (2008). The change of the relationship paradigm between China and the world. Contemporary International Relations, 2008(9):20-21.

Mo, Lifeng (2017). The modern meaning of traditional culture. Jiangsu Zhengxie, 2017(5):33-34.

Movement. Journal of Chongqing City Management Vocational College, Vol.12 No. 1 (General No. 45): 13-15.

Naughton, B (2007). The Chinese Economy: Transitions and Growth. Cambridge, MA: The MIT Press.

Ni, Shixiong (2001). Contemporary Theory of International Relations. Shanghai, PRC: Fudan University Press.

Nishijima, Sadao (1985). The international environment of Japanese history, Tokyo, Japan: University of Tokyo Press.

Perry, Elizabeth (2014). Growing Pains: Challenges for a Rising China. Daedalus, 143(2):5-13.

Pierre Picquart (2012). 20 years later, China and the world. Jiangsu, PRC: Jiangsu People's Publishing House.

Qian, Daqun (2007). The New Commentary of Criminal Law in Tang Dynasty, Nanjing, China: Nanjing Normal University Press.

Qing, Ying (2017). Trump's immigrant ban was blocked. Caixin Weekly, 2017(6):22-24.

Qiu, Haiping, Zhao, Min (2017). The dollar and the new imperialism under the logic of capital accumulation. Studies on Marxism, 2017(6):47-54.

Robert, Triffin, translated by Chen, Shanglin, Lei, Da (1997). Gold and Dollar Crisis. China, Beijing: The Commercial Press, 1997.

Sanderson, John (2008). Doing Business in China, London, U.K.: Dorling Kindersley Limited.

Schuman, Michael (2012). Why China will have an economic crisis? Time. 2012.2.27.

Sha, Zhanhua (2010). Analysis of the basic livelihood services by removing Pan-marketization. Chongqing and the World, 2010(11):4-7.

Shang, Chang (2007). From the sea ban policy to close the border — On the evolution of the two generation of overseas trade system in the Ming and Qing Dynasties. Journal of Hubei University of Economics, 2007(10):63-64.

Shi, Hanbing (2009). My line of wealth. World Economist, January 21, 2009.

Shu, Ping. US' moderate economic recovery makes the Fed loose. International Finance, 2012 (2): 20-23.

Song, Chuanwen (2014). Research on the expansion of income gap between urban and rural residents in China from the perspective of social equity. China, Liaoning: Dongbei University of Finance and Economics. 2014.13-16.

Song, Luzheng (2010). Song Luzheng: The Chinese model creates the greatest miracle in the history of mankind. Social Outlook. 2010(12):84-86.

Song, Qiang et al. (1996), China Can Say No. Beijing, PRC: China Federation of Industry and Commerce Press.

Song, Yanhui and Zhang, Shulin (2009). Dialectical Interpretation of The Needham Problem. Journal of Jingdezhen College, 2009(3):41-42.

Sun, Chengwu (2018). The nineteen Party's theoretical innovation of Chinese culture construction in the new era. Journal of Beijing Jiaotong University(Social Sciences Edition), 2018, 17(1):28-32.

Sun, Jianghong (2010). A subtle change in the relationship between Japan and the United States. Watch Newsweek, October 08, 2010.

Sun, Shiwen (2010). How to fight against academic fraud. Outlook Newsweek, Nov. 06, 2010.

Sun, Shubo (2011). The poorest the second in the world: China is embarrassed by per capita GDP. China Business Daily, February 15, 2011.

Sun, Wei (2015). The basic strategy and strategy of "One Belt, One Road". Macroeconomic Management. 2015(4):41-43.

Tang, Hua (2011). Yanzi's Spring and Autumn Annual·Tenth of the Second Miscellany, Beijing, China: Zhonghua Book Company.

Tang, Huaishan (2017). New thinking on "hide one's light under a bushel, keep a low profile" of diplomatic strategy. Chinese and Foreign Communication, 2017(37): 58-59.

Tang, Min (2009). Sixty-year Transition of Crop Production, Beijing, China: Outlook Weekly.

Tao, Li (2003). A dialectical view of ancient Chinese history. Journal of Liaoning normal College, 2003(2):117-118.

The Editorial Board People's Daily (2010). Ding Wu Famine: Drought and man-made disasters that claimed 13 million lives. Literature and History Reference No. 7, April 14, 2010.

Tian, Guang and Dai, Qinqin (2012). Pan-market criticism. Beijing, PRC: China Finance and economy Press.

Tian, Guang and Dai, Qinqin (2014). What the word will be when China become No.1. Beijing, PRC: China Wealth Press.

Tian, Guang and Dai, Qinqin (2014). When China Becomes No. 1 What the World will Be? Beijing, PRC: China Fortune Publisher.

Tian, Guang, Dai Qinqin, Xiaoguang (2012). Strategic Thinking on Management of the State: Based on the criticism of pan-market trend of thought. Journal of Shijiazhuang Institute of Economics, 2012(2):92-95.

Tian, Guang, Dai, Qinqin (2012). Criticism of Pan-market. Beijing, PRC: China Financial and Economic Publishing House.

Tian, Guang, Li, Dekuan (2014). Anthropology of food. China, Ningxia: Ningxia People's Publishing House, 2014.

Tian， Guang, Wang, Ying (2015). China and the World: To the More Sophisticated Integration. Frontiers, 2015(19):17-33.

Walter, Stephen (2011). The End of the American era. National Interest of United States. 2011 (11-12).

Wang, Changwen (2012). The Evolution of self-Cognitive structure in Modern Japan-centered around the Meiji Restoration. Journal of Yunnan University (Social Sciences Edition, Vol 11(3): 93-96.

Wang, Chunyang (2011). On the trilateral relations between China, the United States and Japan from the sovereignty of Diaoyu Island. Baoji Social Sciences, 2011(3):20-22.

Wang, Huning (1993). Culture as a nation's strength: soft power. Fudan Journal, 1993 (2).

Wang, Jiangang (2007). Mattel Toys: Chinese say the US media should apologize to China. International Herald Guide, Sept. 24, 2007.

Wang, Jing (2011). A study on the economic relations between China and Japan under the financial crisis. China's Urban Economy, 2011(24):299.

Wang, Junjie (2012). History and sovereignty-refuting the three bases of Japan's sovereignty over the Diaoyu Islands. Journal of Sichuan University (philosophy and Social Sciences Edition, 2012(3): 130-135.

Wang, Lijun and Zhou, Shijian (2012). An analysis of the trend of American economic development after the financial crisis. International Trade, 2012 (1): 39-42.

Wang, lin, Zhu, Jiemei (2017). Review of “From closed to open: China early modernization and social transformation”. Journal of Historical Science. 2017(3):121-124.

Wang, Qiang and Liu, Lijuan (2004). Industrialization of Education: argument between angels and devil. Business Week, November 11, 2004.

Wang, Shuxia (2007). The establishment, evolution and significance of the Chinese Imperial examination system. Lantai World, 2007(9):70-71.

Wang, Tianjin and Tian, Guang (2012). Environmental Anthropology, Yinchuan, PRC: Ningxia People's Publishing House.

Wang, Xiaojin (2010). On the enlightenment of Einstein's educational thought to the reform of China's educational system. The Entrepreneur World (Theoretical Edition), 2010(05): 191-1921.

Wang, Xiaowu (2018). Ren Zeping: The causes, impacts, prospects and countermeasures of Trade war between China and the United States. NetEase finance and Economics, March 24, 2018.

Wang, Xinbo and Wei, Tao (2009). The pattern of international relations and China's peaceful rise. Learning Theory, 2009 (27): 55-56.

Wang, Yan (2008). The contradiction between Japan and Russia intensified again. China Newsweek, September 4, 2008.

Wang, Yanping (1998). A Comparative study of the historical development of China and the West in the 18th century. Learning Forum, 1998(7): 19-20.

Wang, Yanrong (2008). Perception analysis of the "Group of Two". Economic & Trade Update. 2008(8):31-36.

Wei, Jie and Wang, Ren (2006). The Dilemma of dualism and the reform of China's educational system. Academic Monthly, 2006(8): 22-27.

Wei, Yuzhong (2007). Probe the phenomenon of Adolescent idolatry in Chinese educational system. Journal of Central North University. Vol. 23 (3):86-89.

Wei, Zongyou (2011). The Rise of the Emerging Powers and the Reform of Global Governance. International Forum. 13(2): 8-14.

Wen, Fang (2004). Black Great History-Natural and man-made disasters. Beijing, PRC: China Literature and History Press.

Wen, Jiabao (2012). Report on the Work of the Government - At the Fifth Meeting of the Eleventh National People's Congress in March 5, 2012. Accounting Yearbook of China. 56(1):38-38.

Wen, Jianning (2012). Has the Chinese economy been successfully reached its bottom-line? Shanghai Securities News, July 19, 2012.

Wolfe, Martin (2010). The lessons of the Japanese economy. Financial Times, January 15, 2010.

Wu, Chengliang (2012). Have the foundations of America's economic prowess been shaken? People's Daily, May 14, 2012.

Wu, Fangchun, Wu, Liangcheng, Wu, Yong and Wu, Binghuang (2011). A study on the causes of the decline of commodity economy in Northeast Jiangxi in modern times. Journal of Nanchang Institute of Engineering, 2011(4), Vol.30 (2):11-16.

Wu, Fei (2015). The flow of Chinese national image: The origin and evolution of "China threat theory". Social Sciences in Nanjing. 2015(9):7-16.

Wu, Minggang (2012). Sun Zi: The best way of a war is without a battle. Dazhong Daily, December 13, 2012.

Wu, Xiaoling (2012). Policy options under the hard recovery of the global economy. Financial Development Review. 2012(2):1-5.

Wu, Xing (2016). The Latest Changes of China —- Japan Relations after China's GDP Surpassed Japan. Academic Exploration, 2016(2):25-31.

Xia, Luran (2018). The cultural confidence and cultural consciousness proposed in the Belt and Road initiative. Enterprise Reform and Management, 2018(01):179-180.

Xinhua News Agency (2012). World competitiveness ranking 2012: Hong Kong first, United States second. Economic Times, Changsha Evening News, June 01, 2012: AA01.

Xu, Fei (2017). The other view of science and culture --- Why is Science walking with Democracy. Impact of Science On Society, 2017(2):12-19.

Xu, Guoliang (2014). An Analysis of Deng Xiaoping's Thought on the Relationship between Social Stability and Party Construction. Journal of the Party School of the Central Committee of the C.P.C. 18(1):33-36.

Xu, Guoxiang (2011). Study on Deng Xiaoping 's thought of opening to the outside world. The Party School of the CPC Jilin Provincial Committee. 2011.

Xu, Hui (2006). Looking present capitalism's new change and development trend from economy globalization. Journal of higher Education of South west University of Science and Technology. 2006(4):24-27.

Xu, Lijuan (2010). On the impact of natural and man-made disasters of agricultural production in Wei and Jin dynasties. Historical Records of Heilongjiang, 2010(21):148-149.

Xu, Xiuli (2012). A Brief Discussion on Food Safety, Heilongjiang, China: Vitality.

Xue, Er (2011). The ocean dream cut off by the Empire of Ming dynasty. Business Review.2011(2):44-47.

Yan, Shiye (2012). Analysis and Countermeasures of the advantages and disadvantages of economic globalization. Youth. 2012(06):213.

Yan, Xuetong (1997). International environmental assessment of China's rise. Strategy and Management, 1997 (1).

Yan, Xuetong (2011). One super and multiple strong began to evolve to two super strong. The Global Times, December 30, 2011.

Yang, Liu (2011). Chinese Catering Industry Development Report 2011, Beijing, China: Social Sciences Academic Press.

Yang, Xiaoguang, Bao, Qin (2016). China 's economic transition under the new normal—Move steadily in the throes. Bulletin of Chinese Academy of Sciences. 2016(3):362-375.

Yang, Zhen, Xue, Yuan (1994). Environmental Science: The Establishment of a New Research Paradigm, Beijing, China: China Environmental Science Press.

Ye, Liya (2018). Trade frictions between China and the United States, these "big moves" in China are still behind us! China Economic Net, March 27, 2018.

Yin, Haiquan and Wang Yimin (2006). Geopolitics and the decline of modern China. Journal of Learning, 2006(2):19-20.

Yin, Xiaolin and Yang, Wen (2011). The IMF predicts that China's economy will surpass that of the United States for five years, drawing attention from foreign media.Law System Evening News， May 25， 2011..

You, Hongbing (2011). To face the "China threat." Advance Forum, 2011(4): 35-36.

Yu, Jianguo (1993). Some characteristics of Western state-owned economy and its management. Economic Research Reference, 1993(Z2): 407-415.

Yu, Liangxin (2011). How to save the education in China. Xinmin Evening News (Shanghai) August 21, 2011.

Yu, Yun (2005). The new trend of the world situation. Outlook News Weekly, May 8, 2005.

Yu, Zhongfu (2018). Carrying out Xi Jinping's thought of strong army in an all-round way, running the armed forces by law furtherly. Ideological and Political Education Research, 2018(1):12-14.

Zeng, Liya (2010). A brief comment on Mao Zedong 's thoughts and practice of opening to the outside world. Journal of China Executive Leadership Academy Jinggangshan. 2010(4):47-51.

Zeng, Peiyan (2012). The Global Economic Pattern Changed Dramatically in 2012. News Weekend. 2012.1.7.

Zhan, Ming and Wang, Lei (2012). From the Obama administration's "Innovation Strategy" to see the United States science and technology innovation mechanism. Science and Technology Innovation & Brands, 2012 (01):64-66.

Zhang, Deming (2011). Ding Wu Famine: China 's greatest drought disaster. Jinan Daily, February 16,2011.

Zhang, Fan, Editor (2011). Confucian Analects, Beijing, China: Beijing Yanshan Publishing House.

Zhang, Jingmu (2007). The Prosperity of Ancient Chinese History. The history of political affairs in middle school. 2007(03):24-26.

Zhang, Jinwen (2012). The methods and reasons of negative reporting on China by Western Media and our counteraction. Truth, 2012 (2): 66-69.

Zhang, Kerong (2011). The historical connotation and contemporary implications of the national reconstruction. Journal of Changsha University of Technology (Social Sciences Edition), Vol.26 (4):92-96.

Zhang, Lijun (2011). The Theory of China threat: The generation of American bias against China. Exploration and Contending, 2011(3): 42-46.

Zhang, Muzhi (2017). The propaganda and historical significance of the American prisoners of war in the American Revolution. World History, 2017(5):61-78.

Zhang, Na (2012). CPI breaks 2 in July; More loose policy may be introduced. China Economic Times, Aug. 10, 2012.

Zhang, Ping (2016). The formation of the Northwest market system in Qing Dynasty under the guidance of official trade. Studies in Qing History, 2016(4):78-89.

Zhang, Runzhi (2011). American Sinologist Jonathan Spence: the textbooks of modern Chinese history should not be told from humiliation. Time Weekly. 2011-12-05.

Zhang, Weiying (2009). 30 Years Later, China Surpassed the United States. Business Times. (13): 18-18.

Zhang, Wenhua (2003). Natural disasters and economic decline in the late Han Dynasty. Journal of Heze Teachers College, Vol.25 (3):60-62.

Zhang, Xiang (2016). Exploring the modern value of Confucius's benevolence --- Repair, keep the family, govern the country, and the world. Journal of Hubei University of Economics (Humanities and Social Sciences Edition), 2016, 13(8):24-25.

Zhang, Xiao (2001). International Review: what is the special relationship. Life Times, December 14, 2001.

Zhang, Xiaotong, Wang, Hongyu, Zhao, ke (2013). On the Application of China's Economic Strength. Northeast Asia Forum. 22(1):91-98.

Zhang, Xinmin and Jiang, Qing (2011). Confucianism and the Politics of Kings: A Dialogue on the Development of modernity in the study of the outside King. The Yangming Annual Academic Journal, 2011.

Zhang, Xiqing (1993). Chinese Imperial Examination System. Beijing, PRC: Xinhua Press.

Zhang, Xuezhong (2010). The hidden worries of China's "economic miracle". Lianhe Morning News, Aug. 06, 2010.

Zhang, Yuguo (2017). Trump regime and the American Asia Pacific rebalance strategy. Northeast Asia Forum, 2017(2):13-24.

Zhang, Yuling, Chang, Xue, Xu, Dongxian (2016). The exploration of the soft power of Chinese culture. Economic Research Guide, 2016(13):36-37.

Zhang, Yunling (2018). China's foreign relations for 40 years: Retrospect and Prospect. World Economics and Politics, 2018(1):5-26.

Zhang, Zhiming (2012). From the "Chinese threat theory" to the "China Responsibility Theory": China's development security under the western cold war thinking pattern. Forum of World Economics & Politics, 2012(3):1-14.

Zhao, Dongmei (2008). On the Prosperity of the Chinese Nation. The road to success. 2008(8):51-52.

Zhao, Jingfang (2012). Four strategic misunderstandings in the context of China's peaceful rise. China Review, October 20, 2012.

Zhao, Jingfang (2012). Reasons for the misinterpretation of China's peaceful rise. Learning Times， 2012 edition.

Zhao, Jingfang (2012). The Reasons for the Misreading of China's Peaceful Rise. StudyMonthly. 515(19):39-39.

Zhao, Lingyun (2003). The reasons for the decline of Chinese traditional economy from the paradox of market development and evolution. The Chinese Economic History, 2003(01):21-24.

Zheng, Jinping (2017). Reflection on the construction of harmonious culture and the promotion of national cultural soft power. Think Tank Era, 2017(11) :293-295.

Zhi, Yan (2009). Fifty Years Later, China Will Become the World's Largest Economic. China Chief Financial Officer. 75(10): 13-13.

Zhong, Jiaping (2010). Reflections on the two Sino-Japanese wars in modern history. New College Entrance Examination (political and historical geography) 2010(02):32.

Zhong, Yan (2012). The past life of the Diaoyu Islands. Inside and outside the orchid station, 2012(01):10-11.

Zhou, Di (2016). The influence and countermeasures of economic globalization on China's economic development in the new period. Economics. 2016(9):37-38.

Zhou, Jin, Zhang, Yunbi (2018). Ambassador of Mongolia to China: China has become the second largest economy in the world, and it is the result of reform and opening up. China Daily, April 5, 2018.

Zhou, Shangbing (2000). The change and influence of the open pattern in the Tang Dynasty. Journal of Henan Normal University (Philosophy and Social Sciences). 2000(1):5-9.

Zhu, Feng (2005). The rise of China and the threat of China--The Origin of American Image. American Study, 2005 (3):21-24.

Zhu, Gaolin (2012). Do not get lost in the halo of the world's second largest economy. Red Flag Documents, 2012(07):26-28.

Zhu, Junda (2013). The development of the three United Nations environmental declarations and its impact on China, Sichuan, China: Resources Inhabitant and Environment.

Zhu, Xiangdong and Bei, Qinghua (2008). A critical outline of official standard. Journal of Central South University, 2008(4): 379-482.

Zhu, Xuzi and Liu, Dandan (2011). The world 's second largest economy in their eyes: Based on the study of national media coverage. News World, 2011(12):172-174.

Zhu, Zhengyi, Lin, Kaijia (2011). Selected Translation of the Book of Rites, Nanjing, China: Phoenix Publishing House.

Zhuo, Mingliang (2010). Different interpretations of "when China dominates the world" in foreign academic circles. Social Sciences Abroad, 2010(6):139-142.

Zong, Han (2003). What does the development of state-owned economy in western countries show? Global Perspective, October 24, 2003.

Zou, Dahai (2017). A new probe into the book age of the Nine Chapters on the Mathematical Art and quantity system during the Qin and Han Dynasties --- Research on archaeological materials based on cultural relics. Studies in History of Natural Science, 2017(3):293-315.

Zou, Jianping (2012). The essence of American Democracy from the Occupy Wall Street. Journal of Chong Qing City Management Vocational College, 2012 (1): 13-15.

Zou, Xin and Zhan, Xiangyang (2010). The enlightenment of Japan's economic boom and decline to China. Financial Times, January 25, 2010.

Index

D

E

F

N

O

P

R

S

T

U

V

W

X

Y

Z

About the Authors

Dr. Tian Guang currently serves as a specially appointed professor and the Director of Business Anthropology Institute at School of Business, Shantou University. He also serves as the Dean of Advanced Research Institute for Applied Anthropology at Jishou University and the Doctoral Supervisor at Hebei University. Dr. Tian received his Ph. D. in social anthropology from York University in 1995 and an MBA from Wilfried Laurier University in 1999. He served as the Director of International Education Office and Chair of the Business Department at Coker College 2002-2005, and the Vice President of International Education at Yinchuan University 2006-2007. Dr. Tian authored and co-authored 25 books and published over hundred peer reviewed academic articles. His research interesting is in regional development, cross-cultural marketing, and economic anthropology.

Dr. Chen Gang is currently Chair Professor and Director of Center for Social and Economic Behavior Studies at Yunnan University of Finance and Economics in China, and Chief Editor of International Journal of Business Anthropology. He received a MA in anthropology from Iowa State University in USA in September 1993, and a Ph D in anthropology from The Ohio State University in USA in June 2000. He used to work as lecturer in Xi'an Jiaotong University (1983-1990), post-doc research fellow in Department of Human Nutrition at The Ohio State University

(2000-2004), visiting professor in Department of Sociology and Anthropology of Ohio University (2004-2006). His chief research interests are in the areas of business anthropology, food safety and culture, development anthropology and cultural tourism, globalization and culture change. He has received numerous research grants both in USA and in China.

Made in United States
Orlando, FL
04 November 2026

90200108R00187